D0494001

THE GRAND
QUARREL

THE GRAND QUARREL

WOMEN'S MEMOIRS *of the* ENGLISH CIVIL WAR

EDITED BY
ROGER HUDSON

SUTTON PUBLISHING

For the passage by Lucy Hutchinson
where she uses the phrase,
'the grand quarrel', see p. 213

First published in 1993 by The Folio Society

This edition first published in 2000 by
Sutton Publishing Limited
Phoenix Mill · Thrupp · Stroud · Gloucestershire GL5 2BU

British Library Cataloguing in Publication Data
A catalogue record for this book is available from the British
Library.

ISBN 0 7509 2390 3(pbk)
      0 7509 2589 2 (hbk)

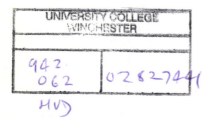
Printed in Great Britain by
MPG, Bodmin, Cornwall

Contents

Introduction

Once wars are over, whether they be civil ones or conventional conflicts between countries, there is the temptation to see the events preceding them as leading inexorably towards them. Thus in the 1900s the great powers of Europe seem so many puppets, their strings becoming more and more entangled, until the guns speak in August 1914. That war then sows the seeds of the Second World War. With the English Civil War, however, it is much more difficult to detect any sense of doom burdening the air in the two decades before it broke out in 1642. The Earl of Clarendon, the earliest and still the greatest historian of the war, (whose first wife was a cousin of Lucy Hutchinson), recalled his youth fondly and contrasted peace at home with wars abroad:

> England enjoyed the greatest measure of felicity that it had ever known; the two crowns of France and Spain worrying each other, by their mutual incursions and invasions of each other, whilst they had both a civil war in their own bowels . . . All Germany weltering in its own blood and contributing to each other's destruction, that the poor crown of Sweden might grow great out of their ruins . . . Italy every year infested by the arms of Spain and France.

Ann Fanshawe's husband Richard, born in 1608 and so an exact contemporary of Clarendon, wrote a somewhat smug poem in 1630 on the same theme:

> *Now war is all the world about . . .*
> *Only the island which we sow*
> *(A world without a world) so far*
> *From present wounds, it cannot show*
> *An ancient scar.*

Charles I's own sister Elizabeth, married to a Rhineland ruler – the Elector Palatine – and mother of Prince Rupert, was one of the earliest victims of the Thirty Years War in Germany. In 1620 she and her husband Frederick were ousted from Bohemia after a brief reign in Prague, and then lost the Palatinate as well.

The trends in Europe were for continuing warfare and upheaval, continuing religious bitterness between Catholics and Calvinists, and the growth of absolutist, centralised royal power at the expense of obsolete medieval institutions. This last tendency was one which Charles I was soon to try and impose on England. The House of Commons was just such a typical medieval left-over and, after some unhappy experiences with three parliaments at the start of his reign, in 1629 he embarked on a period of 'personal rule'. For a decade, it looked as though he were going to get away with it. The country continued prosperous and calm, and enough money with which to pay for a lavish court and the expenses of administration was raised without parliamentary sanction, by such devices as reviving the old laws of knighthood and of the forest, as well as from the Court of Wards, from Ship Money (traditionally a levy on seaside counties only, to build fighting ships for their defence), and from the granting of monopolies for such things as the manufacture of soap. The worst excesses of James I and what Lucy Hutchinson called his 'court caterpillars' were forgotten. As she said:

> King Charles was temperate, chaste, and serious; so that the fools and bawds, mimics and catamites, of the former court, grew out of fashion; and the nobility and courtiers who did not quite abandon their debaucheries, yet so reverenced the king as to retire into corners to practise them. Men of learning and ingenuity in all arts were in esteem, and received encouragement from the king, who was a most excellent judge and a great lover of paintings, carvings, gravings, and other ingenuities. [But he was also] the most obstinate person in his self-will that ever was, and so bent upon being an absolute uncontrollable sovereign, that he was resolved either to be such a king or none.

In Queen Elizabeth's day the royal prerogative had been taken for granted. It was James I who elevated it into the Divine Right of Kings, and then Charles's natural aloofness only made it more offensive. He did not know when to unbend; when to appeal to the loyalty of his people by a show of humanity or a touch of rhetoric; when to flatter the House of Commons so as to get his way. Instead of the public ceremonial and progresses that Elizabeth had used with such effect to promote herself in the eyes of her people, the Stuarts expended their energies on elaborate but ephemeral masques whose only audiences were those at court.

Charles's over-emphasis on Divine Right might have been tolerable had he not, to quote Lucy Hutchinson again,

> had a mistaken principle that kingly government in the state could not stand without episcopal government in the church; and therefore as the bishops flattered him with preaching up his sovereign prerogative, and inveighing against the puritans as factious and disloyal, so he protected them in their pomp and pride and insolent practices against all the godly and sober people of the land.

The 'insolent practices' were the high-church or 'Arminian' style of worship particularly advocated by William Laud, who became Archbishop of Canterbury in 1633. While the many puritans, the 'godly and sober', followed the Calvinist doctrine of predestination and put a heavy emphasis on right behaviour of the individual in following his own conscience, the Arminian stress was much more on the sacramental and ritualistic, what Laud called 'the beauty of holiness'. For them the focus in a church was on the altar, while for the puritans it was on the pulpit, from which the Word could be preached. The puritans substituted a plain table for the railed-off altar, and disapproved of surplices, stained glass, paintings and carving. Many of them were convinced that Laud was merely preparing the ground for a return to full-blown Roman Catholicism, the religion of Charles's French wife, Henrietta Maria.

Laud, according to Lucy Hutchinson 'a fellow of mean extraction and arrogant pride', was determined that not merely the Church of England but also the Church in Scotland should follow the Arminian line. Scotland had gone far futher and more unanimously down the Calvinist path than England, establishing a

Presbyterian, non-episcopal, church government. In 1636 Laud imposed a Book of Canons and Common Prayer north of the border and opposition soon mounted, crystallising round the pledging of the Scottish Covenant to protect the Presbyterian church, in 1638. In the following year Charles rose to the challenge, bringing about the first short Bishops' War between his countries.

It was this that upset the delicately balanced machinery of Charles's personal rule. Inflation had been doing its insidious work (not merely in England but in Europe as a whole) for the previous hundred years, raising prices one hundred per cent in that time. As long as no extra strain was put on his finances, the king could get by, using the various non-parliamentary subterfuges already listed. But he soon found that the attempt to wage war without an income from regular taxation led only to ignominy. The Short Parliament was called in April 1640, but fell out with the king's council about the best way to raise supply, and so was quickly dissolved. The Second Bishops' War followed, and ended even more ignominiously than the first. When the Long Parliament met in November 1640, it was in a strong position to assert itself. As Clarendon put it, a great deal more poetically,

A small, scarce discernible cloud arose in the north, which was shortly after attended with such a storm, that never gave over raging till it had shaken, and even rooted up, the greatest and tallest cedars of the three nations; blasted all its beauty and fruitfulness; brought its strength to decay, and its glory to reproach, and almost to desolation; by such a career and deluge of wickedness and rebellion, as by not being enough foreseen, or in truth suspected, could not be prevented.

The first of the 'tallest cedars' to go was the Earl of Strafford. By his conduct, as president of the Council of the North and then (aided by Alice Thornton's father) as Lord Deputy in Ireland, he had shown himself, in Lucy Hutchinson's words, to be 'a man of deep policy, stern resolution and ambitious zeal to keep up the glory of his own greatness'. He was undoubtedly the most effective of Charles's ministers and the opposition could not rest easy until he was executed in May 1641. The legislation that was now brought in abolished the Courts of Star Chamber and High Commission and the Council of the North, which were seen as the particular tools of the royal prerogative. Ship Money was abolished, Laud was imprisoned, and steps were taken to end episcopacy. Many felt at this point that reform had gone far enough and the balance in Parliament might well have swayed back in Charles's favour, had not Ireland burst into revolt and several thousand Protestants been massacred there in October 1641. Troops needed to be raised to restore order, and neither Charles nor Parliament would concede control of them. At the same time, fears of a similar Catholic uprising in England rapidly spread and the king was persuaded that his Catholic queen was likely to be impeached. So he tried to arrest the five ringleaders within the Commons in January 1642. The coup failed and Charles left a hostile London for York.

The unfolding of the Wars can be followed in the chronological table on pp. xxix–xxxvii and in the linking passages within the main text of the book. Here it only remains to indicate where the two parties were strongest within England, and what the vital turning points were. Charles's strength lay in Wales, the West Country and the North. Parliament was strong in London, the East and the South, but also held a number of ports like Hull, Plymouth, Lyme, Gloucester and Bristol (until July 1643), which were very important to its strategy. The Midlands and parts of Yorkshire and Lancashire were disputed ground. Parliamentary Nottingham, under Colonel Hutchinson, and royalist Newark were vital to each because they controlled crossings over the Trent without which the northern and southern halves of the country would be separated. Just as the royalist Lucas family was isolated in parliamentary Essex, so the parliamentarian Harleys were in strongly royalist Herefordshire.

The early stages of the war offered Charles his best chance of success, but he did not allow Prince Rupert to march on London after the first big battle at Edgehill near Banbury in October 1642. Instead he established his headquarters and court at Oxford. In 1643 the Duke of Newcastle's northern army defeated the parliamentarians of Yorkshire under Fairfax more than once, while those in the West under Sir William Waller were also twice defeated, leading to the fall of Bristol to Prince Rupert in July. When affairs were looking their worst for the roundheads in September, they signed an alliance with the Scots – The Solemn League and Covenant – and the cavaliers failed to gain a resounding victory at Newbury. The following month forces from the royalist stronghold of Newark were defeated by the rising star of the roundheads, Oliver Cromwell, at Winceby in Lincolnshire. The balance really began to swing Parliament's way once the Scottish army crossed the border in January 1644. This gave a numerical superiority which contributed to Prince Rupert's and the Duke of Newcastle's defeat at Marston Moor outside York in July 1644. In 1645 the removal of the old parliamentary commanders by the device of the Self-Denying Ordinance allowed an effective military leadership under Sir Thomas Fairfax and Oliver Cromwell, who then created the New Model Army and led it to overwhelming victory at Naseby in June 1645.

Charles surrendered to the Scots in May 1646, but reached no agreement with them, because they demanded the imposition of Presbyterianism in England. Only when they dropped that condition did he sign a secret treaty at the end of the following year, having in the meantime been in the hands of the New Model and spurned their genuine compromise offer. The Second Civil War followed in 1648, and in spite of an invading Scottish army, Fairfax and Cromwell won it without too much difficulty. But the experience of Charles's duplicity in the previous eighteen months had convinced Cromwell that he must die.

Historians employing Marxist ideas have tried to depict the Civil Wars as the outcome of class conflict between a declining aristocracy and an upthrusting bourgeoisie, but analysis of the protagonists soon rules out this over-neat explanation. Equally, if one looks in 1642 for unhesitant men fighting for reasons of pure ideology or religious belief, they are hard to find. Total abolition of Parliament was no more on the agenda of most royalists than republicanism was the expectation of most roundheads. The Harleys perhaps come closest to having a pure and undeviating motive in their hardline puritanism, but most on their side must have been as unwilling as John Hutchinson to finally take up arms.

It is interesting to see that he did not regard the threat to the puritan style of worship as 'so clear a ground for the war as the defence of the just English liberties'. It was taxation without parliamentary sanction (hitting the gentry in particular) that he regarded as an infringement of the social order and his position in it. Any idea that he was fighting for an extension of liberty downwards is put paid to by Lucy Hutchinson's firm denial of sympathy for those who 'endeavoured the levelling of all estates and qualities'. She is full of scorn for anyone whom she regards as a thrusting parvenu, including parliamentary officers like White and Chadwick at Nottingham or 'the mean sort of people in the House [of Commons], whom to distinguish from the more honourable gentlemen, they called *worsted-stocking men*'.

Ideas of democracy and equality only emerged as a result of the upheavals of the war, and were never the cause of it. The same is true of the bid for religous freedom in the later 1640s made by the Independents, among whom Lucy and John Hutchinson numbered themselves. As the war progressed, within the roundhead camp the various Independent sects became clearly distinguishable from the Presbyterian establishment, of which Sir Robert Harley was a typical member. The Presbyterians could think only in terms of monarchy and an all-embracing nationally-organised church – albeit one that dispensed with bishops. The particular breeding-ground of the Independents was the New Model Army, where religous freedom went hand-in-hand with social and political radicalism. It was to keep control of their men that Ireton and Cromwell were gradually forced into more extreme political solutions. Fairfax, the New Model commander, could not follow them and neither could John Hutchinson who, tied to Nottingham, was not a member of that body when it emerged in 1645.

It is time to turn from the 'sad spectacle of war', its causes and effects, to the more immediate concerns of these six ladies: dowries, husbands' and fathers' incomes, childbirth, illness, family ties. Every husband expected his bride to come with a 'portion' or dowry of money. When Sir Robert Harley married the first of his three wives, she brought £2300 with her. Brilliana Conway came with only £1600, which was acceptable because her powerful father was expected to find a lucrative post for Sir Robert. He was not disappointed. Anne Halkett's fearsome mother, the royal governess, refused to countenance any idea of her marrying Thomas Howard (see p. 137) who, as the son of a younger son of the Earl of Suffolk, badly needed a wife with a decent dowry. Anne's portion of money was tied up by a long-standing lawsuit and when she finally married her Scottish widower, Sir James Halkett, in 1656, she said 'that was my regret that I could not bring him a fortune as great as his affection to recompense his long expectation'. Thanks to the war, Ann Fanshawe's promised portion of £10,000 was wanting, and when she married in Oxford in 1644, she and her husband had less than £20 between them.

Sir Robert Harley's annual income at the start of the war was reckoned to be about £3000, and this in spite of having lost his Mastership of the Mint a few years before. From Lucy Hutchinson's description of her father Sir Allen Apsley's lifestyle it is obvious that he had done very well for himself as victualler to James I's navy, as had Ann Fanshawe's father Sir John Harrison in the King's Customs House. But equally, they were expected to lend large sums to the king with little expectation of their speedy return – £50,000 in the case of Sir John Harrison in 1642.

The war cost all the families in this book, whichever side they fought on, a great deal of money. By 1650 Sir Robert Harley estimated it had cost him nearly £20,000. By 1660 the Duke of Newcastle's losses were reckoned to be about £1,000,000. A glance at the names of the estates gives a clue where the deepest origins of their wealth lay: Henry VIII's Dissolution of the Monasteries a hundred years before. The Lucas home was St John's Abbey, the Duke of Newcastle's was Welbeck Abbey and John Hutchinson's Byron mother came from Newstead Abbey.

The rates of infant mortality in the past are one of the hardest statistics for us to grasp in his healthy century. One historian was so unbalanced by them as to claim that parents in the past were less attached to their children than they are today. He could not imagine the regular expenditure of grief, but there seems little doubt it was there. Even among the better-off only one third of those born survived into adulthood. Brilliana Harley's family, with all seven surviving, was exceptional. Her husband's second wife had nine children, all of whom died. A concomitant of this, and of the lack of contraception, was that most married women spent much of their time pregnant. Alice Thornton's sister Catherine, Lady Danby, died aged thirty as a result of childbirth, having had sixteen children, six of whom were stillborn. Ann Fanshawe had fourteen children, of whom five survived. She also had five miscarriages, one of triplets. Even among the aristocracy, forty-five per cent of women died before they were fifty, a quarter of that percentage directly from childbirth; how many more died through what might be called the attrition of childbirth one cannot know.

The diseases to be feared were legion, but the commonest were the plague, which drove John Hutchinson out of London in 1637 and which he avoided catching in Newark after the town finally surrendered in 1646; the ague (most often malaria); and smallpox. Lucy Hutchinson caught this just before she was due to marry, but John Hutchinson was undaunted by the ghastly spectacle she presented and was rewarded, if she is to be believed, by the return of her good looks in due course (see p. 25). (A similar fate befell Dorothy Osborne, the letter writer and wife-to-be of Sir William Temple, in 1654, but her looks did not return.) Alice Thornton also caught smallpox through excessive devotion to her brother (see p. 93). Modern estimates put battle casualties for the war at 100,000 – bad enough in a total population of perhaps 4,500,000. But there were another 200,000 deaths from army-borne diseases, or such complaints as the scurvey which nearly killed Sir Richard Fanshawe in prison after the battle of Worcester in 1651. It was not until the First World War that losses on such a scale had to be faced again.

The network of intermarriage between upper-class families frequently led to relations finding themselves on opposing sides. John Hutchinson confronted an array of fiercely royalist Byron uncles and Stanhope step-cousins in Nottinghamshire. In Herefordshire the Harleys were kinsmen of two of the leading royalist families, the Crofts of Croft Castle and the Scudamores of Holme Lacy. The situation was neatly encapsulated by Colonel Hutchinson's reply to Sir Richard Byron when he suggested the colonel abandon the parliamentary cause: 'He might consider there was, if nothing else, so much of a Byron's blood in him, that he should very much scorn to betray or quit a trust he had undertaken.' In spite of this intransigence, Lucy Hutchinson reveals that Sir Richard's son was allowed to remain at school in Nottingham throughout the First Civil War. The family trees on pp. xxvi-xxviii are there to show these connections, and also to demonstrate the ties between leading families on the same side – or on both sides, in the case of the Pierreponts. This is perhaps seen at its most pronounced in 'The Great Contrivers', that circle of cousins and relations-by-marriage which embraced the cream of the parliamentarian leadership – Hampden, St John, Warwick, Saye and Sele, Manchester, Cromwell.

The absence of atrocities, reprisals and cold-blooded violence at least during the first years of the conflict, when compared to the Thirty Years War in Germany or to the Wars of the Roses two centuries earlier, must have been due in part to these family ties. One likes to think also that womenfolk such as the ladies in this book reminded their men of the claims of humanity and common sense when passions were running high. As the epitaph of another Civil War heroine, Lady Bankes (see p. 80), put it, they certainly bore 'a noble proportion of the late calamities'.

Prince Rupert once dismissed his times as 'this scribbling age', when stung by roundhead propaganda pamphlets accusing him of atrocities. There is no denying that writing – and reading – had spread rapidly out from the cloister and chancery under the stimulus of the printing press in the previous hundred years. This new climate of literacy, and a growing self-consciousness as the values of the Renaissance filtered through, combined with the natural instinct to record the extraordinary upheavals of the Civil Wars and their aftermath to produce the first great period of English biography and memoir. It cannot be fortuitous either that English portraiture suddenly flowered at this time, with painters such as William Dobson and the miniaturists Samuel Cooper and John Hoskins. The list of men who were then moved to record their experiences makes familiar reading for the most part – Samuel Pepys, John Evelyn, John Aubrey, the Earl of Clarendon, Bulstrode Whitelocke, William Blundell, Sir Philip Warwick. Those women in whom the turbulent times implanted the same urge have not become such common currency.

Margaret, Duchess of Newcastle, has been called 'the first English woman writer'. Claims of this sort are always rash, but certainly she was recognised by her own contemporaries as a novelty and a phenomenon. The idea of any woman, let alone one of her station, bursting into print, not once but with increasing regularity, struck her contemporaries as very strange. Her outlandish behaviour, conversation and costume all added to the impact she made. How much of this derived from her crippling shyness and mere artlessness, and how much from studied eccentricity, is hard to say, but it was to earn her the nickname of 'Mad Madge of Newcastle'. John Evelyn patronised her, calling her 'a mighty pretender to learning'; such criticism was out of turn when the Universities and the Inns of Court were closed to women. She poured out poetry, plays, essays, stories, scientific and philosophical works. Virginia Woolf, saw 'something noble and Quixotic and high-spirited, as well as crack-brained and bird-witted about her'. Among her output were her short autobiography in 1656, an appealing mix of pride in her family, self-conceit and self-knowledge; and, eleven years later, her portrait of her husband the duke. This is an unreliable source for the historian, but among much hagiography has a number of lively passages, for instance on the duke's personal habits, about his part in raising the north of England for King Charles, and in the pivotal battle of Marston Moor in 1644. Her motive was to defend her husband's 'noble actions' in the Civil War from 'unjust aspersions', though her effectiveness was limited by Newcastle's command 'not to mention any thing or passage to the prejudice or disgrace of any family or particular person'.

Lucy Hutchinson also sought to defend the part played by her husband, finally on the losing side, in the 'Grand Quarrel'. Indeed, it is claimed that she was inspired to write her *Memoirs of the Life of Colonel Hutchinson* by the publication of the duchess's Memoir of the duke. However, Lucy was writing with no thought of publication in her own lifetime and she put no constraints on what she allowed herself to say about those, whether royalist or parliamentarian, of whose actions she disapproved. This certainly gives her book an invigorating astringency and, since much of her account of the war years was based on notebook entries that she made soon after the events described, it has some of the immediacy of a diary. Ann Fanshawe wrote her memoirs in 1676, also for private, family circulation only, to hold up her husband as a model to her one surviving son, who was only a year old when Richard Fanshawe died in 1666. Virginia Woolf singled out her particular qualities of 'candour and simplicity . . . the atmosphere is singularly clear; you see the detail and solidity of things as in a child's story of adventure'. Anne Halkett wroter hers in 1677–8 largely, one suspects, to try and set the record straight about her involvement with the duplicitous Colonel Bampfield (see p.180). Her repeated insistence (not included here) on the innocence of their relationship has rather the opposite effect to the one she intended. The extracts by Alice Thornton cover the period some time before her marriage in 1651. This turned out to be unhappy and led to a considerable loss of social status for her, as a result of the financial failure of her husband. Her writings can be seen as an attempt to find some meaning in her poverty-stricken widowhood. Like Lucy Hutchinson and Ann Fanshawe, Anne Halkett and Alice Thornton were writing only for their immediate circle. Brilliana Harley's audience was narrower still: simply her beloved son Ned.

Any endeavour to recruit these ladies for the feminist cause is, on the face of it, a defiance of the evidence. In some of the Duchess of Newcastle's other books she occasionally shows a flash of independent spirit, but the prevailing tone is one of submission. Lucy Hutchinson says of herself and the colonel that she was 'a compliant subject . . . to his wise government', and the other five would have applauded her for it. She is also very critical of the undue sway she claims his wife Anne had over Thomas Fairfax. But by the very act of writing or, in Brilliana Harley's case, fighting, these women were in fact doing something to question the submissive stereotype.

The vagaries of seventeenth-century spelling and some of the punctuation have been ironed out. In particular, many of the longer sentences and paragraphs have been broken up. The criterion in selecting passages has been to take those which are most dramatic and moving, which speak most directly to us across the gap of three and a half centuries, and which present the telling detail that immediately puts the reader in touch with those extraordinary years. One element which perhaps has been over-diluted in the process is the intense religiosity of the age. The Providence of God was perceived at every turn. His help was invoked at all times and thanks rendered back. Insofar as things spiritual can be measured, England can seldom if ever have been as devout as it was during the years of the Great Rebellion.

Biographical Notes

Lucy Hutchinson, daughter of Sir Allen Apsley, Lieutenant of the Tower of London. She was born in 1620 and married John Hutchinson of Owthorpe, Nottinghamshire, in 1638. He was the son of Sir Thomas Hutchinson M P, and during the Civil War held Nottingham Castle for Parliament. In 1649 he put his signature to Charles I's death warrant. After the Restoration he was imprisoned without trial and died in 1664. His wife died some time after 1675.

Ann, Lady Fanshawe, daughter of Sir John Harrison M P of Balls, Hertfordshire. She was born in 1625, married Richard Fanshawe in 1644 and had six sons and eight daughters, of whom only one son and four daughters survived infancy. Her husband was Secretary to the English Ambassador to Spain (1635), Secretary of War to the Prince of Wales (1644), Ambassador to Portugal (1662) and Ambassador to Spain (1664). He died in 1666 and she in 1680.

Margaret, Duchess of Newcastle, daughter of Thomas Lucas of St John's, Colchester, Essex. She was born about 1623, and was one of Queen Henrietta Maria's maids of honour in Oxford in 1643 before going to France with her. There she married William Cavendish, Duke of Newcastle, as his second wife, in 1645. He had been royalist commander in the North of England until the Battle of Marston Moor in 1644. She died childless in 1673.

Brilliana, Lady Harley, daughter of Sir Edward Conway of Ragley, Warwickshire. A soldier and diplomat, he was appointed Secretary of State by James I. She was born about 1598 and married Sir Robert Harley M P of Brampton Bryan Castle, Herefordshire in 1623, as his third wife. She had three sons and four daughters and died in 1643 shortly after enduring a seven-week siege at Brampton Bryan Castle by royalist forces.

Anne, Lady Halkett, daughter of Thomas Murray, Provost of Eton and former tutor to Charles I. Her mother was governess to Charles's younger children, the Duke of Gloucester and Princess Elizabeth, from the early 1640s. Anne was born in 1623 and married a Scottish royalist soldier and widower, Sir James Halkett, in 1656. She had four children, of whom one survived, and she died in 1699.

Alice Thornton, daughter of Sir Christopher Wandesford who succeeded his cousin the Earl of Strafford as Lord Deputy of Ireland. She was born in 1626, brought up in Ireland, and moved to Yorkshire during the Civil War, after the death of her father in 1640. She married in 1651, had nine children of whom three survived, and died in 1706.

Family Trees

The Hutchinsons, Byrons
and Stanhopes

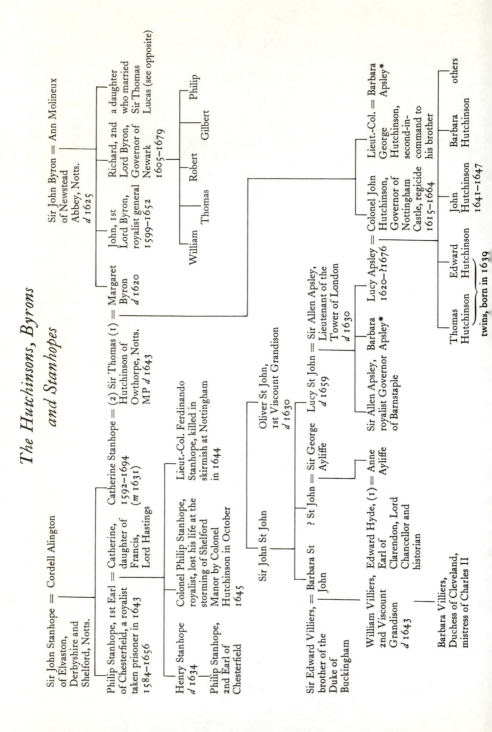

The Cavendishes, Pierreponts and Lucases

Sir William Cavendish of Chatsworth, Derbyshire 1505–1557 = Elizabeth Hardwick 'Bess of Hardwick' later Countess of Shrewsbury 1527–1608

Thomas Lucas of St John's, Colchester = Elizabeth Leighton

Frances Cavendish = Sir Henry Pierrepont of Holme Pierrepont, Nottinghamshire d 1615

Sir Charles Cavendish of Welbeck Abbey, Nottinghamshire 1553–1617 = Katherine, daughter of Cuthbert, Lord Ogle

William Cavendish, 1st Earl of Devonshire 1551–1626

William Cavendish, 2nd Earl of Devonshire 1590–1628

Robert Pierrepont, 1st Earl of Kingston 1584–1643 unwilling royalist killed near Gainsborough = Gertrude Talbot, granddaughter of Earl of Shrewsbury

Sir Charles Cavendish, the mathematician d 1654

William Cavendish, 1st Duke of Newcastle 1593–1676 [by his 1st wife Elizabeth Basset] = Margaret Lucas

John, 1st Lord Lucas

Sir Thomas Lucas, whose wife was a sister of the 1st Lord Byron. Died as a result of a head wound received in Ireland, 1647

Sir Charles Lucas, executed by Lord Fairfax after siege of Colchester 1648

William Cavendish, 3rd Earl of Devonshire 1617–1684 (went abroad in 1642)

Colonel Charles Cavendish, royalist killed at Gainsborough July 1643 aged 23

Henry Pierrepont, Lord Newark, Marques of Dorchester (1645), non-combatant royalist, Lord Lieutenant of Nottinghamshire

Colonel Francis Pierrepont, nominal commander of John Hutchinson's first regiment, parliamentarian

William Pierrepont MP, of Thoresby, distinguished member of the Long Parliament

Frances = Pierrepont Henry Cavendish, 2nd Duke of Newcastle 1630–1691

Charles Cavendish 1629–1659

Mary   Anne   Elizabeth   Catherine

The Harleys, Conways, Veres, and Fairfaxes

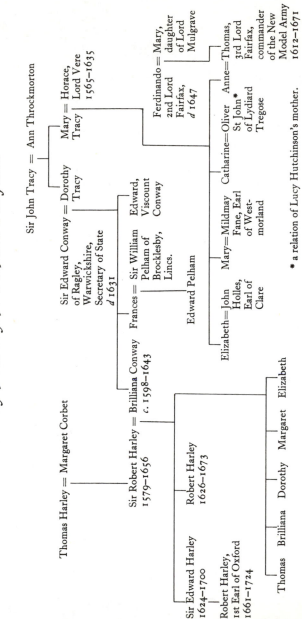

Sir John Tracy = Ann Throckmorton

Mary = Horace,
Tracy   Lord Vere
         1565–1635

Sir Edward Conway = Dorothy
of Ragley,   Tracy
Warwickshire,
Secretary of State
d 1631

Ferdinando = Mary,
2nd Lord   daughter
Fairfax,   of Lord
d 1647   Mulgrave

Edward,
Viscount
Conway

Frances = Sir William
          Pelham of
          Brocklesby,
          Lincs.

Edward Pelham

Catharine = Oliver   Anne = Thomas,
            St John*   3rd Lord
            of Lydiard   Fairfax,
            Tregose   commander
                            of the New
                            Model Army
                            1612–1671

Mary = Mildmay
        Fane, Earl
        of West-
        morland

Elizabeth = John
            Holles,
            Earl of
            Clare

Sir Robert Harley = Brilliana Conway
1579–1656   c. 1598–1643

Thomas Harley = Margaret Corbet

Robert Harley
1626–1673

Sir Edward Harley
1624–1700

Robert Harley,
1st Earl of Oxford
1661–1724

Thomas   Brilliana   Dorothy   Margaret   Elizabeth

* a relation of Lucy Hutchinson's mother.

Chronological Table

The column on the left lists important events on the national scene, while that on the right itemises the lives of the six ladies and their families.

1623		Sir Robert Harley marries Brilliana Conway, his third wife.
1625	James I dies and is succeeded by Charles I.	
1629	Charles begins the 11-year period of 'personal rule' without Parliament.	
1632	Thomas Wentworth, later Earl of Strafford, made Lord Deputy in Ireland.	Alice Thornton's father, Sir Christopher Wandesford, assistant to his cousin Strafford in Ireland.
1633	Charles travels north for his Scottish coronation. Laud becomes Archbishop of Canterbury.	Newcastle entertains Charles on his way north at Welbeck Abbey.
1634		Newcastle entertains Charles and Henrietta Maria at Bolsover Castle.
1635		Richard Fanshawe, future husband of Ann Fanshawe, appointed Secretary to the English Ambassador to Spain.
1636	Book of Canons and Common Prayer issued for Scotland.	
1637	John Hampden refuses to pay Ship Money tax.	
1638	The Scottish Covenant to protect the Presbyterian Church.	Newcastle made Governor to the Prince of Wales. The Harleys' eldest son Edward

1638		goes to Oxford. Richard Fanshawe returns to England. John Hutchinson marries Lucy Apsley.
1639	First Bishops' War between Scotland and England.	Newcastle lends Charles £10,000 for the war and raises a troop of horse. Richard Fanshawe Secretary to the Council of War, Ireland, 1639–41. John Hutchinson contemplates buying a position in the Court of Star Chamber, a hated agency of Royal Prerogative.
1640	The Short Parliament, April to May, followed by the Second Bishops' War. The Long Parliament begins in November.	Members of the Long Parliament: Sir Thomas Hutchinson, father of John; Ann Fanshawe's father, Sir John Harrison and her brother William; Sir Robert Harley, and later his two eldest sons. Edward Harley leaves Oxford to join his father in London. Sir Christopher Wandesford becomes Lord Deputy in Ireland on the recall of the Earl of Strafford, but dies in December 1640.
1641	*May*, execution of Strafford. Archbishop Laud imprisoned. Courts of Star Chamber and High Commission, and Council of the North all abolished. Ship Money tax made illegal. *August*, Parliament prorogued and Charles goes to Scotland. *October*, rebellion in Ireland. *November*, the Grand Remonstrance, a vote of censure on Charles, passed in Commons.	Newcastle ceases being Governor to the Prince of Wales. Richard Fanshawe appointed one of the King's Remembrancers. Sir John Harrison lends the king £50,000 to pay off the Scottish Army. *October*, John and Lucy Hutchinson leave London for his home at Owthorpe in Nottinghamshire.

1642   *January*, Charles attempts to arrest five Members of Parliament and leaves London for Windsor.
February, Queen Henrietta Maria goes abroad.
March, Charles goes to York, and refuses consent to the Militia Ordinance giving control of army to Parliament.
April, Charles tries to take Hull.
August, Royal Standard raised at Nottingham signifies start of the Civil War.
September, Charles in Shrewsbury.

October, Battle of Edgehill in Warwickshire.
November, Royal court and headquarters established in Oxford.
December, Newark in Nottinghamshire garrisoned by royalists.

January, Newcastle sent by Charles to Hull.
June, Newcastle sent to raise the northern counties for the king. Brilliana Harley left in charge of Brampton Bryan Castle in Herefordshire while her husband stays in London as a leading parliamentarian.
August–December, Sir Robert and Edward Harley at Brampton.
August, the family home at Colchester of Margaret Lucas, later Duchess of Newcastle, sacked by a parliamentarian mob. Royalists take over the Nottingham powder magazine.
October, John and George Hutchinson find it safe to return to Nottinghamshire.

December, John Hutchinson enrols as a lieutenant-colonel to garrison Nottingham. Anne Halkett's mother appointed governess to Charles's children, the Duke of Gloucester and Princess Elizabeth.

1643   *February*, Queen Henrietta Maria lands on Yorkshire coast.
March, George Goring leads Newcastle's cavalry to victory over Sir Thomas Fairfax at Seacroft Moor, Yorks.

June, Newcastle defeats the Fairfaxes at Adwalton Moor, Yorks.

February, unsuccessful parliamentary assault on Newark.
March/April, Brilliana Harley under threat of siege at Brampton Bryan Castle, which is lifted when Sir William Waller takes Hereford for Parliament. Royalists win fights at Grantham and Ancaster in Lincolnshire.
June, royalist assault on Nottingham. John Hutchinson appointed Governor of Nottingham Castle.

1643

July, Sir William Waller's parliamentary army defeated at Lansdown and Roundway Down in the West Country. Bristol falls to Prince Rupert.

Edward and young Robert Harley join Waller's army.
July, Alice Thornton and her family besieged in Chester by parliamentary force under Sir William Brereton. Edward Harley's horse shot under him at Battle of Lansdown near Bath.

July/August, Newcastle relieves Gainsborough and Lincoln.

July/August/September, seven-week siege of Brampton Bryan Castle, home of Brilliana Harley. Royalists besiege Gloucester at the same time.

September, Newcastle besieges Fairfaxes in Hull. Parliament signs Solemn League and Covenant with the Scots. Gloucester relieved by parliamentary army under Earl of Essex, followed by inconclusive 1st Battle of Newbury.

September, royalist attempt under Sir Richard Byron on Nottingham.

October, Earl of Manchester, Cromwell and Thomas Fairfax defeat royalists from Newark at Winceby Fight in Lincolnshire. Newcastle abandons siege of Hull and comes south into Nottinghamshire and Derbyshire.

October, Brilliana Harley dies of pneumonia. Margaret Lucas, later Duchess of Newcastle, becomes one of the queen's maids of honour in Oxford.
November, John Hutchinson receives commission to raise his own regiment of foot. Ann Fanshawe joins her father in Oxford. Richard Fanshawe also joins the royal court there.
December, Sir Richard Byron made Governor of Newark.

1644   *January*, Scots army crosses the border in support of Parliament. Lord Byron defeated by Sir Thomas Fairfax at Nantwich in Cheshire.

January, royalist attempt on Nottingham under Sir Charles Lucas.

1644   *February,* Newcastle back in Yorkshire.

March, Hopton's royalists defeated by Waller at Cheriton in the West Country.

March, Prince Rupert defeats besieging parliamentarians under Sir John Meldrum outside Newark and occupies Lincoln. Brampton Bryan Castle finally taken by royalists after a second siege.

April, Newcastle besieged in York.

April, Henrietta Maria leaves Oxford for the West, Margaret Lucas among the party.

May, Lincoln retaken by Eastern Association army. Prince Rupert subdues Lancashire. Richard and Ann Fanshawe marry in Oxford, and he is appointed Secretary for War to the Prince of Wales.

June, Waller defeated at Cropredy Bridge in Warwickshire by the king.

July, Prince Rupert and Newcastle defeated at Battle of Marston Moor by Scots, Eastern Association army under the Earl of Manchester and Cromwell, and the Fairfaxes' Yorkshire forces.

July, Henrietta Maria leaves Falmouth for France.

August, Earl of Essex heavily defeated by the king at Lostwithiel in Cornwall.

October, 2nd Battle of Newbury fails to stop Charles returning to Oxford from the West.

Autumn, unwelcome attention from billeted Scottish soldiers for Alice Thornton in Yorkshire.

1645

January, Sir Richard Willis replaces Sir Richard Byron as Governor of Newark.

March, Richard Fanshawe leaves Oxford for Bristol with the Prince of Wales.

April, resignation of the Earls of Essex and Manchester, Sir William Waller and Ferdinando, Lord Fairfax from

April, Newcastle meets Margaret Lucas in Paris. They are married towards the end of the year.

1645   their commands engineered by
the Self-Denying Ordinance.
New Model Army formed
under Fairfax and Cromwell.
June, Charles defeated at
Battle of Naseby, fought
against Rupert's better
judgement.
July, New Model Army
defeats Goring at Langport in
Somerset.
September, Prince Rupert
surrenders Bristol.
October, Charles and Rupert
both at Newark, quarrelling.
Montrose and Scottish royalists
defeated at Philiphaugh.
November, Charles back in
Oxford.

May, Ann Fanshawe leaves
Oxford to join her husband.
Royalists capture fort at the
Trent bridges outside
Nottingham.

July, the Fanshawes move to
to Barnstaple, then Truro and
Penzance, with the Prince of
Wales.

November, Colonel Hutchin-
son takes Shelford Manor and
Wiverton House in Notts.
Lord Bellasis replaces Sir
Richard Willis as Governor of
Newark. Scots army arrives
outside Newark.

1646

January, Belvoir Castle, south
of Newark, falls to the
parliamentarians.
March, Colonel Hutchinson
elected M P for Nottinghamshire.

April, after finally subduing
the West, Fairfax and the New
Model Army march on
Oxford.
May, Charles surrenders to
the Scottish army outside
Newark.
The end of the First Civil
War.

April, the Fanshawes accom-
pany the Prince of Wales to
the Scilly Isles and then to
Jersey.
May, Newark surrenders.
August, the Fanshawes go to
Caen in northern France and
then Ann Fanshawe crosses
back to London.

1647   *January*, Scots hand over
Charles to Parliament.

January, Richard Fanshawe
returns to London and com-
pounds for his estates. He

1647   *June*, the Army seizes Charles and he is transferred to Hampton Court.
August, Ireton's Heads of Proposals, an attempt to agree a compromise with the king.
November, Charles allowed to escape but soon re-imprisoned on Isle of Wight.
December, Charles signs secret treaty with the Scots.

publishes his translation of *Il Pastor Fido* by Guarini, together with poems by himself.
August, Anne Halkett's mother dies.
September, the Fanshawes visit Charles at Hampton Court.
October, the Fanshawes go to Paris, carrying letters for Henrietta Maria.

1648   *February*, Second Civil War starts.
June, part of the fleet goes over to the royalists and sails for Holland.
August, Scots army under the Duke of Hamilton defeated by Cromwell at Preston.

December, Pride's Purge, the exclusion of the more moderate, Presbyterian, M Ps from the House of Commons by the army.

April, the Fanshawes return to England. Anne Halkett helps Duke of York to escape from St James's Palace.

August, Colchester surrenders to Lord Fairfax who then executes Sir Charles Lucas, the Duchess of Newcastle's brother.
December, the Fanshawes return to Paris. Sir Robert Harley, and his sons Edward and Robert Harley, among those M Ps excluded by Pride's Purge.

1649   *January*, execution of Charles I.

August, Cromwell arrives to subdue Ireland.
October, the royalist fleet under Prince Rupert escapes from Kinsale in southern Ireland to Portugal.

January, Colonel Hutchinson signs Charles I's death warrant. He becomes a member of the Council of State. Ann Fanshawe goes to London.
February, Richard Fanshawe goes to Ireland as Treasurer for the royalist fleet.
May, Ann Fanshawe goes to Cork.
October, Cork declares for Parliament and Ann Fanshawe flees.
November, the Fanshawes in Limerick.

1650

June, Charles II lands in Scotland.

January, the Fanshawes in Galway.
April, the Fanshawes sail for Spain.
August, the Fanshawes leave Madrid.

September, Cromwell defeats Scottish Covenanters' army supporting Charles II at Dunbar.

September, Anne Halkett tends wounded Scottish soldiers from the Battle of Dunbar.
November, the Fanshawes reach Paris.

1651

Ann Fanshawe goes to London and Richard Fanshawe goes to join Charles II in Scotland. Colonel Hutchinson no longer a member of the Council of State and lives in retirement at Owthorpe until 1659.

September, Charles II and his Scottish army defeated by Cromwell at the Battle of Worcester.

September, Richard Fanshawe captured after Battle of Worcester and imprisoned in Whitehall.
November, Richard Fanshawe released on bail. Alice Wandesford marries William Thornton in Yorkshire.

1652   *May*, First Dutch War starts.

Duchess of Newcastle visits London to help Sir Charles Cavendish try and raise money on his brother the duke's estates.

1653   *April*, Cromwell forcibly dissolves Parliament.
July–December, Barebones Parliament.
Cromwell takes title of Lord Protector.

The Fanshawes live in Yorkshire.
The Duchess of Newcastle returns to Antwerp.

1654	Peace with Holland. *September–January*, first Protectorate Parliament.	The Fanshawes in Huntingdonshire.
1655	Rule of the Major-Generals.	The Fanshawes in London. Richard's translation of Camoens's *The Lusiads*, from the Portuguese, is published.
1656	*September*, second Protectorate Parliament.	*Nature's Pictures*, containing her short autobiography, is published by the Duchess of Newcastle. *March*, Anne Murray marries Sir James Halkett as his second wife and goes to live in Scotland. *November*, Brilliana Harley's husband, Sir Robert, dies.
1658	*September*, Cromwell dies.	Richard Fanshawe allowed to go abroad.
1659		Colonel Hutchinson becomes Sheriff of Nottinghamshire under Richard Cromwell. Ann Fanshawe forges a pass to join her husband. Colonel Hutchinson resumes seat in 'Rump' of Long Parliament and sides with Monk against Lambert.
1660	*May*, Charles II lands in England.	*April*, Colonel Hutchinson elected to the Convention Parliament that invites Charles II over.
1661		Richard Fanshawe MP for Cambridge University. Sent to Portugal to arrange marriage of Charles II with Catherine of Braganza.

Maps

THE

IRISH

SEA

THE ENGLISH CHANNEL

Battle sites with
dates, thus
1643

0 10 20 30 40 50
miles

Dunbar
1650

Philiphaugh
1645

Newcastle

Marston Moor
1644

1648
Preston

York

Seacroft
Moor
1643

Hull

Adwalton
Moor
1643

Chester

Winceby
1643

Nantwich
1644

Newark

Nottingham

1643, 1644
Brampton
Bryan

Leicester

Naseby 1645

Ely

Worcester
1651

Edgehill 1642

Gloucester
1643

Cropredy Bridge
1644

Colchester
1648

Oxford

Bristol

1643
Lansdown

LONDON

Langport
1645

Roundway
Down
1643

Newbury
1643, 1644

Lyme Regis
1644

Lostwithiel
1642 1644

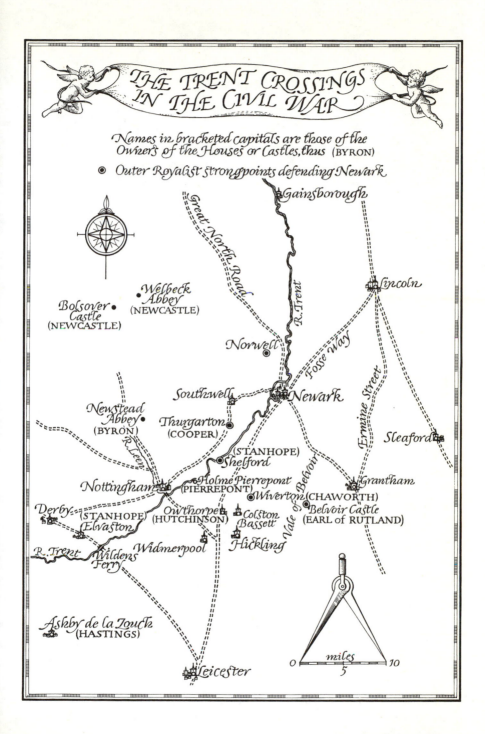

THE TRENT CROSSINGS IN THE CIVIL WAR

Names in bracketed capitals are those of the Owners of the Houses or Castles, thus (BYRON)

⊚ Outer Royalist strongpoints defending Newark

Gainsborough

Great North Road

R. Trent

Lincoln

Welbeck Abbey (NEWCASTLE)

Bolsover Castle (NEWCASTLE)

Norwell

Fosse Way

Southwell

Newark

Newstead Abbey (BYRON)

Thurgarton (COOPER)

Ermine Street

Sleaford

R. Leen

(STANHOPE) Shelford

Nottingham

Holme Pierrepont (PIERREPONT)

Wiverton (CHAWORTH)

Grantham

Derby

(STANHOPE) Elvaston

Owthorpe (HUTCHINSON)

Colston Bassett

Belvoir Castle (EARL of RUTLAND)

Vale of Belvoir

R. Trent

Wildens Ferry

Widmerpool

Hickling

Ashby de la Zouch (HASTINGS)

Leicester

0   miles   10
      5

The Grand Quarrel

The Ladies' Upbringing

Five out of the six ladies have left accounts of their upbringing. Brilliana Harley's is the missing one, she being much older than the others and in any case leaving behind letters to her son rather than a memoir recalling her past. There are no surprises in the descriptions they give of their education and of what were considered the accomplishments suitable for young ladies in the 1630s. Lucy Hutchinson, the only parliamentarian apart from Brilliana Harley, has no monopoly when it comes to piety and regular church-going. Both Margaret Newcastle and Anne Halkett mention Spring Garden in London as a fashionable place of resort. It was in the south-west corner of what is now Trafalgar Square, attached to St James's Park. One wonders how much the tight-knit circle of the Lucas family contributed to the crippling shyness that afflicted Margaret Newcastle in later life.

Lucy Hutchinson's (Apsley's) paternal grandfather was a gentleman 'of a competent estate' in Sussex, member of a cadet branch of the Apsleys of Apsley 'where they had been seated before the Conquest'. Her father was the youngest of seven sons and 'got a place in the household of Queen Elizabeth'. He went on the Earl of Essex's expedition against Cadiz in 1596 and then to Ireland; married twice and then under James I became Victualler to the Navy.

Her mother was of the noble St John family. She came under the influence of a French Calvinist minister when in Jersey, where 'she was instructed in their Geneva discipline, which she liked so much better than our more superstitious service'. She married the forty-eight-year-old widower Sir Allen Apsley in 1615, and two years later he was appointed Lieutenant of the Tower of London.

Lucy Hutchinson

He was a father to all his prisoners, sweetening with such compassionate kindness their restraint, that the affliction of a prison was not felt in his days. He had a singular kindness for all persons that were eminent either in learning or arms, and when, through the ingratitude and vice of that age, many of the wives and children of Queen Elizabeth's glorious captains were reduced to poverty, his purse was their common treasury, and they knew not the inconvenience of decayed fortunes till he was dead. Many of those valiant seamen he maintained in prison, many he redeemed out of prison, and cherished with an extraordinary bounty. He was severe in the regulating of his family, especially would not endure the least immodest behaviour or dress in any woman under his roof. There was nothing he hated more than an insignificant gallant, that could only make his legs and preen himself, and court a lady, but had not brains to employ himself in things more suitable to man's nobler sex. Fidelity in his trust, love and loyalty to his prince, were not the least of his virtues, but those wherein he was not excelled by any of his own or succeeding times. The large estate he reaped by his happy industry, he did many times over as freely resign again to the king's service, till he left the greatest part of it at his death in the king's hands.

Never did any two better agree in magnanimity and bounty than he and my mother, who seemed to be actuated by the same soul, so little did she grudge any of his liberalities to strangers, or he contradict any of her kindness to all her relations; her house being a common home to all of them, and a nursery to their children. He gave her a noble allowance of £300 a year for her own private expense, and had given her all her own portion [dowry] to dispose of how she pleased, as soon as she was married; which she suffered to increase in her friends' hands. What my father allowed her she spent not in vanities, although she had what was rich and requisite upon occasions, but she laid most of it out in pious and charitable uses. Sir Walter Raleigh and Mr Ruthven* being prisoners in the Tower, and addicting themselves to chemistry, she suffered them to make their rare experiments at her cost, partly to comfort and divert the poor prisoners, and partly to gain the knowledge of their experiments, and the medicines to help such poor people as were not able to seek physicians. By these means she acquired a great deal of skill, which was very profitable to many all her life. She was not only to these, but to all the other prisoners that came into the Tower, as a mother.

All the time she dwelt in the Tower, if any were sick she made them broths and restoratives with her own hands, visited and took care of them, and provided them all necessaries; if any were afflicted she comforted them, so that they felt not the inconvenience of a prison who were in that place. She was not less bountiful to many poor widows and orphans, whom officers of higher and lower rank had left behind them as objects of charity. Her own house was filled with distressed families of her relations, whom she supplied and maintained in a noble way. The worship and service of God, both in her soul and her house, and the education of her children, were her principal care. She was a constant frequenter of weekday lectures, and a great lover and encourager of good ministers, and most diligent in her private reading and devotions.

After my mother had had three sons, she was very desirous of a daughter, and when the women at my birth told her I was one, she received me with a great deal of joy; and the nurses fancying, because I had more complexion and favour than is usual in so young children, that I should not live, my mother became fonder of me, and more endeavoured to nurse me. As soon as I was weaned a French woman was taken to be my

---

* Patrick Ruthven had fled to England from Scotland after the Gowrie Conspiracy against James I in 1600, in which his brother the 3rd Earl of Gowrie was killed. James ordered Ruthven's arrest and imprisonment in the Tower when he succeeded to the English throne in 1603.

dry-nurse, and I was taught to speak French and English together. The time of my coming into the world was a considerable mercy to me. It was not in the midnight of popery, nor in the dawn of the gospel's restored day, when light and shades were blended and almost undistinguished, but when the sun of truth was exalted in his progress, and hastening towards a meridian glory.

My father and mother fancying me then beautiful, and more than ordinarily apprehensive, applied all their cares, and spared no cost to improve me in my education, which procured me the admiration of those that flattered my parents. By the time I was four years old I read English perfectly, and having a great memory, I was carried to sermons; and while I was very young could remember and repeat them exactly, and being caressed, the love of praise tickled me, and made me attend more heedfully. When I was about seven years of age, I remember I had at one time eight tutors in several qualities, languages, music, dancing, writing, and needlework; but my genius was quite averse from all but my book, and that I was so eager of, that my mother thinking it prejudiced my health, would moderate me in it. Yet this rather animated me than kept me back, and every moment I could steal from my play I would employ in any book I could find, when my own were locked up from me. After dinner and supper I still had an hour allowed me to play, and then I would steal into some hole or other to read. My father would have me learn Latin, and I was so apt that I outstripped my brothers who were at school, although my father's chaplain, that was my tutor, was a pitiful dull fellow.

My brothers, who had a great deal of wit, had some emulation at the progress I made in my learning, which very well pleased my father; though my mother would have been contented if I had not so wholly addicted myself to that as to neglect my other qualities. As for music and dancing, I profited very little in them, and would never practise my lute or harpsichords but when my masters were with me; and for my needle I absolutely hated it. Play among other children I despised, and when I was forced to entertain such as came to visit me, I tired them with more grave instructions than their mothers, and plucked all their babies to pieces, and kept the children in such awe, that they were glad when I entertained myself with elder company. Living in the house with many persons that had a great deal of wit, and very profitable serious discourses being frequent at my father's table and in my mother's drawing-room, I was very attentive to all, and gathered up things that I would utter again, to great admiration of many that took my memory and imitation for wit.

It pleased God that, through the good instructions of my mother, and the sermons she carried me to, I was convinced that the knowledge of God was the most excellent study, and accordingly applied myself to it, and to practise as I was taught. I used to exhort my mother's maids much, and to turn their idle discourses to good subjects; but I thought, when I had done this on the Lord's day, and every day performed my due tasks of reading and praying, that then I was free to anything that was not sin; for I was not at that time convinced of the vanity of conversation which was not scandalously wicked. I thought it no sin to learn or hear witty songs and amorous sonnets or poems, and twenty things of that kind, wherein I was so apt that I became the confidante in all the loves that were managed among my mother's young women; and there was none of them but had many lovers, and some particular friends beloved above the rest.

The Duchess of Newcastle

We were bred virtuously, modestly, civilly, honourably, and on honest principles: as for plenty, we had not only for necessity, conveniency, and decency, but for delight and pleasure to a superfluity. 'Tis true we did not riot, but we lived orderly. As for our garments, my mother did not only delight to see us neat and cleanly, fine and gay, but rich and costly; maintaining us to the height of her estate, but not beyond it. We were so far from being in debt, before these wars, as we were rather beforehand with the world; buying all with ready money, not on the score. Although after my father's death the estate was divided between my mother and her sons, she lived not in a much lower condition than when my father lived. My mother might have increased her daughters' portions by a thrifty sparing, yet she chose to bestow it on our breeding, honest pleasures, and harmless delights, out of an opinion, that if she bred us with needy necessity, it might chance to create in us sharking qualities, mean thoughts, and base actions, which she knew my father, as well as herself, did abhor. Likewise we were bred tenderly, for my mother naturally did strive to please and delight her children, not to cross or torment them, terrifying them with threats, or lashing them with slavish whips.

My mother was of an heroic spirit, in suffering patiently where there is no remedy, or to be industrious where she thought she could help. She was of a grave behaviour, and had such a majestic grandeur, as it were continually hung about her, that it would strike a kind of an awe to the beholders, and command respect from the rudest. Though she would often complain that her family was too great for her weak management, and often pressed my brother to take it upon him, yet I observe she took a pleasure, and some little pride, in the governing thereof: she was very skilful in leases, and setting of lands, and court-keeping, ordering of stewards, and the like affairs. Neither my mother, nor brothers, before these wars, had ever any law-suits, but what an attorney dispatched in a term with small cost. She suffered not her servants either to be rude before us, or to domineer over us, which all vulgar servants are apt, and oft-times which some have leave to do; likewise she never suffered the vulgar serving-men to be in the nursery among the nurse-maids, lest their rude love-making might do unseemly actions, or speak unhandsome words.

As for tutors, although we had for all sorts of virtues [accomplishments], as singing, dancing, playing on music, reading, writing, working, and the like, yet we were not kept strictly thereto; they were rather for formality than benefit, for my mother cared not so much for our dancing and fiddling, singing and prating of several languages, as that we should be bred virtuously, modestly, civilly, honourably, and on honest principles.

Two of my three brothers were excellent soldiers, and martial discipliners, being practised therein, for though they might have lived upon their own estates very honourably, yet they rather chose to serve in the wars under the States of Holland, than to live idly at home in peace: my brother, Sir Thomas Lucas, there having a troop of horse; my brother, the youngest Sir Charles Lucas, serving therein. But he served the States not long, for after he had been at the siege and taking of some towns, he returned home again. My other brother, the Lord Lucas, who was heir to my father's estate, and as it were the father to take care of us all, is not less valiant than they were, although his skill in the discipline of war was not so much, being not bred therein, yet he had more skill in the use of the sword, and is more learned in other arts and sciences than they were, he being a great scholar, by reason he is given much to studious contemplation.

Their practice was, when they met together, to exercise themselves with fencing, wrestling, shooting, and suchlike exercises, for I observed they did seldom hawk or hunt, and very seldom or never dance, or play on music, saying it was too effeminate for masculine spirits. Neither had they skill, or did use to play, for aught I could hear, at cards or dice, or the like games, nor given to any vice, as I did know, unless to love a mistress were a crime. Not that I know any they had, but what report did say, and usually reports are false, at least exceed the truth.

As for the pastimes of my sisters when they were in the country, it was to read, work, walk, and discourse with each other; for though two of my three brothers were married, likewise, three of my four sisters, yet most of them lived with my mother, especially when she was at her country house, living most commonly at London half the year. When they were at London, they were dispersed into several houses of their own, yet for the most part they met every day, feasting each other like Job's children.

But to rehearse their recreations. Their customs were in

wintertime to go sometimes to plays, or to ride in their coaches
about the streets to see the concourse and recourse of people;
and in the springtime to visit the Spring Garden, Hyde Park,
and the like places; and sometimes they would have music, and
sup in barges upon the water. They did seldom make visits,
nor never went abroad with strangers in their company, but
only themselves in a flock together agreeing so well, that there
seemed but one mind amongst them.

Ann Fanshawe

I was born in London in the year 1625, on our Lady Day,
25th of March. My mother, being sick to death of a fever three
months after I was born, which was the occasion she gave me
suck no longer, her friends and servants, thought to all outward appearance that she was dead, and so lay almost two days
and a night.* But Dr Winston coming to comfort my father,
went into my mother's room and, looking earnestly on her face,
said she was 'so handsome, and now looks so lovely, I cannot
think she is dead'; and suddenly took a lancet out of his pocket
and with it cut the sole of her foot, which bled. Upon this, he
immediately caused her to be laid upon the bed again and to
be rubbed, and such means as she came to life, and opening
her eyes, saw two of her kinswomen stand by her, my Lady
Knollys and my Lady Russell, both with great wide sleeves, as
the fashion then was. She said, 'Did not you promise me
fifteen years, and are you come again?' Which they not understanding, persuaded her to keep her spirits quiet in that great
weakness wherein she then was. Some hours after she desired
my father and Dr Howlsworth might be left alone with her, to
whom she said, 'I will acquaint you, that during the time of
my trance I was in great quiet, but in a place I could neither
distinguish nor describe; but the sense of leaving my girl, who
is dearer to me than all my children, remained a trouble upon

* Ann's mother Margaret's maiden name was Fanshawe, her father being
Ann's husband Richard Fanshawe's great uncle.

my spirits. Suddenly I saw two by me, clothed in long white garments, and methought I fell down with my face in the dust. They asked why I was troubled in so great happiness. I replied, "O let me have the same grant given to Hezekiah, that I may live fifteen years, to see my daughter a woman": to which they answered, "It is done"; and then, at that instant, I awoke out of my trance.' Dr Howlsworth did affirm [at her funeral in July 1640], that that day she died made just fifteen years from that time. My dear mother was of excellent beauty and good understanding, a loving wife, and most tender mother; very pious, and charitable to that degree, that she relieved, besides the offals of the table, which she constantly gave to the poor, many with her own hand daily out of her purse, and dressed many wounds of miserable people, when she had health, and when that failed, as it did often, she caused her servants to supply that place.

She left behind her three sons, all much older than myself. I was the fourth and my sister Margaret the fifth. My father was a handsome gentleman of great natural parts, a great accomptant, of vast memory, an incomparable penman, of great integrity and service to his prince; had been a member of several Parliaments; a good husband and father, especially to me, who never can sufficiently praise God for him. He was born at Bemond, in Lancashire, the twelfth son of his father. He was placed with my Lord Treasurer Salisbury, then Secretary of State, who gave him a small place in the Custom House, to enable him for the employment. He being of good parts and capacity in some time raised himself, by God's help, to get a very great estate, for I have often heard him say that, besides his education, he never had but twenty marks, which his father gave him when he came to London, and that was all he ever had for a portion.

Now it is necessary to say something of my mother's education of me, which was with all the advantages that time afforded, both for working all sorts of fine works with my needle, and learning French, singing, lute, the virginals and dancing, and notwithstanding I learned as well as most did, yet was I wild to that degree, that the hours of my beloved recreation took up too much of my time, for I loved riding in the first place, running, and all active pastimes. In short, I was that which we graver people call a hoyting girl; but to be just to myself, I never did mischief to myself or people, nor one immodest word or action in my life, though skipping and activity was my delight. Upon my mother's death, I then began to reflect, and, as an offering to her memory, I flung away those little child-nesses that had formerly possessed me, and, by my father's command, took upon me charge of his house and family, which I so ordered by my excellent mother's example as found accept-ance in his sight. I was very well beloved by all our relations and my mother's friends, whom I paid a great respect to, and I ever was ambitious to keep the best company, which I have done, I thank God, all the days of my life. My father and mother were both great lovers and honourers of clergymen, but all of Cambridge. We lived in great plenty and hospitality, but no lavishness in the least, nor prodigality, and, I believe, my father never drank six glasses of wine in his life in one day.

Alice Thornton

It pleased God to give my dear mother, my two younger brothers, and myself a safe passage into Ireland about the year 1632, my father being there a year before, and my eldest brother George. In which place I enjoyed great easiness and comfort during my honoured father's life, having the fortunate opportunity in that time, and after when I stayed there, of the best education that kingdom could afford, having the advantage of society in the sweet and chaste company of the Earl of Strafford's daughters, the most virtuous Lady Anne, and the Lady Arabella Wentworth, learning those qualities with them which my father ordered, namely—the French language, to write and speak the same; singing; dancing; playing on the lute and theorbo;* learning such other accomplishments of

* A large double-necked lute.

working silks, gummework, sweetmeats, and other suitable housewifery, as, by my mother's virtuous provision and care, she brought me up in what was fit for her quality and my father's child. But above all things, I accounted it my chiefest happiness wherein I was trained in those pious, holy, and religious instructions, examples, admonitions, teachings, reproofs, and godly education, tending to the welfare and eternal happiness and salvation of my poor soul, which I received from both my honoured father and mother, with the examples of their chaste and sober, wise and prudent conversations in all things of this world.

Anne Halkett

My mother spared no expense in educating all her children. If I made not the advantage I might have done, it was my own fault and not my mother's, who paid masters for teaching my sister and me to write, speak French, play on the lute and virginals, and dance, and kept a gentlewoman to teach us all kinds of needlework, which shows I was not brought up in an idle life. But my mother's greatest care, and for which I shall ever owe to her memory the highest gratitude, was the great care she took that even from our infancy we were instructed never to neglect to begin and end the day with prayer, and orderly every morning to read the Bible, and ever to keep the church as often as there was occasion to meet there either for prayers or preaching. So that for many years together I was seldom or never absent from divine service at five o'clock in the morning in the summer and six o'clock in the winter till the usurped power put a restraint to that public worship so long owned and continued in the Church of England.

2

The Husbands' Early Years

After the ladies we must turn to the upbringing and early years of their menfolk. The Duchess of Newcastle's description of her husband begins with his education, examples of his 'natural wit and judgment' and personal habits, before she passes on to an account of the entertainments he laid on for Charles in the early 1630s. This was a calculated investment (of some £20,000) in the hope of being rewarded with a high court office in return, which eventually materialised when he was made Governor to the Prince of Wales in 1638. The arms and ammunition that as Lord Lieutenant he caused to be bought for Nottinghamshire were no doubt those that John Hutchinson was to prevent Newcastle's successor as Lord Lieutenant, the royalist Lord Newark, from seizing at the start of the Civil War (see pp. 48–50). The episode the duchess recounts from the First Bishops' War is symptomatic of that whole futile campaign.

In the accounts of John Hutchinson and Richard Fanshawe it is interesting to see the future parliamentarian and the royalist both looking towards public offices in the king's gift as a source of private income. John Hutchinson tried to get a post in Star Chamber, a court which his own wife called 'unjust and arbitrary'. Richard Fanshawe tried for the post of King's Remembrancer in the Court of Exchequer, a job once held by his father. Sir Robert Harley's Mastership of the Mint, secured for him by his father-in-law Secretary Conway in 1626, was worth nearly £500 a year, until he lost it as a result of his support of non-conformist ministers in 1635. To spend time at one of the Inns of Court (Lincoln's Inn, the Inner Temple, etc.) completing one's education after university was the normal procedure for the sons of those families that could afford it.

Brilliana Harley's letters to her eldest son Edward, newly gone up to Magdalen Hall, Oxford, are full of concern for his diet, wardrobe, health, and spiritual welfare—particularly the last. While imbued with the authentic puritan tone, they also show endearing evidence of more worldly concerns and pleasures—reading Don Quixote, *asking her son to search the Oxford shops for looking glasses and fruit dishes.*

The Duchess of Newcastle

His education was according to his birth; for as he was born a gentleman, so he was bred like a gentleman. To school-learning he never showed a great inclination; for though he was sent to the University, and was a student of St John's College in Cambridge, and had his tutors to instruct him, yet they could not persuade him to read or study much, he taking more delight in sports, than in learning. His father being a wise man, and seeing that his son had a good natural wit, and was of a very good disposition, suffered him to follow his own genius; whereas his other son Charles,* in whom he found a greater love and inclination to learning, he encouraged as much that way, as possibly he could.

One time it happened that a young gentleman, one of my lord's relations, had bought some land, at the same time when my lord had bought a singing-boy for £50, a horse for £50 and a dog for £2, which humour his father Sir Charles liked so well, that he was pleased to say, that if he should find his son to be so covetous, that he would buy land before he was twenty years of age, he would disinherit him. But above all the rest, my lord had a great inclination to the art of horsemanship

---

* 'A little, weak, crooked man, and nature having not adapted him for the Court nor Camp, he betook himself to the study of mathematics.' John Aubrey, *Brief Lives.*

and weapons, in which latter, his father Sir Charles, being a most ingenious and unparalleled master of that age, was his only tutor, and kept him also several masters in the art of horsemanship, and sent him to the Mews to Mons. Antoine, who was then accounted the best master in that art. But my lord's delight in those heroic exercises was such, that he soon became master thereof himself, which increased much his father's hopes of his future perfections.

Although my lord has not so much of scholarship and learning as his brother Sir Charles Cavendish had, yet he hath an excellent natural wit and judgment, and dives into the bottom of everything; as it is evidently apparent in the fore-mentioned art of horsemanship and weapons, which by his own ingenuity he has reformed and brought to such perfection, as never any one has done heretofore. Though he is no mathematician by art, yet he hath a very good mathematical brain, to demonstrate truth by natural reason, and is both a good natural and moral philosopher, not by reading philosophical books, but by his own natural understanding and observation, by which he hath found out many truths.

To pass by several other instances, I will but mention, that when my lord was at Paris, in his exile, it happened one time, that he discoursing with some of his friends, amongst whom was also that learned philosopher Hobbes, they began amongst the rest, to argue upon this subject, namely, whether it were possible to make man by art fly as birds do. When some of the company had delivered their opinion, that they thought it probable to be done by the help of artificial wings, my lord declared that he deemed it altogether impossible, and demonstrated it by this following reason. Man's arms are not set on his shoulders in the same manner as birds' wings are; for that part of the arm which joins to the shoulder, is in man placed inward, as towards the breast, but in birds outward, as toward the back. This difference and contrary position or shape, hinders so that man cannot have the same flying-action with his arms, as birds have with their wings; which argument Mr Hobbes liked so well, that he was pleased to make use of it in one of his books called *Leviathan*, if I remember well.

Some other time they falling into a discourse concerning witches, Mr Hobbes said, that though he could not rationally believe there were witches, yet he could not be fully satisfied to believe there were none, by reason they would themselves confess it, if strictly examined.

To which my lord answered, that though for his part he cared not whether there were witches or no, yet his opinion was, that the confession of witches, and their suffering for it, proceeded from an erroneous belief, that they had made a contract with the Devil to serve him for such rewards as were in his power to give them. It was their religion to worship and adore him, in which religion they had such a firm and constant belief, that if anything came to pass according to their desire, they believed the Devil had heard their prayers, and granted their requests, for which they gave him thanks. But if things fell out contrary to their prayers and desires, then they were troubled at it, fearing they had offended him, or not served him as they ought, and asked him forgiveness for their offences. Also (said my lord) they imagine that their dreams are real exterior actions; for example, if they dream they fly in the air, or out of the chimney top, or that they are turned into several shapes, they believe no otherwise, but that it is really so. This wicked opinion makes them industrious to perform such ceremonies to the Devil, that they adore and worship him as their God, and choose to live and die for him. Thus my lord declared himself concerning witches, which Mr Hobbes was also pleased to insert in his fore-mentioned book.

My lord's discourse is as free and unconcerned, as his behaviour, pleasant, witty, and instructive. He is quick in repartees or sudden answers, and hates dubious disputes, and premeditated speeches. He loves also to intermingle his discourse with some short pleasant stories, and witty sayings, and always names the author from whom he hath them; for he hates to make another man's wit his own.

He accouters [dresses] his person according to the fashion, if it be one that is not troublesome and uneasy for men of heroic exercises and actions. He is neat and cleanly, which makes him to be somewhat long in dressing, though not so long as many effeminate persons are. He shifts [changes his linen] ordinarily once a day, and every time when he uses exercise, or his temper is more hot than ordinary.

In his diet he is so sparing and temperate, that he never eats nor drinks beyond his set proportion, so as to satisfy only his natural appetite. He makes but one meal a day, at which he drinks two good glasses of small-beer, one about the beginning, the other at the end thereof, and a little glass of sack in the middle of his dinner; which glass of sack he also uses in the morning for his breakfast, with a morsel of bread. His supper consists of an egg, and a draught of small-beer. And by this temperance he finds himself very healthful, and may yet live many years, he being now of the age of seventy-three, which I pray God from my soul, to grant him.

When His Majesty was going into Scotland to be crowned, he took his way through Nottinghamshire; and lying at Worksop Manor, hardly two miles distant from Welbeck, where my lord then was, my lord invited His Majesty thither to a dinner, which he was graciously pleased to accept of. This entertainment cost my lord between four and five thousand pounds. His Majesty liked it so well, that a year after his return out of Scotland, he was pleased to send my lord word, that Her Majesty the Queen was resolved to make a progress into the northern parts, desiring him to prepare the like entertainment for her, as he had formerly done for him. This my lord did, and endeavoured for it with all possible care and industry, sparing nothing that might add splendour to that feast, which both Their Majesties were pleased to honour with their presence. Ben Jonson he employed in fitting such scenes and speeches as he could best devise; and sent for all the gentry of the country to come and wait on Their Majesties; and in short, did all that ever he could imagine, to render it great, and worthy their royal acceptance.

This entertainment he made at Bolsover Castle in Derbyshire, some five miles distant from Welbeck, and resigned Welbeck for Their Majesties' lodging; it cost him in all between fourteen and fifteen thousand pounds.

Besides these two, there was another small entertainment

which my lord prepared for His late Majesty, in his own park at Welbeck, when His Majesty came down, with his two nephews, the now Prince Elector Palatine, and his brother Prince Rupert, into the Forest of Sherwood; which cost him fifteen hundred pounds.

Not long after his being made Lord Lieutenant of Nottinghamshire, there was found so great a defect of arms and ammunition in that county, that the Lords of the Council being advertised thereof, as the manner then was, His Majesty commanded a levy to be made upon the whole county for the supply thereof. Whereupon the sum of £500 or thereabout, was accordingly levied for that purpose, and three persons of quality, then deputy lieutenants, were desired by my lord to receive the money, and see it disposed. This being done accordingly, and a certain account rendered to my lord, he voluntarily ordered the then Clerk of the Peace of that county, that the same account should be recorded amongst the Sessions Rolls, and be published in open sessions, to the end that the county might take notice how their monies were disposed of, for which act of justice my lord was highly commended.

In the year 1638, His Majesty called him up to court, and thought him the fittest person whom he might entrust with the government of his son Charles, then Prince of Wales, and made him withal a Member of the Lords of His Majesty's most honourable Privy Council. As it was a great honour and trust, so he spared no care and industry to discharge his duty accordingly; and to that end, left all the care of governing his own family and estate, with all fidelity attending his master not without considerable charges, and vast expenses of his own.

In this present employment he continued for the space of three years, during which time there happened an insurrection and rebellion of His Majesty's discontented subjects in Scotland, which forced His Majesty to raise an army, to reduce them to their obedience. His treasury being at that time exhausted he was necessitated to desire some supply and assistance of the noblest and richest of his loyal subjects; amongst the rest, my lord lent His Majesty £10,000 and raised himself a volunteer troop of horse. This consisted of 120 knights and gentlemen of quality, who marched to Berwick by His Majesty's command, where it pleased His Majesty to set this mark of honour upon that troop, that it should be independent, and not commanded by any general officer, but only by His Majesty himself; the reason thereof was upon this following occasion.

His Majesty's whole body of horse, being commanded to march into Scotland against the rebels, a place was appointed for their rendezvous. Immediately upon their meeting, my lord sent a gentleman of quality of his troop to His Majesty's then General of the Horse [the Earl of Holland, see p. 143], to know where his troop should march; who returned this answer, that it was to march next after the troops of the general officers of the field. My lord conceiving that his troop ought to march in the van, and not in the rear, sent the same messenger back again to the general, to inform him that he had the honour to march with the prince's colours, and therefore he thought it not fit to march under any of the officers of the field; yet nevertheless the general ordered that troop as he had formerly directed. Whereupon, my lord thinking it unfit at that time to dispute the business, immediately commanded his cornet to take off the prince's colours from his staff, and so marched in the place appointed, choosing rather to march without his colours flying, than to lessen his master's dignity by the command of any subject.

Immediately after the return from that expedition the general made a complaint thereof to His Majesty; who being truly informed of the business, commended my lord's discretion for it, and from that time ordered that troop to be commanded by none but himself.

At last when the whole army was disbanded, then, and not before, my lord thought it a fit time to exact an account from the said general for the affront he passed upon him, and sent him a challenge. The place and hour being appointed by both their consents, where and when to meet, my lord appeared there with his second, but found not his opposite. After some while his opposite's second came all alone, by whom my lord perceived that their design had been discovered to the king by some of his opposite's friends, who presently caused them both to be confined until he had made their peace.

Lucy Hutchinson

John Hutchinson was the eldest surviving son of Sir Thomas Hutchinson and the Lady Margaret, his first wife, one of the daughters of Sir John Byron, of Newstead in Nottinghamshire. The Hutchinsons have been in the same county for generations;* though none of them before Sir Thomas advanced beyond an esquire, yet they successively matched into all the most eminent and noble families in the country. I spoke with one old man who had known five generations of them in these parts, where their hospitality, their love to their country, their plain and honest conversation with all men, their generous and unambitious inclinations, had made the family continue as well beloved and reputed as any of the prouder houses in the country.

Sir Thomas Hutchinson, as I have heard, was not above eight years of age when his father died, and his wardship fell into the hands of an unworthy person, Sir Germaine Poole, who did him so many injuries, that he was fain, after he came of age, to have suits with him. This so raised the malice of the wicked man that he watched an opportunity to assassinate him unawares, and as Sir Thomas was landing out of a boat at the Temple Stairs in London, Poole having on a private coat, with some wicked assistants, before he was aware, gave him some cuts on the head and his left hand that was upon the boat; but he full of courage drew his sword, run at Poole and broke his weapon, which could not enter his false armour; whereupon he run into him, resolved not to be murdered without leaving some mark on the villain, and bit off his nose; and then, by the assistance God sent him of an honest waterman, being rescued,

* A Thomas Hutchinson bought Owthorpe in Nottinghamshire in 1523.

he was carried away so sorely wounded that his life was in some danger: but the fact being made public, his honourable carriage in it procured him a great deal of glory, and his adversary carried the mark of his shame to the grave.

After this, returning into the country, he there lived with very much love, honour, and repute; but having been tossed up and down in his youth, and interrupted in his studies, he grew into such an excessive humour for books, that he wholly addicted himself to them; and deeply engaging in school divinity, spent even his hours of meat and sleep among his books. When he was entered into this studious life, God took from him his dear wife, who left him only two weak children; and then being extremely afflicted for so deplorable a loss, he entertained his melancholy among the old fathers and schoolmen, instead of diverting it; and having furnished himself with the choicest library in that part of England, it drew to him all the learned and religious men thereabouts, who found better resolutions from him than from any of his books. Living constantly in the country, he could not be exempted from administering justice among them, which he did with such equity and wisdom, and was such a defender of the country's interest, that, without affecting it at all, he grew the most popular and most beloved man in the country, even to the envy of those prouder great ones that despised the common interest. What others sought, he could not shun, being still sought by the whole county, to be their representative, to which he was several times elected, and ever faithful to his trust and his country's interest, though never approving violence and faction. He was a man of a most moderate and wise spirit, but still so inclined to favour the oppressed saints and honest people of those times that, though he conformed to the government, the licentious and profane encroachers upon common native rights branded him with the reproach of the world, though the glory of good men—puritanism; yet notwithstanding he continued constant to the best interest, and died at London in the year 1643, a sitting member of that glorious Parliament that so generously attempted, and had almost effected, England's perfect liberty.

Mr John Hutchinson was born at Nottingham in the month of September in the year 1616. Two years and a half after this Mr George Hutchinson, his younger brother, was born at Owthorpe; and half a year after his birth the two children lost their mother, who died of a cold she had taken. As soon as she was dead, her brother, Sir John Byron, carried away Sir Thomas and John Hutchinson towards his own house, leaving George at his nurse's. But the horses of the coach being mettled, in the halfway between Owthorpe and Nottingham they ran away, overthrew it, and slightly hurt all that were in the coach; who all got out, one by one, except the maid that had the child in her arms, and she stayed as long as there was any hope of preventing the coach from being torn to pieces. But when she saw no stop could be given to the mad horses, she lapped him as close as she could in the mantle, and flung him as far as she could from the coach into the ploughed lands, whose furrows were at that time very soft. By the good providence of God the child, reserved to a more glorious death, had no apparent hurt.

When it was time for them to go to school, Sir Thomas sent his sons to the free school at Lincoln, where there was a master very famous for learning and piety, Mr Clarke. But he was such a supercilious pedant, and so conceited of his own pedantic forms, that he gave Mr Hutchinson a disgust of him, and he profited very little there. An advantage he did have at this school was that, there being very many gentlemen's sons there, an old Low Country soldier was entertained to train them in arms, and they all bought themselves weapons. Instead of childish sports, when they were not at their books, they exercised in all their military postures and in assaults and defences; which instruction was not useless a few years after, to some of them.

Mr Hutchinson was removed from Lincoln to the free school at Nottingham, where his father married a second wife, and for a while went up to London with her, leaving his son at board in a very religious house, where new superstitions and pharisaical holiness, straining at gnats and swallowing camels, gave him a little disgust. It was for a while a stumbling block in his way of purer profession, when he saw among professors such unsuitable miscarriages. [Later,] the familiar kindness [of a new] schoolmaster made him now to love that which the other's austerity made him loathe, and in a year's time he advanced exceedingly in learning and was sent to Cambridge. He was made a fellow-commoner of Peterhouse and betook himself with such delight to his studies that he attained to a great height of learning, performed public exercises in his college with much applause, and upon their importunity took a degree in the University; whereof he was at that time the grace, there not being any gentleman in the town that lived with such regularity in himself, and such general love and good esteem of all persons as he did. He kept not company with any of the vain young persons, but with the graver men, and those by whose conversation he might gain improvement. He was constant at their chapel, where he began to take notice of their stretching superstition to idolatry; and was courted much into a more solemn practice of it than he could admit, though as yet he considered not the emptiness and carnality, to say no more, of that public service which was then in use. For his exercise he practised tennis, and played admirably well at it; for his diversion, he chose music, and got a very good hand, which afterwards he improved to a great mastery on the viol. There were masters that taught to dance and vault, whom he practised with, being very agile and apt for all such becoming exercises. His father stinted not his expense, which the bounty of his mind made pretty large, for he was very liberal to his tutors and servitors, and to the meaner officers of the house. He was enticed to bow to their great idol, learning, and had a higher veneration for it a longer time than can strictly be allowed; yet he then looked upon it as a handmaid to devotion, and as the great improver of natural reason. His tutor and the masters that governed the college while he was there, were of Arminian [high-church] principles, and that college was noted above all for popish superstitious practices; yet through the grace of God, notwithstanding the mutual kindness the whole household had for him and he for them, he came away, after five years' study there, untainted with those principles or practices, though not yet enlightened to discern the spring of them in the rites and usages of the English church.*

When he came from the University, he was about twenty years of age, and returned to his father's house, who had now settled his habitation at Nottingham; but he there enjoyed no great delight, another brood of children springing up in the house, and the servants endeavouring with tales and flatteries to sow dissension on both sides. Therefore, having a great reverence for his father, and being not willing to disturb him with complaints, as soon as he could obtain his leave he went to London. There, he was admitted of Lincoln's Inn, where he was soon coveted into the acquaintance of some gentlemen of the house. But he found them so frothy and so vain, and could so ill centre with them in their delights, that the town began to be tedious to him. He tried a little the study of the law, but finding it unpleasant and contrary to his genius, and the plague that spring beginning to drive people out of town, he began to think of leaving it, but had no inclination to return home. While he was in this deliberation, his music master came in and told him to go to Richmond, where the Prince of Wales's court was. He had a house there where he might be accommodated, and there was very good company and recreations, the king's hawks being kept near the place, and several other conveniences. Mr Hutchinson resolved to accept his offer, and went to Richmond where he found a great deal of good young company. The man being a skilful composer in music, the rest of the king's musicians often met at his house to practise new airs.

In the same house there was a young daughter of Sir Allen Apsley, tabled [boarding] for the practice of her lute, staying till the return of her mother who was gone into Wiltshire for

---

* There is no exaggeration in Lucy Hutchinson's characterisation of her husband's college. High Anglicanism at this time essentially derived from Cambridge and, within the University, Peterhouse led the way. Its new chapel was designed for worship in this style, harking back to Catholic practices. John Hutchinson's emergence from Peterhouse with his puritanism intact demonstrates that independence of mind which was his most pronounced characteristic.

the accomplishment of a treaty about the marriage of her elder daughter with a gentleman of that country. This gentlewoman, that was left in the house with Mr Hutchinson, was a very child, her elder sister being at that time scarcely passed it; but a child of such pleasantness and vivacity of spirit, and ingenuity in the quality she practised, that Mr Hutchinson took pleasure in hearing her practise, and would fall in discourse with her. She having the keys of her mother's house, some half a mile distant, would sometimes ask Mr Hutchinson, when she went over, to walk along with her. One day when he was there, looking upon an odd by-shelf in her sister's closet, he found a few Latin books; asking whose they were, he was told they were her elder sister's; whereupon, enquiring more after her, he began first to be sorry she was gone, before he had seen her, and gone upon such an account that he was not likely to see her. Then he grew to love to hear mention of her, and the other gentlewomen who had been her companions used to talk much to him of her, telling him how reserved and studious she was, and other things which they esteemed no advantage. But it so much inflamed Mr Hutchinson's desire of seeing her, that he began to wonder at himself, that his heart, which had ever entertained so much indifference for the most excellent of womankind, should have such strong impulses towards a stranger he never saw.

Lucy Hutchinson continues with the story of her husband's growing infatuation for herself, until finally he met her.

She was not ugly in a careless riding-habit; she had a melancholy negligence both of herself and others, as if she neither affected to please others, nor took notice of anything before her. Yet, in spite of her indifference, she was surprised in some unusual liking in her soul when she saw this gentleman. The next day, to his joy he found that she was wholly disengaged from that treaty which he so much feared had been accomplished; he found withal that though she was modest, she was accostable, and willing to enter his acquaintance. He daily frequented her mother's house, and had the opportunity of conversing with her in those pleasant walks which, at that sweet season of the spring, invited all the neighbouring inhabitants to seek their joys. He prosecuted his love with so much discretion, duty, and honour, that at the length, through many difficulties, he accomplished his design.

The day that the friends on both sides met to conclude the marriage, she fell sick of the smallpox, which was in many ways a great trial upon him. First her life was almost in desperate hazard, and then the disease made her the most deformed person that could be seen for a great while after she recovered. Yet he was nothing troubled by it, but married her as soon as she was able to quit the chamber, when the priest and all that saw her were affrighted to look on her. God recompensed his justice and constancy by restoring her, though it was longer than ordinary before she recovered to be as well as before.

Four months were scarcely past after their marriage before he was in great danger of losing her, when she lost two children she had conceived by him. Soon after conceiving again she grew so sickly, that her indulgent mother and husband, for the advantage of her health, removed their dwelling out of the city, to a house they took in Enfield Chase, called the Blue House, where, upon the 3rd of September, 1639, she was brought to bed of two sons, whereof the elder he named after his own father, Thomas, the younger was called Edward, who both survived him. September, 1641, she brought him another son, called by his own name, John, who lived scarce six years, and was a very hopeful child, full of his father's vigour and spirit, but death soon nipped that blossom.

Mr Hutchinson employed his time in making an entrance upon the study of school divinity, wherein his father was the most eminent scholar of any gentleman in England, and had a most choice library, valued at a thousand pounds; which Mr Hutchinson, mistakingly expecting to be part of his inheritance, thought it would be very inglorious for him not to understand how to make use of his father's books. Having therefore gotten into the house with him an excellent scholar in that kind of learning, he for two years made it the whole employment of his time. The gentleman that assisted him he converted to a right belief in that great point of predestination, he having been before of the Arminian judgment. At that time, this great doctrine grew much out of fashion with the prelates, but was generally embraced by all religious and holy persons in the land.

It was a remarkable providence of God in his life, that must not be passed over without special notice, that he gave him these two years' leisure, and a heart so to employ it, before the noise of war and tumult came upon him. Yet about the year 1639, the thunder was heard afar off rattling in the troubled air, and even the most obscured woods were penetrated with some flashes, the forerunners of the dreadful storm which the next year was more apparent; but Mr Hutchinson was not yet awakened till it pleased God to deliver him from a danger into which he had run himself, had not mercy prevented him. His wife having already two sons, and being again with child, considered that it would be necessary to seek an augmentation of revenue, or retire into a cheaper country; and more inclining to the first, than to leave at once her mother, and all the rest of her dear relations, she had propounded to him to buy an office, which he was not of himself very inclinable to; but, to give her and her mother satisfaction, he hearkened to a motion that was made him in that kind.

Sir William Pennyman, who had married his cousin-german, a very worthy gentleman, who had great respect both for and from his father, had purchased the chief office in the Star Chamber; the gentleman who held the next to him was careless and debauched, and thereby a great hindrance of Sir William's profits, who apprehended that if he could get an honest man into that place, they might mutually much advantage each other; whereupon he persuaded Mr Hutchinson to buy the place, and offered him any terms, to go any share with him, or any way he could desire. Mr Hutchinson treated with the gentleman, came to a conclusion, went down into the country, provided the money, and came up again, thinking presently to enter into the office; but the gentleman that should have sold it, being of an uncertain humour, thought to make the benefit of another term before he sold his place; and it pleased God, in the mean time, that arbitrary court was, by the Parliament then sitting, taken away. Mr Hutchinson was very sensible of a peculiar providence to him herein, and resolved to adventure no more such hazards; but to retire to that place whither God seemed to have called him by giving him so good an interest there, and to study how he was to improve that talent. His wife went along with him, and about October 1641, they came to their house at Owthorpe.

Ann Fanshawe

He [Richard Fanshawe] was but seven years old when his father* died, and his mother, my lady, designed him for the law, having bred him first in Jesus College in Cambridge, from whence, being a most excellent Latinist, he was admitted into the Inner Temple; but it seemed so crabbed a study, and disagreeable to his inclinations, that he rather studied to obey his mother than to make any progress in the law. Upon the death of his mother, whom he dearly loved and honoured, he went into France to Paris. After a year's stay, he travelled to Madrid in Spain, there to learn that language. Having spent some years abroad, he returned to London, and gave so good an account of his travels, that he was about the year 1635 made Secretary of the Embassy, when my Lord Aston went ambassador [to Madrid]. Upon the return of the ambassador, your father was left resident until Sir Arthur Hopton went ambassador, and then he came home about the year 1637 or 1638.

After being here a year or two, and no preferment coming (Secretary Windebank calling him puritan, being his enemy, because himself was a papist), he was, by his elder brother, put into the place of the King's Remembrancer. But the war breaking out presently after, put an end to this design; for, being the king's sworn servant, he went to the king at Oxford, as well as his fellows, to avoid the fury of this madness of the people.

* Richard Fanshawe was the fifth and youngest son of Sir Henry Fanshawe, Kt., of Ware Park, Hertfordshire. He was born in 1608.

Brilliana Harley

2 November 1638: I earnestly desire you [Edward Harley] may have that wisdom, that from all the flowers of learning you may draw the honey and leave the rest. I am glad you find any that are good, where you are. I believe that there are but few noblemen's sons in Oxford; for now, for the most part they send their sons into France, when they are very young, there to be bred.

13 November 1638: I beseech the Lord to bless you with those choice blessings of his Spirit, which none but his dear elect are partakers of. I have sent you some juice of liquorice, which you may keep to make use of, if you should have a cold.

17 November 1638: I am glad you find a want of that ministry you did enjoy: labour to keep a fresh desire after the sincere milk of the word, and then in good time you shall enjoy that blessing again. My dear Ned, as you have been careful to choose your company, be so still, for pitch will not easily be touched without leaving some spot. I hope the news of the Swedes [fighting for the Protestant cause in the Thirty Years War] is not true. Great troubles and wars must be, both to purge his church of hypocrites and that his enemies at the last may be utterly destroyed. Yet I look with joy beyond those days of trouble, considering the glory that the Lord will bring his church to; and happy are they that shall live to see it, which I hope you will do. I heard that there was a cardinal's cap brought to the Custom House, valued at a high rate, but none would own it.

Undated: I have sent you by the carrier eight bottles of cider in a box. Pray send me one of your socks, to make you new ones by.

30 November 1638: I believe that indisposition you felt was caused by some violent exercise: if you use to swing, let it not be violently; for exercise should be rather to refresh than tire nature. You did well to take some balsam; it is a most sovereign thing, and I purpose, if please God, to write you the virtues of it. Dear Ned, if you would have anything, send me word; or if I thought a cold pie, or such a thing, would be of any pleasure to you, I would send it you. But your father says you care not for it, and Mrs Pierson tells me, when her son was at Oxford, and she sent him such things, he prayed her that she would not. I thank you for the *Man in the Moon*. I had heard of the book, but not seen it; by as much as I have looked upon, I find it is some kind of *Don Quixote*. I would willingly have the French book you write me word of; but if it can be had, I desire it in French, for I had rather read anything in that tongue than in English.

14 December 1638: I bless my God, for those good desires you have, and the comfort you find in the serving your God. Be confident, he is the best master, and will give the best wages, and they wear the best livery, the garment of holiness, a clothing which never shall wear out, but is renewed every day. Dear Ned, be careful to use exercise; and for that pain in your back, it may be caused by some indisposition of the kidneys. I would have you drink in the morning beer boiled with liquorice; it is a most excellent thing for the kidneys. Dear Ned, it is very well done, that you submit to your father's desire in your clothes; and that is a happy temper, both to be contented with plain clothes and, in the wearing of better clothes, not to think oneself the better for them, nor to be troubled if you be in plain clothes, and see others of your rank in better.

14 January 1639: None tastes of his love but his chosen ones; and if we be loved of the Lord, what need we care what the men of the world think of us? I believe, before this, you have read some part of Mr Calvin; send me word how you like him. I have sent you a little purse with some small money in it, all the pence I had, that you may have a penny to give a poor body, and a pair of gloves; not that I think you have not better in Oxford, but that you may sometimes remember her, that seldom has you out of my thoughts.

29 November 1639: If there be any good looking glasses in Oxford, choose me one about the bigness of that I use to dress me in, if you remember it. I put it to your choice, because I think you will choose one, that will make a true answer to one's face. All my fruit dishes are broken; therefore, good Ned, if there be any such blue and white dishes as I used to have for fruit, buy me some; they are not porcelain, nor are they of the ordinary metal of blue and white dishes. I see your sister has a new hood; it seems she lost hers and durst not tell, and so, as I guess, wrote to you for one, which I will pay you for. I have sent you my watch, and I believe it may be mended. I do willingly give you the ring of gold that was about the agate.

25 April 1640: I should be glad to hear from you a relation how the king went to Parliament [the Short Parliament] and at what ease you heard his speech; for I did fear there would be a great crowd, which made me desire your father not to be there. I hear your father had a fit of the [pastion?] of the heart, the day before you went from London. I beseech the Lord preserve him from them. Here is great pressing.* Mr Harberd is gone with his troop of horse; one of his soldiers killed a man in Shrewsbury, but they say he was provoked to it. They are gallant and merry. The trained band it is thought must go, or else provide men to go in their places. I cannot yet hear for certain where their rendezvous is.

I have sent you some violet cakes. Dear Ned, be careful of yourself, especially be watchful over your heart.

Edward Piner's children's bed was set on fire, and it was God's mercy they had not been smothered. Piner in putting it out, having none to help him but Phoebe, who is with his wife, took cold, for he was in his shirt, and the smoke almost took away his breath, that he is very ill, and I fear has a fever.

3 July 1640: The soldiers from Hereford were at Leominster last Thursday on their march to their rendezvous; the captain not paying them all their pay, they would have returned into

* Forcible recruitment of men for the army to fight the Scots in the Second Bishops' War.

the town again, but all the town rose, and those that were come out of church, with those arms they had, beat them back. But there being a great heap of stones out of town, the soldiers made use of them as long as they lasted. The townsmen did but little good, till that powder was spent, and then the townsmen were too hard; many were hurt on both sides. The captain would have come into the town, but was kept out.

December 1640: The last night I heard from your father. He saw Mr Prynne and Mr Burton come into London;* they were met with 2000 horse and 150 Scotch, and the men wore rosemary that met them. I have here sent you the seven articles against my Lord Strafford; your father sent them me. The Parliament goes on happily; I pray God continue it. I have sent your father a snipe pie and a teal pie, and a collar of brawn, or else I had sent you something this week.

March 1641: I am glad the bishops begin to fall and I hope it will be with them as it was with Haman;† when he began to fall, he fell indeed.

21 May 1641: I am glad justice is executed on my Lord Strafford, who I think died like a Seneca,‡ but not like one that had tasted the mystery of godliness.

5 June 1641: I much rejoice that it is come so far that the bishops and all their train is voted against. I trust in God they will be enacted against, which I long to hear, and I pray God take all those things away which have so long offended.

2 July 1641: I fear, as you do, that it will be August before

---

* They had been sentenced to have their ears cropped and then to be imprisoned, by the Court of Star Chamber in 1637, for libelling the bishops.
† Favourite of Ahasuerus and oppressor of the Jews, until Esther's accusation led to his execution. The story is told in the Book of Esther in the Old Testament.
‡ Tutor to the Emperor Nero who fell into disfavour and was ordered to commit suicide.

your father will have time to come down. I hope you will ride sometimes in Hyde Park to take the air.* I thank you for giving me some hope of the bishops' bill passing this week.

* By this time Edward Harley had joined his father in London.

The Approach of War
1641-2

The Irish Revolt and the accompanying massacre of Protestants in October 1641, which many thought presaged a similar Popish uprising in England; Parliament's passing of the Grand Remonstrance, in effect a vote of no confidence in Charles, the next month; and Charles's bungled attempt to arrest the five ringleaders amongst the Members of Parliament in January 1642—these three events drove an unbridgeable gap between the two sides. From now on the prime consideration for both was to raise troops and arm themselves for the coming war.

Here we see Newcastle sent on a special mission to try and secure Hull, with its big magazine, for Charles. When Newcastle failed, Charles did not give up, arriving himself outside the walls of the town in April. Sir John Hotham, the Governor of Hull (at this time faithful to Parliament but later executed for treachery), in Lucy Hutchinson's words 'kneeling upon the wall, entreated the king not to command that which, without breach of trust, he could not obey'. The king left humiliated, only to return in July with a besieging force. Sir John Meldrum, a professional Scottish soldier fighting for Parliament whom we will meet often in Lucy Hutchinson's account, sallied out from the town and drove them off.

Brilliana Harley, in her letter to her son in May 1642, gives us the first taste of that most tragic effect of civil war, when close relatives find themselves on opposing sides. Sir William Pelham of

Brocklesby in Lincolnshire, a widower after the death of her sister Frances, had gone off to join the king. Later Brilliana is arranging for the family plate and horses to be sent to London for the parliamentary cause. In return she is sent powder and muskets by her son and husband, but she has to buy her own lead shot via the plumber who happens to be mending the castle roof at the time. One sympathises with the note of long-suffering in Brilliana Harley's letters. She obviously felt somewhat abandoned by her husband, and yet he felt free to criticise her management of the estate in his absence.

Next year Sir Robert Harley distinguished himself as chairman of the parliamentary committee for 'the destruction of monuments of superstition and idolatry'. John Hutchinson's bit of iconoclasm in a local Nottinghamshire church is hard for us to square with Lucy's later account of his purchasing pictures from the royal collection after Charles's death. But he was certainly not in the same league as Sir Robert, who personally helped to smash statues and stained glass in Westminster Abbey and various royal chapels.

The picture that Lucy gives of the Hutchinsons and their home county in the early stages of the war underlines again the splits within families: meeting her cavalier brother Sir Allen Apsley when she is a refugee; using the good offices of her smart Villiers relation Lord Grandison to secure George Hutchinson's release; her husband's cousin Henry Ireton setting off on his career, which was to end with him second only to Cromwell in the Commonwealth and married to his daughter; the numerous Byron cousins of the Hutchinsons, 'all passionately the king's'. In this they were unlike the other major Nottinghamshire family, the Pierreponts. Its head, the Earl of Kingston, 'divided his sons between both parties and concealed himself'. All the time John Hutchinson was himself reluctant to take up arms formally, and only at the end of 1642 did he become a lieutenant-colonel.

The Duchess of Newcastle

My lord having hitherto attended the prince, his master, with all faithfulness and duty befitting so great an employment, for the space of three years, in the beginning of that rebellious and unhappy Parliament, which was the cause of all the ruins and misfortunes that afterwards befell this kingdom, was privately advertised, that the Parliament's design was to take the government of the prince from him, which he apprehending as a disgrace to himself, wisely prevented. He obtained the consent of His late Majesty, with his favour, to deliver up the charge of being governor to the prince, and retire into the country; which he did in the beginning of the year 1641. He settled himself, with his lady, children and family, to his great satisfaction, with an intent to have continued there, and rested under his own vine, and managed his own estate. He had not enjoyed himself long, but an express came to him from His Majesty [in January 1642], who was then unjustly and unmannerly treated by the said Parliament, to repair with all possible speed and privacy to Kingston upon Hull, where the greatest part of His Majesty's ammunition and arms then remained in that magazine, it being the most considerable place for strength in the northern parts of the kingdom.

Immediately upon the receipt of these orders and commands, my lord prepared for their execution, and about twelve of the clock at night, hastened from his own house when his family were all at their rest, save two or three servants which he appointed to attend him. The next day early in the morning he arrived at Hull, in the quality of a private gentleman, which place was distant from his house forty miles. None of his family that were at home, knew what was become of him, till he sent an express to his lady to inform her where he was.

Thus being admitted into the town, he fell upon his intended design, and brought it to so hopeful an issue for His Majesty's service, that he wanted nothing but His Majesty's further commission and pleasure to have secured both the town and magazine for His Majesty's use. By a speedy express he gave His

Majesty, who was then at Windsor, an account of all his transactions therein, together with his opinion of them, hoping His Majesty would have been pleased either to come thither in person, which he might have done with much security, or at least have sent him a commission and orders how he should do His Majesty further service. But instead thereof he received orders from His Majesty to observe such directions as he should receive from the Parliament then sitting. Whereupon he was summoned personally to appear at the House of Lords, and a committee chosen to examine the grounds and reasons of his undertaking that design; but my lord showed them his commission, and that it was done in obedience to His Majesty's commands, and so was cleared of that action.

Not long after, my lord obtained the freedom from His Majesty to retire again to his country life, which he did with much alacrity. He had not remained many months there, but His Majesty was forced by the fury of the said Parliament, to repair in person to York, and to send the queen beyond the seas for her safety.

No sooner was His Majesty arrived at York [in March 1642] but he sent his commands to my lord to come thither to him; which, according to his wonted custom and loyalty, he readily obeyed, and after a few days spent there in consultation, His Majesty was pleased to command him to Newcastle upon Tyne, to take upon him the government of that town, and the four counties next adjoining; that is to say, Northumberland, Cumberland, Westmorland, and the Bishopric of Durham. My lord did accordingly, although he wanted men, money and ammunition for the performance of that design; for when he came thither he neither found any military provision considerable for the undertaking that work, nor generally any great encouragement from the people in those parts, more than what his own interest created in them. Nevertheless, he thought it his duty rather to hazard all, than to neglect the commands of his sovereign. He resolved to show his fidelity, by nobly setting all at stake, as he did, though he well knew how to have secured himself, as too many others did, either by neutrality or adhering to the rebellious party; but his honour and loyalty was too great to be stained with such foul adherencies.

As soon as my lord came to Newcastle, in the first place he sent for all his tenants and friends in those parts, and presently raised a troop of horse consisting of 120, and a regiment of foot, and put them under command, and upon duty and exercise in the town of Newcastle. With this small beginning he took the government of that place upon him; where with the assistance of the townsmen, particularly the mayor and the rest of his brethren, within few days he fortified the town, and raised men daily, and put a garrison of soldiers into Tynemouth Castle, standing upon the River Tyne, betwixt Newcastle and the sea, to secure that port, and armed the soldiers as well as he could. Thus he stood upon his guard, and continued them upon duty; playing his weak game with much prudence, and giving the town and country very great satisfaction by his noble and honourable deportment. In the meantime, there happened a great mutiny of the trainband soldiers of the Bishopric at Durham, so that my lord was forced to remove thither in person, attended with some forces to appease them; where at his arrival (I mention it by the way, and as a merry passage) a jovial fellow used this expression, that he liked my lord very well, but not his company (meaning his soldiers).

My lord effected that which never any subject did, nor was (in all probability) able to do; for though many great and noble persons did also raise forces for His Majesty, yet they were brigades, rather than well-formed armies, in comparison to my lord's. The reason was, that my lord, by his mother, the daughter of Cuthbert, Lord Ogle, being allied to most of the most ancient families in Northumberland, and other the northern parts, could pretend a greater interest in them, than a stranger. They, through a natural affection to my lord as their own kinsman, would sooner follow him, and under his conduct sacrifice their lives for His Majesty's service, than anybody else, well knowing that by deserting my lord, they deserted themselves. By this means my lord raised an army of 8000 horse, foot and dragoons, in those parts. Afterwards upon this ground, at several times, and in several places, he raised so many several troops, regiments and armies, that in all from the first to the last, they amounted to above 100,000 men, and those most upon his own interest, and without any other considerable help or assistance; which was much for a particular subject, and in such a conjuncture of time.

Amongst the rest of his army, my lord had chosen for his own regiment of foot, 3000 of such valiant, stout and faithful men (whereof many were bred in the moorish grounds of the northern parts) that they were ready to die at my lord's feet, and never gave over, whensoever they were engaged in action, until they had either conquered the enemy, or lost their lives. They were called Whitecoats, for this following reason: my lord being resolved to give them new liveries, and there being not red cloth enough to be had, took up so much of white as would serve to clothe them, desiring withal, their patience until he had got it dyed; but they impatient of stay, requested my lord, that he would be pleased to let them have it un-dyed as it was, promising they themselves would dye it in the enemy's blood. Which request my lord granted them, and from that time they were called Whitecoats.

My lord received from Her Majesty the Queen, out of Holland, a small supply of money, *viz.* a little barrel of ducatoons, which amounted to about £500; which my lord distributed amongst the officers of his new raised army, to encourage them the better in their service; as also some arms, the most part whereof were consigned to His late Majesty. About the same time the King of Denmark was likewise pleased to send His Majesty a ship, which arrived at Newcastle, laden with some ammunition, arms, regiment pieces, and Danish clubs.*

* War-maces originally used by the Danes instead of swords.

Brilliana Harley

17 February 1642: In Hereford they have turned the table in the cathedral,* and taken away the copes and basins and all such things. I hope they begin to see that the Lord is about to purge his church of all such inventions of men.

23 April 1642: I am persuaded things are now come to their ripeness, and if God be not very merciful to us, we shall be in a distressed condition. Doctor Wright [a local puritan] desires you would do him the favour to buy him two muskets and rests and bandoleers,† and fifteen or sixteen pounds of powder in a barrel. He desires you would send them by the Leominster carrier.

29 April 1642: I see the distance is still kept between the king and Parliament. The Lord in his mercy make them one, and in his good time incline the king to be fully assured in the faithful counsel of the Parliament.

17 May 1642: This day I heard out of Lincolnshire. I thank God they are all well, but I see my brother [-in-law] Pelham is not of my mind. He writes me word that he has given up his lieutenancy and is going to York, to the king; being his servant, as he writes me word, and so bound by his oath. I think now my dear sister was taken away that she might not see that which would have grieved her heart.

4 June 1642: At Ludlow they set up a maypole, and a thing like a head upon it, and so they did at Croft, and gathered a great many about it, and shot at it in derision of roundheads. At Ludlow they abused Mr Bauge's son very much, and are so insolent that they durst not leave their house to come to the

* Puritans regarded the altar as a popish piece of equipment and substituted a plain communion table. They then went a step further, as here, and aligned it west–east rather than north–south within the church.
† A shoulder belt for ammunition.

fast. I acknowledge I do not think myself safe where I am. I lose the comfort of your father's company, and am in but little safety, but that my trust is in God. What is done in your father's estate pleases him not, so that I wish myself, with all my heart, at London, and then your father might be a witness of what is spent. But if your father think it best for me to be in the country, I am very well pleased with what he shall think best. I have sent you by this carrier, in a box, three shirts; there is another, but it was not quite made; one of them is not washed; I will, and please God, send you another the next week, and some handkerchiefs.

11 June 1642: Your father's horses could not be sold at the fair, therefore I think and please God, to send them up on Monday or Tuesday, when I hope to write to you more at large, for now I have deferred writing till it be late, that I might let you know how the fair went. I thank God hitherto it has passed quietly, but I was something afraid, because they are grown so insolent. I hope this night will be as quiet as the day has been.

17 June 1642: I doubt not but that your father will give to his utmost for the raising of the horse, and in my opinion it were better to borrow money, if your father will give any, than to give his plate. For we do not know what straits we may be put to, and therefore I think it is better to borrow whilst one may, and keep the plate for a time of need, without your father had so much plate, that he could part with some, and keep some to serve himself another time. This I do not say, that I am unwilling to part with the plate or anything else in this case; if your father cannot borrow money, I think I might find out some in the country to lend him some. Dear Ned, tell your father this, for I have not written to him about it.

20 June 1642: Since your father thinks Herefordshire as safe as any other country, I will think so too; but when I considered how long I had been from him, and how this country was affected, my desire to see your father, and my care to be in a place of safety, made me earnestly desire to come up to London. But since it is not your father's will, I will lay aside that desire.

This day Mr Davis came from Hereford, where he went to preach, by the entreaty of some in the town, and this befell him: when he had ended his prayer before the sermon, which he was short in, because he was loth to tire them, two men went out of the church and cried, 'pray God bless the king; this man does not pray for the king.' Upon which, before he read his text, he told them that ministers had that liberty, to pray before or after the sermon for the church and state. For all that, they went to the bells and rang, and a great many went into the churchyard and cried 'roundheads', and some said, 'let us cast stones at him!' He could not look out of doors, nor Mr Lane, but they cried 'roundhead'. In the afternoon they would not let him preach; so he went to the cathedral. Those that had any goodness were much troubled and wept much.

24 June 1642: I hope the horses are come well to your father: and by this carrier I purpose, and please God, to send the two pistols you write me word your father would have, and the gilt plate which he has sent for.

Mr William Littellton being at Ludlow last week, as he came out of the church, a man came to him and looked him in the face and cried 'roundhead'. He gave the fellow a good box of the ear, and stepped to one that had a cudgel and took it from him and beat him soundly. They say, they are now more quiet in Ludlow.

25 June 1642: Dear Ned—I love to write to you, and therefore, my dear Ned, be something glad to receive my letter. Sir William Croft* came to see me: he never asked how your father did; spoke slighty, and stayed but a little. I hear that he has commanded the beacon new furnished, and new pitch put into it. I have sent to enquire after it; if it be so, I will send your father word.

* Of Croft Castle, a local royalist.

2 July 1642: At first when I saw how outrageously this country carried themselves against your father, my anger was so up, and my sorrow, that I had hardly patience to stay. But now, I have well considered, if I go away I shall leave all that your father has to the prey of our enemies, which they would be glad of; so that, and please God, I purpose to stay as long as it is possible, if I live. This is my resolution, without your father contradict it. I have received this night the hamper with the powder and match,* but I have not yet the muskets, but will enquire after them.

5 July 1642: The reason why I send this bearer to your father is, to let him know that the king has sent a commission to twelve of the justices to settle the militia. I have written your father their names. I did not hear it till late this night. I heard it presently after dinner, but it was but a flying report. I pray God direct your father and the Parliament what to do, and I think, if any country had need of some to have been sent down into it, it is this. Your father they are grown to hate. I pray God forgive them. My dear Ned, I am not afraid, but sure I am, that we are a despised company.

8 July 1642: They go on with the militia in this country; the sheriff has sent out warrants that they appear on the 15th of this month at Hereford. Your father's company, I hear, they mean to make offer of to you, and if you will not have it, they will give it to another. They triumph bravely, as they say, and threaten poor Brampton; but we are in the hand of our God, who I hope will keep us safe.

9 July 1642: I have been so long in putting up the plate to send your father, that I have no time to write any more than that I long to see you. I am confident you are not troubled to see the plate go this way; for I trust in our gracious God, you will have the fruit of it. I do long almost to be from Brampton. In the hamper with the plate, I have sent your father a cake.

* Cord impregnated with some inflammable substance so, once lit, it kept smouldering. Used in matchlock muskets, the standard firearm of the Civil War.

15 July 1642: I have received the box with twenty bandoleers, but the boxes with the muskets and rests the carrier has left to come in a waggon to Worcester; he promises I shall have them shortly. I pray you tell your father, the reason why I did not send the trunk of plate by the Leominster carrier was, because the last I sent to Leominster, they said it was plate. But Bagly, that went with it, not knowing what it was, only I told him there was a cake in it, and so he told the carrier's wife.

17 July 1642: I sent Samuel to Hereford to observe their ways. He had come home last night, but that he had a fall from his horse and put out his shoulder. He tells me that they all at Hereford cried out against your father, and not one said anything for him, but one man, Mr Phillips of Ledbury said, when he heard them speak so against your father, 'Well,' said he, 'though Sir Robert Harley be low here, yet he is above, where he is.' My dear Ned, I cannot think I am safe at Brampton, and by no means I would have you come down. I should be very glad if your father could get some religious and discreet gentleman to come for a time to Brampton, that he might see sometimes what they do in the country. I trust the Lord will direct your father what way is best, and I doubt not that we shall pray, one for another.

19 July 1642: Had I not had this occasion to send to your father, yet I had sent this boy up to London. He is such a roguish boy that I dare not keep him in my house, and as little do I dare to let him go in this country, lest he join with the company of volunteers, or some other such crew. I have given him no more money than will serve to bear his charges up; and because I would have him make haste and be sure to go to London, I have told him that you will give him something for his pains, if he come to you in good time and do not loiter. Here enclosed I have sent you half a crown. Give him what you think fit, and I desire he may not come down any more, but that he may be persuaded to go to sea, or some other employment.

My cousin Davis tells me that none can make shot but those

whose trade it is, so I have made the plumber write to Worcester for fifty weight of shot. I sent to Worcester, because I would not have it known. If your father thinks that is not enough, I will send for more.

Lucy Hutchinson

Mr Hutchinson was of a middle stature, of a slender and exactly well-proportioned shape in all parts, his complexion fair, his hair of light brown, very thickset in his youth, softer than the finest silk, and curling into loose great rings at the ends; his eyes of a lively grey, well-shaped and full of life and vigour, graced with many becoming motions; his visage thin, his mouth well made, and his lips very ruddy and graceful, although the nether chap shut over the upper, yet it was in such a manner as was not unbecoming; his teeth were even and white as the purest ivory; his chin was something long, and the mould of his face; his forehead was not very high; his nose was raised and sharp; but withal he had a most amiable countenance, which carried in it something of magnanimity and majesty mixed with sweetness, that at the same time bespoke love and awe in all that saw him; his skin was smooth and white, his legs and feet excellently well-made; he was quick in his pace and turns, nimble and active and graceful in all his motions; he was apt for any bodily exercise, and any that he did became him; he could dance admirably well, but neither in youth nor riper years made any practice of it; he had skill in fencing, such as became a gentleman; he had a great love of music, and often diverted himself with a viol, on which he played masterly; and he had an exact ear and judgment in other music; he shot excellently in bows and guns, and much used them for his exercise; he had great judgement in paintings, graving, sculpture, and all liberal arts, and had many curiosities of value in all kinds; he took great delight in perspective glasses, and for his other rarities was not so much affected with the antiquity as the merit of the work; he took much pleasure in improvement of grounds,

in planting groves, and walks, and fruit-trees, in opening springs
and making fish-ponds; of country recreations he loved none
but hawking, and in that was very eager and much delighted
for the time he used it, but soon left it off; he was wonderfully
neat, cleanly, and genteel in his habit, and had a very good
fancy in it, but he left off very early the wearing of anything
that was costly, yet in his plainest negligent habit appeared
very much a gentleman; he had more address than force of
body, yet the courage of his soul so supplied his members that
he never wanted strength when he found occasion to employ it;
his conversation was very pleasant, for he was naturally cheerful, had a ready wit and apprehension; he was eager in everything he did, earnest in dispute, but withal very rational, so that
he was seldom overcome; everything that it was necessary for
him to do he did with delight, free and unconstrained; he hated
ceremonious compliment, but yet had a natural civility and
complaisance to all people; he was of a tender constitution, but
through the vivacity of his spirit could undergo labours, watch-
ings, and journeys, as well as any of stronger compositions; he
was rheumatic, and had a long sickness and distemper occasioned thereby, two or three years after the war ended, but else,
for the latter half of his life, was healthy though tender; in his
youth and childhood he was sickly, much troubled with weakness and toothaches, but then his spirits carried him through
them; he was very patient under sickness or pain, or any common accidents, but yet, upon occasions, though never without
just ones, he would be very angry, and had even in that such a
grace as made him to be feared, yet he was never outrageous in
passion; he had a very good faculty in persuading, and would
speak very well, pertinently, and effectually without premedita-
tion upon the greatest occasions that could be offered, for indeed, his judgment was so nice, that he could never frame any
speech beforehand to please himself; but his invention was so
ready, and wisdom so habitual in all his speeches, that he never
had reason to repent himself of speaking at any time without
ranking the words beforehand; he was not talkative, yet free of
discourse; of a very spare diet, not given to sleep, and an early
riser when in health; he never was at any time idle, and hated

to see any one else so; in all his natural and ordinary inclinations and composure, there was something extraordinary and tending to virtue, beyond what I can describe, or can be gathered from a bare dead description; there was a life of spirit and power in him that is not to be found in any copy drawn from him. To sum up, therefore, all that can be said of his outward frame and disposition, we must truly conclude, that it was a very handsome and well furnished lodging prepared for the reception of that prince, who in the administration of all excellent virtues reigned there a while, till he was called back to the palace of the universal emperor.

To take up my discourse of Mr Hutchinson where I left it: he was now come to his own house at Owthorpe, about the time when the Irish massacre was acted [October 1641], and finding humours begin to be very stirring, he applied himself to understand the things then in dispute, and read all the public papers that came forth between the king and Parliament, besides many other private treatises, both concerning the present and foregoing times. Hereby he became abundantly informed in his understanding, and convinced in conscience of the righteousness of the Parliament's cause in point of civil right; and though he was satisfied of the endeavours to reduce [revive] popery and subvert the true protestant religion, which indeed was apparent to everyone that impartially considered it, yet he did not think that so clear a ground for the war as the defence of the just English liberties; and although he was clearly swayed by his own judgment and reason to the Parliament, he, thinking he had no warrantable call at that time, to do anything more, contented himself with praying for peace.

At that time Mr Henry Ireton was in the country, and being a kinsman of Mr Hutchinson's, and one that had received so much advantage to himself and his family in the country by Sir Thomas Hutchinson's countenance and protection, that he seemed a kind of dependant upon him, and being besides a very grave, serious, religious person, there was a great league of kindness and good-will between them. Mr Ireton being very active in promoting the Parliament, and the godly interest in the country, found great opposition from some projectors, and others of corrupt interest that were in the commission of the peace. Making complaint at the Parliament, he procured some of them to be put out of the commission, and others, better affected, to be put in their rooms, of which Mr Hutchinson was one; but he then forbore to take his oath, as not willing to launch out rashly into public employments, while such a storm hung threatening overhead. Yet his good affections to godliness and the interest of his country, being a glory that could not be concealed, many of his honest neighbours made applications to him, and endeavoured to learn his conduct, which he at first in modesty and prudence would not too hastily rush into.

The Parliament had made orders to deface the images in all churches. Within two miles of his house there was a church, where Christ upon the cross, the Virgin, and John, had been fairly set up in a window over the altar, and sundry other superstitious paintings, of the priest's own ordering, were drawn upon the walls. When the order for rasing out those relics of superstition came, the priest only took down the heads of the images, and laid them carefully up in his closet, and would have had the church officers to have certified that the thing was done according to order; whereupon they came to Mr Hutchinson, and desired him that he would take the pains to come and view their church, which he did, and upon discourse with the parson, persuaded him to blot out all the superstitious paintings, and break the images in the glass; which he consented to, but being ill-affected, was one of those who began to brand Mr Hutchinson with the name of puritan.

At that time most of the gentry of the country were disaffected to the Parliament; most of the middle sort, the able substantial freeholders, and the other commons, who had not their dependence upon the malignant* nobility and gentry, adhered to the Parliament. These, when the king was at York, made a petition to him to return to the Parliament, which, upon their earnest entreaty, Mr Hutchinson went, with some others, and presented at York; where, meeting his cousins the Byrons,

* This, in the puritan vocabulary, meant a royalist.

they were extremely troubled to see him there on that account. After his return, Sir John Byron being likewise come to his house at Newstead, Mr Hutchinson went to visit them there, and not finding him, returned to Nottingham, five miles short of his own house. There going to the mayor to hear some news, he met with such as he expected not, for as soon as he came in, the mayor's wife told him, that the sheriff of the county was come to fetch away the magazine that belonged to the trained bands of the county, which was left in her husband's trust; and that her husband had sent for the country to acquaint them, but she feared it would be gone before they could come in. Mr Hutchinson, taking his brother from his lodgings along with him, presently went to the town hall, and going up to my Lord Newark,* Lord Lieutenant, told him that, hearing some dispute concerning the country's powder, he was come to wait on his lordship, to know his desires and intents concerning it. My lord answered him, that the king, having great necessities, desired to borrow it of the country. Mr Hutchinson asked my lord what commission he had from His Majesty. My lord told him he had one, but he had left it behind. Mr Hutchinson replied that my lord's affirmation was satisfactory to him, but the country would not be willing to part with their powder in so dangerous a time, without an absolute command. My lord urged that he would restore it in ten days. Mr Hutchinson replied, they might have use for it sooner, and he hoped my lord would not disarm his country in such a time of danger. My lord condemned the mention of danger, and asked what they could fear while he was their lord lieutenant, and ready to serve them with his life. Mr Hutchinson told him they had some grounds to apprehend danger by reason of the daily passing of armed men through the country, whereof there was now one troop in the town, and that before they could repair to my lord, they might be destroyed in his absence, and withal urged to him examples of their insolence; but my lord replied to all, the urgency of the king's occasions for it, which were such that he could not dispense with it. It was in vain to argue with him the

* Eldest son of the Earl of Kingston, see p. 51.

property the country had in it, being bought with their money, and therefore not to be taken without their consent; my lord declared himself positively resolved to take it, whereupon Mr Hutchinson left him.

There were in the room with him Sir John Digby, the high sheriff of the county, who was setting down the weight of the powder and match, and two or three captains and others, that were busy weighing the powder. By the time Mr Hutchinson came down, a good company of the country was gathered together; whom Mr Hutchinson acquainted with what had passed between him and my lord, and they told him that if he would but please to stand by them, they would part with all their blood before he should have a corn of it; and said, moreover, they would go up and tumble my lord and the sheriff out of the windows. Mr Hutchinson, seeing them so resolved, desired them to stay below while he went up yet once again to my lord, which they did; and he told my lord some of the country were come in, at whose request he was again come to beseech his lordship to desist from his design, which if pursued might be of dangerous consequence. My lord replied, it could not be, for the king was very well assured of the cheerful compliance of the greatest part of the country with his service. Mr Hutchinson told him, whatever assurance His Majesty might have, if his lordship pleased to look out, he might see no inconsiderable number below that would not willingly part with it. My lord replied, they were but a few factious men; whereupon Mr Hutchinson told him, since it was yet the happiness of these unhappy times that no blood had been spilt, he should be sorry the first should be shed upon my lord's occasion, in his own country. My lord scornfully replied, 'Fear it not, it cannot come to that, the king's occasions are urgent and must be served.' Whereupon Mr Hutchinson, looking out at the countrymen, they came very fast up the stairs; and Mr Hutchinson told him, however he slighted it, not one was there but would part with every drop of his blood before they would part with it, except he could show a command or request for it under the king's hand, or would stay till the country were called in to give their consent; for it was their property, and all had interest in it, as bought with their money for the particular defence of the country.

Then my lord fell to entreaties to borrow part of it, but that being also denied, he took the sheriff aside, and, after a little conference, they put up their books and left the powder; when my lord, turning to the people, said to them, 'Gentlemen, His Majesty was by some assured of the cheerfulness of this country's affections to him, whereof I am sorry to see so much failing, and that the county should fall so much short of the town, who have cheerfully lent His Majesty one barrel of powder, but it seems he can have none from you; I pray God you do not repent this carriage of yours towards His Majesty, which he must be acquainted withal.' A bold countryman then stepping forth, by way of reply, asked my lord, whether, if he were to take a journey with a charge into a place where probably he should be set upon by thieves, if any friend should ask to borrow a sword he would part with it: 'My lord,' said he, 'the case is ours; our lives, wives, children, and estates, all depend upon this country's safety; and how can it be safe in these dangerous times, when so many rude armed people pass daily through it, if we be altogether disarmed?' My lord made no reply, but bade the men who were weighing the powder desist, and went down.

Mr Hutchinson followed him down the stairs, when an ancient gentleman, that was sitting with my lord, came and whispering him, commended his and the country's zeal, and bade them stand to it, and they would not be foiled. As they passed through a long room below, my lord told Mr Hutchinson he was sorry to find him at the head of a faction. Mr Hutchinson replied, he could not tell how his lordship could call that a faction which arose from the accident of his being at that time in the town; where, hearing what was in hand, and out of respect to his lordship, he only came to prevent mischief and danger, which he saw likely to ensue. My lord replied, he must inform the king, and told him his name was already up; to which Mr Hutchinson answered, that he was glad, if the king must receive an information of him, that it must be from so honourable a person; and for his name, as it rose, so in the name of God let it fall; and so took his leave and went home.

The rest of the country that were there, determined to give my lord thanks for sparing their ammunition, and locked it up with two locks, whereof the key of the one was entrusted with the Mayor of Nottingham, the other with the sheriff of the county, which accordingly was done.

Before the flame of the war broke out in the top of the chimneys, the smoke ascended in every country; the king had sent forth commissions of array, and the Parliament had given out commissions for their militia, and sent off their members into all counties to put them in execution. Between these, in many places, there were fierce contests and disputes, almost to blood, even at the first; for in the progress every county had the Civil War, more or less, within itself. Some counties were in the beginning so wholly for the Parliament, that the king's interest appeared not in them; some so wholly for the king, that the godly, for those generally were the Parliament's friends, were forced to forsake their habitations, and seek other shelters: of this sort was Nottinghamshire. All the nobility and gentry, and their dependants, were generally for the king; the chief of whose names I shall sum up here, because I shall often have occasion to mention them.

The greatest family was the Earl of Newcastle's,* a lord once so much beloved in his country, that when the first expedition was against the Scots, the gentlemen of the country set him forth two troops, one all of gentlemen, the other of their men, who waited on him into the north at their own charges. He had, indeed, through his great estate, his liberal hospitality, and constant residence in his country, so endeared them to him, that no man was a greater prince in all that northern quarter; till a foolish ambition of glorious slavery carried him to court, where he ran himself much into debt, to purchase neglects of the king and queen, and scorns of the proud courtiers. Next him was the Earl of Kingston, a man of vast estate, and no less covetous, who divided his sons between both parties, and concealed himself; till at length his fate drew him to declare himself absolutely on the king's side, wherein he behaved himself

* He was only created duke in 1665.

honourably, and died remarkably. His eldest son was lord lieutenant of the county, and at that time no nobleman had a greater reputation in the court for learning and generosity than he; but he was so high in the king's party, that the Parliament was very much incensed against him. Lord Chesterfield, and all his family, were high in the royal party; so was the Lord Chaworth. The Earl of Clare was very often of both parties, and, I think, never advantaged either.* Sir John Byron, afterwards Lord Byron, and all his brothers, bred up in arms, and valiant men in their own persons, were all passionately the king's. Mr William Pierrepont, second son of the Earl of Kingston, was of the Parliament, though he served not for his own country, to which notwithstanding he was an ornament, being one of the wisest counsellors and most excellent speakers in the house, and by him was that bill promoted and carried on which passed for the continuation of this Parliament.† He had a younger brother living at Nottingham, who coldly owned the Parliament.‡

Sir Thomas Hutchinson continued with the Parliament, was firm to their cause, but infinitely desirous that the difference might rather have been composed by accommodation, than ended by conquest; and therefore did not improve his interest to engage the country in the quarrel, which, if he could have prevented, he would not have had come to a war. He was, however, clearly on the Parliament's side, and never discouraged his two sons, who thought this prudential tardiness in their father was the declension of that vigour which they derived from him, and which better became their youth. Mr Henry Ireton, their cousin, was older than they, and having had an education in the strictest way of godliness, and being a very grave and solid person, a man of good learning, great understanding, and other abilities, to which was joined a willing and zealous heart in the cause and his country, he was the chief promoter of the Parliament's interest in the county; but finding it generally disaffected, all he could do, when the king

* His wife was a first cousin of Brilliana Harley and a sister of Lady Fairfax, see p. xxviii.
† In May 1641.
‡ Francis Pierrepoint, see p. 59.

approached it, was to gather a troop of those godly people which the cavaliers drove out, and with them to go into the army of my Lord of Essex; which he, being a single person, could better do. Mr Hutchinson was not willing so soon to quit his house, to which he was so lately come, if he could have been suffered to live quietly in it; but his affections to the Parliament being taken notice of, he became an object of envy to the other party.

Sir Thomas Hutchinson, a little before the standard was set up [there, in August 1642], had come to Nottingham, where his house was, to see his children and refresh himself; when, hearing of the king's intentions to come to the town, he, some days before his coming, went over to Owthorpe, his son's house, to remain there till he could fit himself to return to the Parliament. One day, as Mr Hutchinson was at dinner, the Mayor of Nottingham sent him word that the high sheriff had broken open the lock of the country's ammunition, which was left in his trust, and was about to take it away. Mr Hutchinson immediately went in all haste to prevent it, but before he came to the town it was gone, and some of the king's soldiers were already come to town, and were plundering all the honest men of their arms. As one of them had taken a musket, seeing Mr Hutchinson go by, he said he wished it loaded for his sake, and hoped the day would shortly come when all such roundheads would be fair marks for them.

This name of roundhead coming so opportunely in, I shall make a little digression to tell how it came up. When puritanism grew into a faction few of the puritans, what degree soever they were of, wore their hair long enough to cover their ears, and the ministers and many others cut it close round their heads, with so many little peaks, as was something ridiculous to behold. From this custom of wearing their hair, that name of roundhead became the scornful term given to the whole Parliament party, whose army indeed marched out as if they had been only sent out till their hair was grown. Two or three years after, any stranger that had seen them, would have enquired the reason of that name. It was very ill applied to Mr Hutchinson, who, having naturally a very fine thickset head of hair, kept it clean and handsome, so that it was a great ornament to him. The godly of those days, when he embraced their party, would not allow him to be religious because his hair was not in their cut, nor his words in their phrase, nor such little formalities altogether fitted to their humour. Many of them were so weak as to esteem such insignificant circumstances, rather than solid wisdom, piety, and courage, which brought real aid and honour to their party.

When he found the powder gone, and saw the soldiers taking up quarters in the town, and heard their threats and revilings, he went to his father's house in the town, where he had not been long before an uncivil fellow stepped into the house, with a carabine in his hand. Mr Hutchinson asked what he would have; the man replied, he came to take possession of the house; Mr Hutchinson told him, he had the possession of it, and would know on what right it was demanded from him; the man said, he came to quarter the general there; Mr Hutchinson told him, except his father and mother, and their children, were turned out of doors, there was no room. The quarter-master, upon this, growing insolent, Mr Hutchinson thrust him out of the house, and shut the doors upon him. Immediately my Lord of Lindsey* came himself, in a great chafe, and asked who it was that denied him quarter? Mr Hutchinson told him, he that came to take it up for him deserved the usage he had, for his uncivil demeanour; and those who had quartered his lordship there had much abused him, the house being no ways fit to receive a person of his quality, which, if he pleased to take a view of it, he would soon perceive. Whereupon my lord, having seen the rooms, was very angry they had made no better provision for him, and would not have lain in the house, but they told him the town was so full that it was impossible to get him room anywhere else. Hereupon he told Mr Hutchinson, if they would only allow him one room, he would have no more; and when he came upon terms of civility, Mr Hutchinson was as civil to him, and my lord only employed one room, staying

* Robert Bertie, Earl of Lindsey, nominally royalist General-in-Chief, killed at Edgehill.

there, with all civility to those that were in the house. As soon as my lord was gone, Mr Hutchinson was informed by a friend, that the man he had turned out of doors was the quarter-master general, who, upon his complaint, had procured a warrant to seize his person; whereupon Mr Hutchinson, with his brother, went immediately home to his own house at Owthorpe.

About four or five days after, a troop of cavaliers, under the command of Sir Lewis Dives, came to Stanton, near Owthorpe, and searched Mr Needham's house, who was a noted puritan in those days, and a colonel in the Parliament's service, and Governor of Leicester: they found not him, for he hid himself in the gorse, and so escaped them. His house being lightly plundered, they went to Hickling, and plundered another puritan house there, and were coming to Owthorpe, of which Mr Hutchinson having notice, went away to Leicestershire; but they, though they had orders to seize Mr Hutchinson, came not at that time because the night grew on. But some days after he was gone, another company came and searched for him and for arms and plate, of which finding none, they took nothing else.

Two days after Mr Hutchinson was in Leicestershire, he sent for his wife, who was then big with child, to come thither to him; where she had not been a day, but a letter was brought him from Nottingham, to give him notice that there was a warrant sent to the Sheriff of Leicestershire to seize his person. Upon this he determined to go the next day into Northamptonshire, but at five of the clock that evening, the sound of their trumpets told him a troop was coming into the town. He stayed not to see them, but went out at the other end as they came in; who, by a good providence for his wife (somewhat afflicted to be so left alone in a strange place), proved to be commanded by her own brother, Sir Allen Apsley, who quartered in the next house to that where she was, till about two or three days before all the king's horse that were thereabouts marched away, being commanded upon some service to go before the rest.

Mr Hutchinson, in the meantime, was carried by a servant that waited on him, to the house of a substantial honest yeoman,

who was bailiff to the lord of the town* of Kelmarsh, in
Northamptonshire. This man and his wife, being godly, gave
Mr Hutchinson very kind entertainment, and prevailed upon
him to be acquainted with their master, who had just then made
plate and horses ready to go in to the king, that had now set up
his standard at Nottingham; but Mr Hutchinson diverted him,
and persuaded him and another gentleman of quality, to carry in
those aids they had provided for the king, to my Lord General
Essex,† who was then at Northampton, where Mr Hutchinson
visited him, and would gladly at that time have engaged with
him, but that he did not then find a clear call from the Lord.

Intelligence being brought of the king's removal, he was
now returning to his wife, when unawares he came into a town,
where one of Prince Rupert's troops was; which he narrowly
escaped, and returning to his former honest host, sent a letter
to his wife, to acquaint her what hazard he was in by attempting
to come to her, but that as soon as the horse was marched away,
he would be with her. This letter was intercepted at Prince
Rupert's quarters, and opened and sent her. There was with
Prince Rupert, at that time, one Captain Welch, who having
used to come to Captain Apsley, and seen Mrs Hutchinson
with him, made a pretence of civility to visit her that day that
all the prince's horse marched away. They marched by the door
of the house where she was, and all the household having gone
out to see them, had left her alone in the house, with Mr George
Hutchinson, who was in her chamber when Captain Welch
came in, and she went down into the parlour to receive him.
He, taking occasion to tell her of her husband's letter, by way
of compliment, said it was a pity she should have a husband so
unworthy of her, as to enter into any faction which should make
him not dare to be seen with her; whereat she being piqued,
and thinking they were all marched away, told him he was mistaken, she had not a husband that would at any time hide himself from him, or that durst not show his face where any honest
man durst appear; and to confirm you, said she, he shall now

* It was customary, in Nottinghamshire, to call every village of any size
a town.
† Robert Devereux, Earl of Essex, parliamentary commander.

come to you. With that she called down her brother-in-law, who, upon a private hint, owned the name of husband, which she gave him, and received a compliment from Welch, that in any other place he had been obliged to make him a prisoner, but here he was in sanctuary; and so, after some little discourse, went away.

When the gentleman of the house and the rest of the family, that had been seeing the march, were returned, and while they sat laughing together, at those that went to see the prince, telling how some of the neighbouring ladies were gone along with him, and Mrs Hutchinson telling how she had abused the captain, with Mr Hutchinson instead of her husband, the captain came back, bringing another gentleman with him; and he told Mr Hutchinson, that his horse having lost a shoe, he must be his prisoner till the smith released him. But they had not sat long, ere a boy came in with two pistols, and whispered the captain, who desiring Mr Hutchinson and the gentleman of the house to walk into the next room, seized Mr George, in the name of Mr John Hutchinson. It booted not for them both to endeavour to undeceive him, by telling him Mr John was still at Northampton, for he would not, at least would seem not, to believe them, and carried him away, to be revenged of Mrs Hutchinson, at whom he was vexed for having deluded him. So, full of wicked joy, to have found an innocent gentleman, whom he knew the bloodhounds were after, he went and informed the prince, and made it of such moment, as if they had taken a much more considerable person.

The prince had sent back a troop of dragoons to guard him to them, which troop had beset the house and town, before Welch came in to them the second time; and, notwithstanding all informations of his error, he carried away Mr Hutchinson, and put his sister-in-law into affright and distemper with it; which, when the women about her saw, they railed at him for his treachery and baseness, but to no purpose. As soon as he overtook the body of horse with his prisoner, there was a shout from one end to the other of the soldiers. Mr Hutchinson, being brought to the prince, told him he was the younger brother, and not the person he sent for, which three or four of the

Byrons, his cousin-germans, acknowledged to be so; yet Welch outswore them all that it was Mr John Hutchinson. The Lord Viscount Grandison, a cousin-german of Mrs Hutchinson's, was then in the king's army, to whom she immediately despatched a messenger, to entreat him to oblige her by the procurement of her brother-in-law's liberty, who, upon her imprudence, had been brought into that trouble. My lord sent her word, that, for the present, he could not obtain it, but he would endeavour it afterwards; and in the meantime he gave her notice that it was not safe for her husband to return, there being forty men left to lie close in the country, and watch his coming to her. So Mr George Hutchinson was carried to Derby, and there, with some difficulty, his liberty was obtained by the interposition of my Lord Grandison* and the Byrons. They would have had him give them an engagement, that he would not take arms with the Parliament; but he refused, telling them that he lived peaceably at home, and should make no engagement to do anything but what his conscience led him to; that if they pleased, they might detain him, but it would be no advantage to them, nor loss to the other side. Upon which considerations they were persuaded to let him go.

Immediately after his release, he went to London to his father, where his elder brother was before him; for as soon as he understood from his wife what his brother suffered in his name, he took post to London to procure his release. There they both stayed till they received assurance that the king's forces were quite withdrawn from the country, and then they together returned to Leicestershire, where Mrs Hutchinson, within a few days after her brother-in-law was taken, was brought to bed of her eldest daughter. By reason of the mother's and the nurse's griefs and frights, in those troublesome times, it was so weak a child that it lived not four years, dying afterwards in Nottingham Castle. When Mr Hutchinson came to his wife, he carried her and her children, and his brother, back again to his house, about the time that the battle was fought at Edgehill [October 1642]. After this the two brothers, going to Nottingham, met there most of the godly people, who had been

* He died in 1643 of wounds received at the siege of Bristol.

driven away by the rudeness of the king's army, and plundered on account of their godliness. These now returned to their families, and were desirous to live in peace; but having, by experience, found they could not do so, unless the Parliament interest was maintained, they were consulting how to raise some recruits for the Earl of Essex, to assist in which, Mr Hutchinson had provided his plate and horses ready to send in.

After the battle at Edgehill, Sir John Digby, the High Sheriff of Nottinghamshire, returned from the king, and had a design of securing the county against the Parliament; whereupon he sent out summons to all the gentlemen resident in the country to meet him at Newark. Mr Hutchinson was at the house of Mr Francis Pierrepont, the Earl of Kingston's third son, when the letter was delivered to him, and another of the same to Mr Pierrepont. Mr Pierrepont was a man of good natural parts, but not of education according to his quality, who was in the main well affected to honest men; but his goodness received a little allay by a vainglorious pride, which could not well brook that any other should outstrip him in virtue and estimation. While they were reading them, and considering what might be the meaning of this summons, an honest man, of the sheriff's neighbourhood, came and gave them notice, that the sheriff had some design in agitation; for he had assembled and armed about fourscore of his neighbours, to go out with him to Newark, and, as they heard, from thence to Southwell, and from thence to Nottingham, through which town many armed men marched day and night, to their great terror. Mr Hutchinson, upon this intimation, went home and, instead of going to meet the sheriff, sent an excuse by an intelligent person, well acquainted with all the country, who had orders to find out their design; which he did so well, that he assured Mr Hutchinson if he and some others had gone in, they would have been made prisoners. For the sheriff came into Newark with a troop of eighty men, with whom he was gone to Southwell, and was to go the next day to Nottingham, to secure those places for the king.

Mr Hutchinson immediately went with his brother and acquainted them at Nottingham with his intelligence, which they had likewise received from other hands. Although the town was generally more malignant than well affected, yet they cared not much to have cavalier soldiers quarter with them, and therefore agreed to defend themselves against any force which should come against them; and being called hastily together, as the exigence required, about seven hundred listed themselves, and chose Mr George Hutchinson for their captain, who having lived among them, was very much loved and esteemed by them. The sheriff hearing this, came not to Nottingham, but those who were now there thus became engaged to prosecute the defence of themselves, the town, and country, as far as they could. They were but few, and those not very considerable, and some of them not very hearty; but it pleased God here, as in other places, to carry on his work by weak and unworthy instruments. There were seven aldermen in the town, and of these only Alderman James, then mayor, owned the Parliament. He was a very honest, bold man, but had no more than a burgher's discretion; he was yet very well assisted by his wife, a woman of great zeal and courage, and with more understanding than women of her rank usually have. All the devout people of the town were very vigorous and ready to offer their lives and families, but there was not a quarter of the town that consisted of these; the ordinary civil sort of people coldly adhered to the better, but all the debauched, and such as had lived upon the bishops' persecuting courts, and had been the lackeys of projectors and monopolisers and the like, they were all bitterly malignant.

Sir John Digby having notice that they had prevented him, by getting arms in their hands before, came not to Nottingham; where they, having now taken up the sword, saw it was not safe to lay it down again, and hold a naked throat to their enemy's whetted knives. Wherefore, upon the Parliament's commission for settling the militia sometime before, there having been three colonels nominated, *viz.* Sir Francis Thornhagh, Sir Francis Molineux, and Mr Francis Pierrepont, they propounded to them to raise their regiments. Sir Francis Molineux altogether declined; Sir Francis Thornhagh appointed his son for his lieutenant-colonel, and began to raise a regiment of horse, with whom many of the honest men that first enlisted themselves with Mr George Hutchinson, became troopers. Mr John Hutchinson and his brother were persuaded to be lieutenant-colonel and major to Colonel Pierrepont's regiment of foot; and accordingly Mr George Hutchinson had immediately a very good standing company of foot, formed out of those townsmen who first came in to enlist under him. Mr John Hutchinson had a full company of very honest, godly men, who came for love of him and the cause, out of the country. It was six weeks before the colonel could be persuaded to put on a sword, or to enlist any men, which at length he did, of substantial honest townsmen; and Mr Poulton, a nephew of Sir Thomas Hutchinson, a stout young gentleman, who had seen some service abroad, was his captain-lieutenant. They also sent to the Earl of Essex, to desire that Captain Ireton, with a troop of horse, which he had carried out of the country into his excellency's army, might be commanded back, for the present service of his country, till it was put into a posture of defence; which accordingly he was, and was major of the horse regiment.

The high sheriff and the malignant gentry, finding an opposition they expected not, wrote a letter to Mr Francis Pierrepont and Mr John Hutchinson, excusing the sheriff's force, that he brought with him, and desiring a meeting with them, to consult for the peace of the country, security of their estates, and such like fair pretences. At length a meeting was appointed at a village in the country, on the forest side, where Mr Sutton should have met Mr John Hutchinson. Mr Hutchinson came to the place, but found not Mr Sutton there, only the Lord Chaworth came in and called for sack, and treated Mr Hutchinson very kindly. Mr Hutchinson, telling my lord he was come according to appointment, to conclude the treaty which had been between Nottingham and Newark, my lord told him he knew nothing of it. Whereupon, Mr Hutchinson being informed that some of my Lord Newcastle's forces were to be in that town that night, and that Mr Sutton was gone to meet them, and conduct them into the country, returned to Nottingham, where he received a kind of lame excuse from Mr Sutton for his disappointing of him, and for their bringing strange soldiers into Newark, which they pretended was to save the town from the plunder of some Lincolnshire forces. But Mr Hutchinson, seeing all their treaties were but a snare for him, would no longer amuse himself about them. Being certainly informed that Henderson, who commanded the soldiers at Newark, if he were not himself a papist, had many Irish papists in his troops, he, with the rest of the gentlemen, sent notice to all the towns about Nottingham, desiring the well-affected to come in to their assistance. The ministers pressing them to do [so], upon Christmas Day, 1642, many came to them, and stayed with them till they had put themselves into some posture of defence.

As soon as these strange soldiers were come into Newark, they presently began to block up and fortify the town, as on the other side, they at Nottingham began works about that town; but neither of them being yet strong enough to assault each other, they contented themselves to stand upon their own defence. The Earl of Chesterfield had raised some horse for the king, and was in the Vale of Belvoir with them, where he had plundered some houses near Mr Hutchinson's; whereupon Mr Hutchinson sent a troop of horse in the night, for they were not strong enough to march in the day, and fetched away his wife and children to Nottingham.

The preservation of this town was a special service to the Parliament, it being a considerable pass into the north, which, if the enemy had first possessed themselves of, the Parliament would have been cut off from all intercourse between the north and south; especially in the winter time, when the River Trent is not fordable, and only to be passed over by the bridges of Nottingham and Newark, and higher up at a place called Wilden Ferry, where the enemy also had a garrison.

The attempting to preserve this place, in the midst of so many potent enemies, was a work of no small difficulty; and nothing but an invincible courage, and a passionate zeal for the interest of God and his country, could have engaged Mr Hutchinson, who did not, through youthful inconsideration and improvidence, want a foresight of those dangers and travails he then undertook. He knew well enough that the town was more than half disaffected to the Parliament; that had they been all otherwise, they were not half enough to defend it against any unequal force; that they were far from the Parliament and their armies, and could not expect any timely relief or assistance from them; that he himself was the forlorn hope of those who were engaged with him, and had then the best stake among them; that the gentlemen who were on horseback, when they could no longer defend their country, might at least save their lives by a handsome retreat to the army; but that he must stand victorious, or fall, tying himself to an indefensible town. Although his colonel (Pierrepont) might seem to be in the same hazard, yet he was wise enough to content himself with thè name, and leave Mr Hutchinson to act in all things, the glory of which, if they succeeded, he hoped to assume; if they failed, he thought he had a retreat. But Mr Hutchinson, though he knew all this, yet was he so well persuaded in his conscience of the cause, and of God's calling him to undertake the defence of it, that he cast by all other considerations, and cheerfully resigned up his life, and all other particular interests, to God's disposal, though in all human probability he was more likely to lose than to save them.

He and his brother were so suddenly called into this work, that they had not time beforehand to consult their father; but they sent to him to buy their armour and useful swords, which he did, giving them no discouragement, but promoting all their desires to the Parliament very effectually.

The First Hostilities
1642-3

Brilliana Harley was joined at Brampton Bryan Castle by both her husband and her son in the autumn of 1642, so there are no more letters until December of that year. While he was at home, Edward was commended by the local parliamentary commander for capturing some royalist troops. Hereford, which had been in Parliament's hands, was occupied by the royalists in January 1643 and Lord Hertford passed through with 2000 Welsh recruits for the king. In February 1643 the royalist commander Lord Herbert began preparing for a siege of Brampton, but his forces were diverted to attack Gloucester, where they were defeated by Sir William Waller at the end of March. In April some royalist troops entered Brampton Park, took four oxen, beat up some workmen and then opened fire, killing one man. Later in the month Waller took Hereford briefly again for Parliament, but then had to march away to reinforce Bristol. It was at this time that Edward Harley and his brother Robert joined Waller's forces as officers.

The equivocal behaviour of Ballard, the commander of the unsuccessful assault by the parliamentary forces of Lincolnshire, Derbyshire and Nottinghamshire on Newark, echoes that of the Earl of Kingston and his son Colonel Francis Pierrepont, as described by Lucy Hutchinson on pp. 51 and 63. Ann Fanshawe movingly describes the civilian refugee's lot during wartime: 'the perpetual discourse of losing and gaining towns and men; at the windows the sad spectacle of war.'

The Duke of Newcastle won his first sizeable victory over Ferdinando, Lord Fairfax, the northern parliamentary commander and father of the famous Thomas Fairfax, at Tadcaster near York in December 1642. In February 1643 Queen Henrietta Maria landed at Bridlington on the Yorkshire coast and was escorted by the duke to York. In March the young Fairfax was defeated at Seacroft Moor by Newcastle's cavalry under George Goring. In May the tables were turned at Wakefield and Goring was captured in a night attack. In June the queen left York to join Charles in Oxford, with an escort of 7000 men. Two thousand of these went to reinforce Newark. Thus Newcastle had 'to recruit again his army'.

Brilliana Harley

13 December 1642: My heart has been in no rest since you went. I confess I was never so full of sorrow. I fear the provision of corn and malt will not hold out, if this continue; and they say they will burn my barns; and my fear is that they will place soldiers so near me that there will be no going out. My comfort is that you are not with me, lest they should take you; but I do most dearly miss you. I wish, if it pleased God, that I were with your father. I would have written to him, but I durst not write upon paper. Dear Ned, write to me, though you write upon a piece of cloth, as this is. I pray God bless you, as I desire my own soul should be blessed. There were 1000 dragoneers came into Hereford five hours after my lord Hertford.

25 December 1642: I must now tell you how gracious our God has been to us. On the sabbath day after I received the letter from the Marquis [of Hertford], we set that day apart to speak to our God, and then on Monday we prepared for a siege; but our good God called them another way. And the marquis sent me word he remembered him to me, and that I need not fear him, for he was going away, but bid me fear him that came after him.

Mr Coningsby is the Governor of Hereford, and he sent to

me a letter by Mr Wigmore. I did not let him come into my house, but I went into the garden to him. Your father will show you the letter; they are in a mighty violence against me; they revenge all that was done upon me, so that I shall fear any more Parliament forces coming into this country. Dear Ned, when it is in your power, show kindness to them, for they must be overcome so. I pray you advise with your father whether he thinks it best that I should put away most of the men that are in my house, and whether it be best for me to go from Brampton, or by God's help to stand it out. I will be willing to do what he would have me do. I never was in such sorrows, as I have been since you left me. I hope the Lord will deliver me; but they are most cruelly bent against me.

28 January 1643: Poor Griffiths was cruelly used, but he is now set at liberty. But the poor drummer is still in the dungeon [at Hereford], and Griffiths says he fears he will die. I cannot send to release him. I know it will grieve you to know how I am used. It is with all the malice that can be. Mr Wigmore will not let the fowler bring me any fowl, nor will not suffer any of my servants to pass. They have forbid my rents to be paid. They drove away the young horses at Wigmore, and none of my servants dare go scarce as far as the town. If God were not merciful to me, I should be in a very miserable condition. I am threatened every day to be beset with soldiers. My hope is, the Lord will not deliver me or mine into their hands; for surely they would use all cruelty towards me. I am told that they desire to leave your father neither root nor branch. You and I must forgive them.

14 February 1643: We are still threatened and injured as much as my enemies can possible. But our God still takes care of us, and has exceedingly showed His power in preserving us. Nine days past my Lord Herbert was at Hereford, where he stayed a week. There was held a council of war, what was the best way to take Brampton; it was concluded to blow it up, and which counsel pleased them all. The Sheriff of Radnorshire, with the trained bands of that county and some Herefordshire soldiers, were to come against me. My Lord Herbert had appointed a day to come to Presteigne, that so his presence might persuade them to go out of their county. He had commanded them to bring pay for victuals for ten days. The soldiers came to Presteigne, but it pleased God to call my Lord Herbert another way, for those in the Forest of Dean grew so strong, that they were afraid of them.

Now they say, they will starve me out of my house; they have taken away all your father's rents, and they say they will drive away the cattle, and then I shall have nothing to live upon. All their aim is to enforce me to let those men I have go, that then they might seize upon my house and cut our throats by a few rogues, and then say, they knew not who did it. For so they say, they knew not who drove away the six colts, but Mr Coningsby keeps them, though I have written to him for them.

23 February 1643: Mr Hill has undertaken to bring the water into the moat. I ventured but 20*s.* but he has had many opponents, but Mr Gower was for him. I hope it will be done.

25 February 1643: I am in the same condition as I was; still amongst my enemies, who now threaten me not with force, because the soldiers are gone before Gloucester. My dear Ned, desire your father to send me word what he thinks I had best do; for if I should put away the men in my house, I should be every day plundered, and as basely used as it is possible, and I can receive no rents.

8 March 1643: Dear Ned, find some way or other to write to me that I may know how the world goes, and how it is with your father and yourself; for it is a death to be amongst my enemies, and not to hear from those I love so dearly.

Here I have sent you a copy of the summons that was sent me. I wish with all my heart that everyone would take notice what way they take: that if I do not give them my house, and what they would have, I shall be proceeded against as a traitor. It may be everyone's case to be made traitors; for I believe everyone will be as unwilling to part with their houses as I am.

I desire your father would seriously think what I had best do; whether stay at Brampton, or remove to some other place. I hear there are 600 soldiers appointed to come against me. I know not whether this cessation of arms will stay them.

11 March 1643: The judges came not to Hereford, so that there was nothing down against me at the bench. They sent for the trained bands and have taken away their arms; some say to give the arms to my Lord Herbert's soldiers that want. They say that they gave half-a-crown to every soldier to look for enemies every day. They have taken More's lad and he is in prison at Hereford, because he was with me.* If I had money to buy corn and meal and malt I should hope to hold out, but then I have three shires against me. I thank God we are well, though all would not have it so.

6 May 1643: Let this tell you, God has mightily been seen in Herefordshire. Mr Coningsby and Sir William Croft and Sir Walter Pye are [imprisoned] at Gloucester.

To my grief I must tell you that honest Petter is taken. Six set upon him; three shot at him as he was opening a gate not far from Mortimer's Cross. He fought with them valiantly and acquitted himself with courage: he hurt two of them, and if there had not been six to one, he had escaped. He is wounded in the head and shoulder, but not mortally; he is in prison at Ludlow. I have done all that is possible to get him out, but it cannot be; but I hope the Lord will deliver him. I have found him very faithful to me, and he desired to have come to you.

9 May 1643: Since God has put into your heart that you have taken this employment upon you, the Lord in much mercy bless you, and make you to do wisely and valiantly. You may be confident my very soul goes along with you and because I cannot be with you myself, I have sent you one, to be of your

---

* Samuel, son of Richard More, the MP for Bishop's Castle, who was one of the besieged at Brampton Bryan Castle later that year. No doubt he was released from prison when Sir William Waller took Hereford briefly for Parliament at the end of April 1643.

troop, and have furnished him with a horse which cost me £8. I hope it will come safe to your hand, with his rider.

I pray you, consider that Mr Hill is much given to keep company and so to drink, and I fear he will put his mind much to plundering.

Mr More is come to stay at Brampton, which I am very glad of. Your brother Robin [Robert] goes about as if he were discontented, but I know not for what. Mr Phillips carries himself very honestly and carefully, and is impatient to have you come to Brampton, where I should be glad to see you. Petter is still in prison at Ludlow.

28 May 1643: The water is brought quite into the green court, and I think you will like the work well. Poor Petter is used better now than he was at Ludlow.

3 June 1643: We are still threatened. Some soldiers are billeted in Purslo[w]. I pray God send the fair well passed over. The work about the court is almost ended, and I think you will like it well. I wrote to my nephew Pelham, who is cornet to my Lord Capel, but he has not got Petter's release. He wrote me an answer with some hope of his release. I am very sorry for him; he has been used pitifully.

11 June 1643: I heard from Gloucester on Thursday last, by one I sent on purpose. Sir William Waller went on Tuesday towards the west. Lieutenant-Colonel Massey is commanded to be Governor of Gloucester by my Lord General. I have been and am exceedingly beholden to Colonel Massey, as much as I was ever to one I did not know. I pray you tell your father so, and pray him to give him thanks. I sent to him to desire him to send me an able soldier, that might regulate the men I have, and he has sent me one that was a sergeant, an honest man, and I think an able soldier; he was in the German wars.

Honest Petter is come out of prison. He was grievously used in Ludlow. Turks could have used him no worse; a Lieutenant-Colonel Marrow would come every day and kick him up and down, and they laid him in a dungeon upon foul straw. In Shrewsbury he was used well for a prisoner; but he is very glad he is come home again, and so am I. I shall be full of doubts till the fair be passed. Some soldiers are come to Knighton; my old friends that were there before.

June 1643: I received your letter dated the 17th of this month, which was dearly welcome to me, because it brought me word that you were safely come to Sir William Waller. My heart is with you, and I know you believe it; for my life is bound up with yours. My dear Ned, since you desire your brother to come to you, I cannot be unwilling he should go to you, to whom I pray God make him a comfort. If Mr Hill be with you, and you would be free of him, you may if please you, tell him I desire he should come to me, and so you may send him to me.

30 June 1643: That you left me with sorrow, when you went last from Brampton, I believe; for I think, with comfort I think of it, that you are not only a child, but one with childlike affections to me, and I know you have so much understanding that you did well weigh the condition I was in. But I believe it, your leaving of me was more sorrow than my condition could be. I hope the Lord will in mercy give you to me again, for you are both a Joseph and a Benjamin to me, and dear Ned, long to see me. In this country they begin to raise new troops, and they have assessed the country at £1200 a month. My Lord Herbert and Colonel Vavasour who is to be Governor of Hereford, is gone up into Montgomeryshire to raise soldiers. All of them [the Herefordshire cavaliers] are returned. They say that besides the £1200 a month, there must be free quarter for soldiers. They counsel, but the Lord in mercy defeat their counsels. I must look for new onsets, but I hope I shall look to my rock of defence, the Lord my God, from whom is deliverance. Out of Cheshire, I hear from a sure hand, that on the 19th of this month Sir William Brereton sent out a party of horse into Shropshire, but when they were plundering at Hanmer, the Lord Capel's troops surprised them;* they hastened to their horses and fled, but there was taken prisoners of them the

* Brereton later besieged Chester (p. 92). For Capel, see pp. 155, 177, 179.

Lieutenant-Colonel and Captain-Lieutenant Sanky, and thir-
teen more taken prisoners, and about twelve slain, and many
more wounded. They used the prisoners very barbarously. All
Lancashire is cleared, only Lathom House.* My Lord of Derby
has left that county, which they take ill. My dear Ned, I know
you love to hear how I do. I thank God, beyond my expectation or that of some in my house, my provisions has held out;
and I have borrowed yet not much money, though my tenants
will not pay me. As you desired to have some honest men sent
you, I did as much desire to send you some. Those that I
thought would have gone gladly, find out excuses, but these
three desired to go, to venture their lives with you, or else they
would not go from me. Doctor Wright asked his man the question, but the poor gardener and Stangy desired it of themselves,
and they set forward with good courage. I will endeavour to see
whether any will contribute to buy a horse; but those that have
hearts have not means, and they that have means have not hearts.
I do not send you Jack Griffiths, because I thought you might
like Philip Luke, who is a pretty ingenious fellow, but if you
would have Griffiths, I pray you let me know by Ralph, and I
will, if please God, send him to you. By Ralph and the rest I
have sent you your books. Dear Ned, I could say much more
to you, but I have run out my paper. I am confident you will
hate all plundering and unmercifulness. I pray you ask your
brother what I bid him tell you concerning Mr Hill.

Lucy Hutchinson

By reason of the coldness of the colonel [Pierrepont], the affairs
of the war at Nottingham went on more tardily than otherwise
they would have done; but the gentlemen there, thinking it
would be easier to prevent Newark from being made a fortified
garrison, than to take it when it was so, sent over to Lincoln

---

* Cleared of royalist forces thanks to the success of Colonel Shuttleworth's troops, see pp. 93–4. Lathom House held out for the king under
its redoubtable commander, the Countess of Derby.

and Derby, to propound the business to them. At length, about Candlemas [2 February 1643], it was agreed and appointed that the forces of Nottingham and Derby should come on their side of the town [Newark], and those of Lincoln on the other. All the disaffected [cavalier] gentry of both those counties, were at that time gone into Newark, and one Ballard, a gentleman who, decayed in his family, and owing his education to many of them, had been bred up in the wars abroad, was commander-in-chief for the Parliament in Lincolnshire. Much ado had the [parliamentarian] gentlemen of that county to engage him in the design against Newark; but when he could not divert them, he was resolved to cast them away rather than ruin his old benefactors.

He had appointed the forces of Nottingham and Derby to come to a rendezvous within a mile of Newark, upon Saturday, upon which day, all the persuasion the Lincolnshire gentlemen could use, could not prevail with him to march out, according to appointment; which those at Newark had notice of, and had prepared an ambuscade to have cut off all those forces if they had then come to the place. By providence of an extraordinary stormy season, they marched not till the next day, and so were preserved from that danger, which no doubt was treacherously contrived. As soon as they came, being about a thousand horse, foot, and dragoons, the Lincolnshire commanders informed ours of the sloth and untoward carriage of Ballard, and told them how that day he had played his ordinance [fired his artillery] at a mile's distance from the town. When the Newark horse came out to face them, upon the Beacon Hill, he would not suffer a man of the Lincolnshire troops to fall upon them, though the Lincoln horse were many more in number than they, and in all probability might have beaten them.

The next day, notwithstanding Mr Hutchinson went to him, to give him an account of the forces they had brought, and to receive orders, he could have none, but a careless answer to stand at such a side of the town and fall on as they saw occasion. Accordingly they did, and beat the enemy from their works, with the loss of only four or five men, and entrenched themselves. The night coming on upon them, they provided straw to have lodged in their trenches all the night. On the other side of the town, Captain King, of Lincolnshire, had taken a street, cut up a chain, and placed a drake* in a house. The Newark gentlemen were almost resolved to yield up the town, and some of them began to fly out of it, but Ballard would not suffer the horse to pursue them. One captain went out without his leave and took fifty horses, and turned back Mr Sutton and many others that were flying out of the town. At length, when he could no other way preserve his old patrons, but by betraying his friends, he ordered Captain King to retreat; whereupon the whole force of Newark fell upon the forces of Nottingham and Derby, in their trenches, where they fought very resolutely, till a Lincolnshire trooper came and bade them fly for their lives, or else they were all lost men. At this, 200 Lincolnshire men, whom Ballard with much entreaty had sent to relieve them, first ran away, and then Sir John Gell's greycoats [from Derby] made their retreat after them. Major Hutchinson and Captain White all this while kept their trenches, and commanded their Nottingham men not to stir, who accordingly shot there, till all their powder was spent. The lieutenant-colonel in vain importuned Ballard to send them ammunition and relief, but could obtain neither, and so they were forced, unwillingly, to retreat, which they did in such good order, the men first, and then their captains, that they lost not a man in coming off. The town was sallying upon them, but they discharged a drake and beat them back. The next day all the captains importuned Ballard that they might fall on again, but he would neither consent nor give any reason for his denial; so that the Nottingham forces returned with great dissatisfaction, though Ballard, to stop their mouths, gave them two pieces of ordnance.

* A small cannon.

Ann Fanshawe

About 1641, my second brother, William Harrison, was chosen
Burgess of Queenborough, Kent, and sat in the Commons'
House of Parliament, but not long, for when the king set up
his standard he went with him to Nottingham. Yet he, during
his sitting, undertook that my father should lend £50,000 to
pay the Scots who had then entered England, and, as it seems,
were to be both paid and prayed to go home, but afterwards
their plague infected the whole nation, as to all our sorrows
we know, and that debt of my father's remained to him until
the restoration of the king. In 1642 my father was taken
prisoner at his house, called Montague House, in Bishopgate
Street, and threatened to be sent on board a ship with many
more of his quality. They plundered his house, but he getting
loose, under pretence to fetch some writings they demanded in
his hands concerning the public revenue, he went to Oxford in
1643. Thereupon the Long Parliament, of which he was a
member for the town of Lancaster, plundered him out of what
remained, and sequestered his whole estate, which continued
out of his possession until the happy restoration of the king
[Charles II].

My father commanded my sister and myself to come to him
to Oxford, where the court then was. We, that had till that hour
lived in great plenty and great order, found ourselves like fishes
out of the water, and the scene so changed, that we knew not
at all how to act any part but obedience. From as good a house
as any gentleman of England had, we came to a baker's house
in an obscure street, and from rooms well furnished, to lie in a
very bad bed in a garret, to one dish of meat, and that not the
best ordered, no money, for we were as poor as Job, nor clothes
more than a man or two brought in their cloak bags. We had
the perpetual discourse of losing and gaining towns and men;
at the windows the sad spectacle of war, sometimes plague,
sometimes sicknesses of other kind, by reason of so many
people being packed together, as, I believe, there never was
before of that quality; always in want, yet I must needs say that

most bore it with a martyr-like cheerfulness. For my own part, I began to think we should all, like Abraham, live in tents all the days of our lives. The king sent my father a warrant for a baronet, but he returned it with thanks, saying he had too much honour of his knighthood which His Majesty had honoured him with some years before, for the fortune he now possessed.

As in a rock the turbulence of the waves disperses the splinters of the rock, so it was my lot. My brother, William, died at Oxford with a bruise on his side, caused by the fall of his horse, which was shot under him, as he went out with a party of horse against a party of the Earl of Essex, in 1643. He was a very good and gallant young man; and they are the very words the king said of him, when he was told of his death.

The Duchess of Newcastle

After Her Majesty's departure out of Yorkshire, my lord was forced to recruit again his army, and within a short time, *viz.* in June 1643, took a resolution to march into the enemy's quarters, in the western parts; in which march he met with a strong stone house well fortified, called Howley House, wherein was a garrison of soldiers, which my lord summoned. But the governor* disobeying the summons, he battered it with his cannon, and so took it by force. The governor having quarter given him contrary to my lord's orders, was brought before my lord by a person of quality. For this the officer that brought him received a check; and though he resolved then to kill him, yet my lord would not suffer him to do it, saying it was inhumane to kill any man in cold blood. Hereupon the governor kissed the key of the house door, and presented it to my lord; to which my lord returned this answer: 'I need it not, for I brought a key along with me, which yet I was unwilling to use, until you forced me to it.'

At this house my lord remained five or six days, till he had refreshed his soldiers; and then a resolution was taken to march

* Sir John Savile.

against a garrison of the enemy's called Bradford, a little but a strong town. In the way he met with a strong interruption by the enemy [under the Fairfaxes] drawing forth a vast number of musketeers, which they had very privately gotten out of Lancashire, the next adjoining county to those parts of Yorkshire, which had so easy an access to them at Bradford, by reason the whole country was of their party, that my lord could not possibly have any constant intelligence of their designs and motions. In their army there were near 5000 musketeers, and eighteen troops of horse, drawn up in a place full of hedges, called Adwalton Moor, near to their garrison at Bradford, ready to encounter my lord's forces, which then contained not above half so many musketeers as the enemy had. Their chiefest strength consisted in horse, and these made useless for a long time together by the enemy's horse possessing all the plain ground upon that field, so that no place was left to draw up my lord's horse, but amongst old coal-pits. Neither could they charge the enemy, by reason of a great ditch and high bank betwixt my lord's and the enemy's troops, but by two on a breast, and that within musket shot. The enemy were drawn up in hedges, and continually playing upon them, which rendered the service exceeding difficult and hazardous.

In the meanwhile the foot of both sides on the right and left wings encountered each other, who fought from hedge to hedge, and for a long time together overpowered and got ground of my lord's foot, almost to the environing of his cannon. My lord's horse all this while were made, by reason of the ground, incapable of charging. At last the pikes of my lord's army having had no employment all the day, were drawn against the enemy's left wing, and particularly those of my lord's own regiment, which were all stout and valiant men, who fell so furiously upon the enemy, that they forsook their hedges, and fell to their heels. At which very instant my lord caused a shot or two to be made by his cannon against the body of the enemy's horse, drawn up within cannon shot, which took so good effect, that it disordered the enemy's troops. My lord's horse got over the hedge, not in a body (for that they could not), but dispersedly two on a breast; and as soon as some considerable number was gotten over, and drawn up, they charged the enemy, and routed them. In an instant there was a strange change of fortune, and the field totally won by my lord, notwithstanding he had quitted 7000 men, to conduct Her Majesty, besides a good train of artillery, which in such a conjuncture would have weakened Caesar's army. In this victory the enemy lost most of their foot, about 3000 were taken prisoner, and 700 horse and foot slain, and those that escaped fled into their garrison at Bradford, amongst whom was also their general of the horse [Sir Thomas Fairfax].

After this my lord caused his army to be rallied, and marched in order that night before Bradford, with an intention to storm it the next morning. But the enemy that were in the town, it seems, were so discomfited, that the same night they escaped all various ways, and amongst them the said general of the horse, whose lady being behind a servant on horseback, was taken by some of my lord's soldiers, and brought to his quarters.* She was treated and attended with all civility and respect, and within few days sent to York in my lord's own coach, and from thence very shortly after to Kingston upon Hull, where she desired to be, attended by my lord's coach and servants.

The whole county of York, save only Hull, being now cleared and settled by my lord's care and conduct, he marched to the city of York, and having a competent number of horse well armed and commanded, he quartered them in the East Riding, near Hull, there being no visible enemy then to oppose them. In the meanwhile, my lord receiving news that the enemy had made an invasion into the next adjoining county of Lincoln, where he had some forces, he presently dispatched his lieutenant-general of the army [Lord Ethyn] away with some horse and dragoons, and soon after marched thither himself with the body of the army, being earnestly desired by His Majesty's party there. The forces which my lord had in the same county, commanded by the then lieutenant-general of the

* This was Thomas Fairfax's wife, Anne, first cousin of Brilliana Harley. Lucy Hutchinson mentions her on several occasions (pp. 169–70, 192, 195–6), usually in a somewhat critical tone.

horse, Mr Charles Cavendish, second brother to the now Earl of Devonshire, though they had timely notice, and orders from my lord to make their retreat to the lieutenant-general of the army and not to fight the enemy, yet the said lieutenant-general of the horse being transported by his courage (he being a person of great valour and conduct), and having charged the enemy, unfortunately lost the field, and himself was slain in the charge, his horse lighting in a bog.* Which news being brought to my lord when he was on his march, he made all the haste he could, and was no sooner joined with his lieutenant-general, but fell upon the enemy, and put them to flight.

My lord drawing near Gainsborough, there appeared on the top of a hill above the town, some of the enemy's horse drawn up in a body. He immediately sent a party of his horse to view them; who no sooner came within their sight, but they retreated fairly so long as they could well endure; but the pursuit of my lord's horse caused them presently to break their ranks, and fall to their heels, where most of them escaped, and fled to Lincoln, another of their garrisons. Hereupon my lord summoned the town of Gainsborough; but the governor thereof refusing to yield, caused my lord to plant his cannon, and draw up his army on the mentioned hill. Having played some little while upon the town, [these cannon] put the enemy into such a terror, that the governor sent out and offered the surrender of the town upon fair terms, which my lord thought fit rather to embrace, than take it by force. According to the articles of agreement made between them, both the enemy's arms and the keys of the town should have been fairly delivered to my lord. Yet it being not performed as it was expected, the arms being in a confused manner thrown down and the gates set wide open, the prisoners that had been kept in the town began first to plunder; which my lord's forces seeing, did the same, although it was against my lord's will and orders.

---

* At Gainsborough, on 28 July 1643. 'He was the soldiers' mignon and His Majesty's darling . . . the rebels surround him and take him prisoner; and after he was so, a base rascal comes behind him and runs him through.' Aubrey: *Brief Lives*.

5

Some Sieges
1643

*After the abortive attack on Newark in February 1643, the next
alarm for the Hutchinsons was Henrietta Maria, 'She-Majesty
Generalissima over all' as she called herself, passing by Nottingham
with an escort of 5000 troops on her way to Oxford in June. At the
end of that month, John Hutchinson was officially appointed
Governor of Nottingham Castle. Lucy Hutchinson's account of the
fighting at Gainsborough in Lincolnshire in July includes the ironic
story of the time-serving Earl of Kingston's death, as well as a different view of the eventual surrender of the town to that given by
the Duchess of Newcastle (see p. 78).*

*The 'so sharp a fight' in which Edward Harley's horse was
killed under him was at Lansdown near Bath, an incident in
Waller's western campaign which eventually ended in his defeat at
Roundway Down and the fall of Bristol to the royalists in July. This
allowed the royalists to start their long-delayed siege of Brampton
Bryan Castle at the end of that month. Brilliana Harley managed to
get virtually no letters out to her son during it, and for an account of
the siege and its sad aftermath we must turn to her aptly-named
kinsman Captain Priam Davies, who was present throughout.*

*Although Brilliana Harley's stubborn defence forced the royalists
to raise their siege of Brampton in 1643, the castle was to fall in
March 1644 following another three-week siege, its surrender
hastened by the slaughter of twenty-five men after they had been*

taken prisoner at Hopton Castle, an outpost two miles away from Brampton. Prince Rupert's demand that all Brampton's inhabitants be put to the sword fortunately was not obeyed, thus sparing Brilliana's children Thomas, Dorothy and Margaret. Her own body buried in the castle did not fare so well, 'being taken up under pretence to search for jewels, but the jewels being gone, the cabinet was raked up again in close cinders, from where it will one day rise against the monsters and usurpers of the name Christian'.

Brilliana Harley's ordeal was not unique; several royalist ladies endured similar sieges. Lady Arundell was besieged at Wardour Castle in Wiltshire in May and June 1643, Lady Bankes at Corfe Castle in Dorset in June 1643 and again in 1645, the Countess of Derby at Lathom House in Lancashire from February 1644 until relieved by Prince Rupert in May, and the Marchioness of Winchester at Basing House in Hampshire from August 1643 until October 1645.

Alice Thornton gives some curious details of another siege, that of Chester, which ended a few days before Brampton's began. She then recounts her family's adventures, passing through enemy lines at the end of their protracted journey back from Dublin to her mother's home county of Yorkshire.

Lucy Hutchinson

Now the queen was preparing to march up with the assistance she had gotten to the king. Those countries through which she was to pass, could not but be sensible of their danger, especially the gentlemen at Nottingham, who were but a few young men, environed with garrisons of the enemy, and scarcely firm among themselves, and hopeless of relief from above, where the Parliament, struggling for life, had not leisure to bind up a cut finger. But God was with them in these difficulties, and gave an unexpected issue.

A house of my Lord Chaworth's [Wiverton House] in the vale was fortified, and some horse put into it, and another house of the Earl of Chesterfield's [Shelford Manor], both of them within a few miles of Nottingham. Ashby de la Zouch, within eighteen miles of Nottingham, on the other side, was kept by Mr Hastings.* On the forest side of the country, the Earl of Newcastle's house had a garrison, and another castle of his, within a mile, was garrisoned [Welbeck Abbey and Bolsover Castle]. Sir Roger Cooper's house, at Thurgarton, was also kept; so that Nottingham, thus beleaguered with enemies, seemed very unlikely to be able either to resist the enemy or support itself. Therefore the gentlemen, upon the news of my Lord Newcastle's intended approach that way, sent up Mr John Hutchinson to acquaint the Parliament with their condition; who so negotiated their business that he procured an order for Colonel Cromwell, Colonel Hubbard, my Lord Grey, and Sir John Gell, to unite their forces, and rendezvous at Nottingham, to prevent the queen from joining with the king, and to guard those parts against the cavaliers.

As soon as Sir John Meldrum came down to [command these assembled forces at] Nottingham, the queen's forces came and faced the town; whereupon the cannon discharging upon them, the Duke of Vendôme's son and some few others were slain. The Parliament horse drew out of Nottingham to receive the queen's, but they came not on, after this execution of the cannon. In the meantime the queen was passing by, and although the Parliament horse pursued them, yet they would not engage, for it was not their business; so when they saw they had lost their design, the horse returned again to Nottingham, where the foot had stayed all the while they were out.

Sir John Meldrum called the committee of Nottingham together, to consult what was to be done for the settlement of the place, which upon deliberation he had judged it not fit to leave in the hands it was, nor in Colonel Pierrepont's, who, with some appearance, lay under suspicion at that time; and therefore conceiving Mr Hutchinson the most able to manage, and the most responsible for it, both Sir John and the whole committee ordered him to take the castle into his charge.

The castle was built upon a rock, and nature had made it

* Henry Hastings, a son of the Earl of Huntingdon, himself created Lord Loughborough in 1643.

capable of very strong fortification, but the buildings were very ruinous and uninhabitable, neither affording room to lodge soldiers nor provisions. The castle stands at one end of the town, upon such an eminence as commands the chief streets of the town. There had been enlargements made to this castle after the first building of it. There was a strong tower, which they called the old tower, built upon the top of all the rock, and this was that place where Queen Isabel, the mother of King Edward III, was surprised with her paramour Mortimer, who, by secret windings and hollows in the rock, came up into her chamber from the meadows lying low under it, through which there ran a little rivulet, called the Leen, almost under the castle rock. At the entrance of this rock there was a spring, which was called Mortimer's Well, and the cavern Mortimer's Hole. The ascent to the top is very high, and it is not without some wonder that at the top of all the rock there should be a spring of water. In the midway to the top of this tower there is a little piece of the rock, on which a dovecote had been built, but the governor took down the roof of it, and made it a platform for two or three pieces of ordnance, which commanded some streets and all the meadows better than the higher tower. Under that tower, which was the old castle, there was a larger castle, where there had been several towers and many noble rooms, but the most of them were down. The yard of that was pretty large, and without the gate there was a very large yard that had been walled, but the walls were all down, only it was situated upon an ascent of the rock, and so stood a pretty height above the streets; and there were the ruins of an old pair of gates, with turrets on each side.

Before the castle, the town was on one side of a close, which commanded the fields approaching the town; which close the governor afterwards made a platform. Behind it was a place called the Park, that belonged to the castle, but then had neither deer nor trees in it, except one tree, growing under the castle, which was almost a prodigy, for from the root to the top, there was not a straight twig or branch in it; some said it was planted by King Richard III, and resembled him that set it. On the other side the castle, was the little river of Leen, and beyond that, large flat meadows, bounded by the River Trent. In the whole rock there were many large caverns, where a great magazine and many hundred soldiers might have been disposed, if they had been cleansed and prepared for it; and they might have been kept secure from any danger of firing the magazines by any mortar-pieces shot against the castle. In one of these places, it is reported that one David, a Scotch king, was kept in cruel durance, and with his nails, had scratched on the wall the story of Christ and his twelve apostles. The castle was not defended by lateral fortifications, and there were no works about it, when Mr Hutchinson undertook it, but only a little breastwork, before the outermost gate. It was as ill provided as fortified, there being but 10 barrels of powder, 1150 pounds of butter, and as much cheese, 11 quarters of bread corn, 7 beeves, 214 flitches of bacon, 560 fishes, and 15 hogsheads of beer. As soon as the governor received his charge, he made proclamation in the town, that whatsoever honest persons desired to secure themselves or their goods in the castle, should have reception there, if they would repair their quarters; which divers well-affected men accepting, it was presently made capable of receiving 400 men commodiously.

The Earl of Kingston [had, at the start of the Civil War,] a few months stood neuter, and would not declare himself for either party, and being a man of great wealth and dependencies, many people hung in suspense, by his example. When the danger grew more imminent, and my lord lay out a brave prey to the enemy, they sent Captain Lomax, one of the committee, to understand his affections from himself, and to press him to declare for the Parliament, in that so needful a season. My lord, professing himself to him as rather desirous of peace, and fully resolved not to act on either side, made a serious imprecation on himself in these words: 'When', said he, 'I take arms with the king against the Parliament, or with the Parliament against the king, let a cannon bullet divide me between them'; which God was pleased to bring to pass a few months after. For he, going to Gainsborough, and there taking up arms for the king, was surprised by my Lord Willoughby, and, after a handsome defence of himself, yielded, and was put prisoner into a pinnace, and sent down the river to Hull. My Lord Newcastle's army marching along the shore, shot at the pinnace, and being in danger, the Earl of Kingston went up on the deck to show himself and to prevail with them to forbear shooting. But as soon as he appeared, a cannon bullet flew from the king's army, and divided him in the middle, and thus, being then in the Parliament's pinnace, he perished according to his own unhappy imprecation.

Immediately part of my Lord Newcastle's army, with all that Newark could make, besieged my Lord Willoughby in Gainsborough; and General Essex sent a command to Sir John Meldrum to draw all the horse and foot he could out of Nottingham, to relieve my lord, leaving only a garrison in the castle of Nottingham. Sir John Meldrum, joining with Colonel Cromwell's men, marched to Gainsborough, and engaged those that besieged it, and were victorious, killing their general, Sir Charles Cavendish, with many more commanders, and some hundreds of soldiers. This was opportunely done, as my Lord Newcastle was hastening to come over the water and join them. By a bridge of boats, he passed all his army over, and came near Gainsborough, just in a season to behold the rout of all his men. The Parliament's forces expected he would have fallen upon them, and drew up in a body and faced him, but he advanced not; so they contented themselves by relieving Gainsborough, and made a very honourable retreat to Lincoln. But Gainsborough not being fortified, nor provided, this relief did not much advantage them, for my Lord Newcastle again besieged it, which was rendered to him, after eight days, upon conditions honourable for the defendants, though they were not performed by the besiegers. All my Lord Willoughby's men were disarmed contrary to articles, and with them, some of the Nottingham soldiers that had gone into the town to refresh themselves, and so were shut up with them, when my Lord Newcastle laid siege to it. At Lincoln, all the forces that went from Nottingham dispersed into different services. Major Ireton began an inseparable league with Colonel Cromwell, whose son-in-law he afterwards was. None of them could return to Nottingham, by reason of my Lord Newcastle's army, which lay between.

Brilliana Harley

11 July 1643: I acknowledge the great mercy of my God that he preserved you in so sharp a fight, when your horse was killed. I am sorry you have lost so many horses out of your troop; but I hope they will be made up again. I know not what they will do hereafter but, as yet, I can get but very little towards the buying of a horse; what it is, I have sent you enclosed.

An account of the siege of Brampton Bryan Castle by Captain Priamus Davies, who was an eyewitness.

That honourable and gallant Lady Harley put herself into a posture of defence against their insolent and illegal proceedings. The castle being of considerable strength was manned with about fifty musketeers, some gentlemen commanders, with an answerable proportion of powder and match, and thus inoffensively did this noble lady live upon her own in an honourable, resolute and religious way till the malice of her enemies broke forth. A summons was sent from Mr William Coningsby, which contained many threats and vapours, but no storm followed, save only seizing upon her revenues very valiantly. The next summons came from the Lord Marquis of Hertford, whose honour was presently remanded unto a more honourable service than to fight with a lady. The third summons was by Henry Lingen, High Sheriff of the county of Hereford, Sir Walter Pye, knight, and William Smallman, esquire. Upon Wednesday the 26th of July, 1643, these appeared and faced us with a body of horse and foot, stopped our passages and sat down before us, took some of the inhabitants, amongst whom there was one born blind, who [when] they demanded who he was for, he replied for King and Parliament, him they presently murdered.

Upon the 27th the enemy possessed themselves of the town and church; we played upon each other all that day and night with small shot and slew some of the enemy. The 28th we continued shooting till the evening, when another trumpet was sent from Sir William Vavasour, Governor of Hereford, with a letter.

The 29th their horse faced us again; by this time they had plundered us of all horses, fat beef, sheep, etc., which was indeed their business and errand they came about, and then sent a drum with a letter. Upon Sunday the 30th we expected their ordnance, and were compelled to block up our double portcullis, for the loss of the church which stood directly before the castle gate, within sixty or seventy paces, did extremely annoy us. The 1st of August, the enemy made their approaches into our quarters, began to raise breastworks and batteries, whereupon we gave fire and beat them out. The cavaliers presently fired a house in the town, and we for our own defence put fire to all our out-houses, which contained many bays of new building, which was much for our advantage. A trumpeter was again sent with a letter.

Upon the 3rd of August the enemy burnt our mills. This day the greatest part of the town was consumed and burnt. In the afternoon they placed a great gun in the steeple and made five shots which only shattered the battlements but did no execution. It is observable, that in these nine days not one of us was hurt; that all of us took joyfully the spoiling of our goods, that none of us were daunted either by the enemy, or by the malignants of the country, who stood upon hills about us, giving great shouts whenever the ordnance played. Upon the 4th the parsonage house was burnt which was for our advantage, for then they began to raise more batteries. All this day they played with their great gun; twenty-six shots they made which did little execution but upon chimneys and battlements. Upon the 5th the enemy made twenty-three shots more, at last came down a stack of chimneys, at which the cavaliers gave a great shout and cause they had so to do, that with thirty-seven shots no more execution should be done. We pretermitted [omitted] nothing that might strengthen our walls, but all of us laboured, as they say, for life with much cheerfulness. Sunday the 6th they would not let us rest; they made eight shots against us before morning sermon, then left off that day as if they had been ashamed. It was this day observed, that although there were of men, women and children above a hundred all immured up in a close house, and in the dog days, yet there was not one feeble or sick person amongst us.

Upon the 7th in the afternoon they planted another great gun against the west part of our castle. The third shot the bullet came in at a window, shattered the walls, which hurt the Lady Colburn, struck out one of her eyes. Lieutenant-Colonel Wright's wife was hurt, but neither of them mortally. Upon the 8th they planted another great gun against the west part of the castle; this made twenty-nine shots, all which did no further execution. This evening two colonels of foot, the trainbands of Ludlow came before, who at their first approach vapoured, called us roundheads, rogues and traitors, and sat down. Upon the 9th the enemy had planted five great guns, as if they meant this day to have beaten it to dust. They made forty-two shots, which through God's mercy did little hurt. The noble lady was this day more courageous than ever, bid us now play the men, for the enemy was in good earnest. Among the many policies of war it is not the least to hold intelligence with friends abroad, and in this her wisdom was great. This night we had secret intelligence through all their courts of guard to our no small advantage and encouragement.

Upon the 10th they made but three shots which did no execution, but some Venice glasses in a high tower. These had formerly entertained some of those capon-faced cowards who had now unmanned themselves in offering violence to so noble a lady. This night we had secret intelligence that their greatest gun was yesterday broken, which killed their cannoneer; that we had slain many of their men, amongst others our mason as he was pointing with his hand to show the enemy the weakest part of the castle was shot through that hand into his belly and died. Upon the 11th the enemy began very early with their great guns which in the night they had placed nearer to us; this day they made thirty-five shots which did no great execution. Upon the 12th the enemy continued this battery, cursing the roundheads, calling us Essex's bastards, Waller's bastards, Harley's bastards, rogues, thieves, traitors. It is very remarkable that notwithstanding so many thousand great and small shot not a man was hurt. Sunday 13th of August we were necessitated to work, for we found that our wall was battered almost to a breach, very near the ground. Here we made strong barricades and lined the walls with earth. This night we had intelligence that two more of their great iron guns were broken, the cannoneers sore hurt.

Upon the 15th we had secret intelligence that Gloucester was besieged, that the king lay before it, that Bristol was delivered up, that our castle was given to Sheriff Lingen if he could get it. [The bombardment continued.] Upon the 18th our cook was shot into the arm with a poisoned bullet and died, this was the first bullet that touched any of us. This night we had secret intelligence from our friends abroad but no hopes of relief, that we had slain about sixty of the enemy. Sunday, the 20th, we spent in fasting and praying that we might be delivered out of the hands of these bloody enemies, who were by the power of God this day restrained from disturbing us. Upon the 21st the noble lady called a council to advise how those quarters of the enemy should be fired where their grenades were preparing. It was resolved that ten men should sally out upon that quarter suddenly, who were to retreat by a word. These no sooner fell on but, with rockets from the castle, the house was fired, all their materials and grenades burnt; our men slew some of them and retreated back again without any loss, in all which time the enemy were struck with such a panic fear that they could neither fight nor run away. At last recollecting themselves they made four shots with their great gun which did no execution.

Upon the 22nd day the enemy made their approaches nearer to us, cast up breastworks in our garden and walks, where their rotten and poisoned language annoyed us more than their poisoned bullets. This day they made eight shots against another tower of the castle, which did no execution. Upon the 23rd a drum* was sent with a parley; Sir John Scudamore was sent with a letter from His Majesty to the noble lady; she returns an humble petition to His Majesty, then lying before Gloucester. This night we had secret intelligence by letters from London of an insurrection of the malignants there, into what a low condition the Parliament party were throughout the kingdom, this

---

* Drum: a small party, accompanied by a drummer, sent to parley.

exceeding us insomuch that some advised then to deliver up the castle. But then the noble lady protested, that she would rather choose an honourable death, for she was confident that God would own His cause both in the public and private. We needed no better an encouragement.

Upon the 24th the parley continued with a cessation of arms. Sir John Scudamore came up into the castle by a ladder and a rope, had conference with the noble lady, demanded her castle, etc.

Upon the 25th at night intelligence came to us from our friends abroad, that things in the general were not so bad. Gloucester was resolved to fight it out to the last man and such cruelty was exercised at Bristol notwithstanding fair promises, that it was a precedent to the whole kingdom never to believe the cavaliers. This parley continued seven days until an answer of the petition aforesaid should be returned. The seventh night we had secret intelligence through all their courts of guard again, that Gloucester still held out gallantly although the greatest of our enemies with divers oaths affirmed that it was delivered up. Upon the 2nd of September a trumpet was sent by Sir William Vavasour with a letter. Upon the 4th we had intelligence that the enemy meant to undermine us, and that they had prepared 'hoggs' to that end. Upon the 5th a knight came with the king's answer, as they pretended, subscribed by Lord Falkland. Upon the 6th the parley continued. This day the enemy began to remove their carriages whereupon we gave them a warning piece; they answered us with two great guns. Upon the 7th with two more. This night the enemy stole away their great guns. Upon the 8th they carried away our bells, which cost some of them their lives. Upon the 9th of September the enemy fired their barricade and then we were confident they were taking their leave.

This night we had secret intelligence that my lord General [Essex] was with a great army very near Gloucester. That the king had raised the siege to give him battle, and that all his forces were called away. This night the Lord was pleased to take away these bloody enemies and to return them with shame which had now lain before us seven weeks almost, for which we returned humble thanks to God that delivered our poor family

out of the hands of fifteen malignant counties set against it.
During the siege our sufferings were great, the enemy sat down
so suddenly before us. All our bread was ground with a hand
mill, our provisions very scarce, the roof of the castle so battered that there was not one dry room in it; our substance without plundered and all our friends fled, yet this noble lady bore
all with admirable patience, and thus have I truly related the
several passages of our siege from our shutting up to the day of
our deliverance.

The former siege being raised and we set at liberty, the noble
lady instead of revenging herself upon the inhabitants of that
country who were active against her to the utmost of their
might and power, yea none more forward and false than her
own tenants and servants, in a courteous and winning way
gently entreated the part adjacent to come in and level those
works which they pretended the enemy had compelled them to
raise against her, promising to protect them, and that none of
her soldiers should plunder them. All which they barbarously
refused, whereupon we took out a party and compelled them in,
but by her special command that none should take a penny-
worth from any of them, which was as truly observed, I dare
appeal to their own consciences, until their malice broke forth
again. Many that had not paid their rents of some years before
refused; yea they would not let us have provisions nor any of
the conveniences of life which they could hinder us from.

Our necessities and resolutions would no longer brook such
barbarism; we then daily sent our parties only against those
that had been most active against us; whereby our necessities
were in a short time supplied. This exasperated the enemy that
they removed their quarters nearer to us. Whereupon this noble
lady who commanded in chief, I may truly say with such a
masculine bravery, both for religion, resolution, wisdom and
warlike policy, that her equal I never yet saw, commanded that
a party of about forty should go and beat up their quarters in
Knighton, a market town in Radnorshire, four miles off, where
Colonel Lingen's troop, her late antagonist, was quartered.
This was so performed that we brought some prisoners, arms
and horses without the loss of one man; colours also we had, a

hand reaching out of a cloud, holding a sword, with the instruction or motto, *Rex et Regina beati, sibi, suisque.** This struck such a panic fear upon the enemy, that for six weeks after they never appeared, in which time we put ourselves into a considerable posture again, and made good preparation for approaching winter, besides that noble Colonel Massey had sent us one barrel of powder, some men and arms, which was all the encouragement or rescue we had.

By this time the fame of this noble lady was spread over most of the kingdom with admiration and applause, even of her enemies. Those that were commanders-in-chief against her were extremely jeered in the king's army, but herself honourably spoken of. Suddenly, as she was a setting forward the work of God, she unexpectedly fell sick of an apoplexy with a defluxion of the lungs. Three days she continued in great extremity with admirable patience. Never was a holy life consummated and concluded with a more heavenly and happy end. Her body, which she desired might be wrapped in lead, was carefully preserved and placed in a high tower of the castle to attend an honourable funeral.

Alice Thornton

Many and great was the sorrows and sufferings of my dear and honoured mother, with her whole family, upon the sad change by the death of my honoured father. And she continued in her house in Dublin, maintaining the great household in the same condition as it was, at her own charges, for the honour of the same, till about the October after, when, on the 23rd day in the year 1641, that horrid rebellion and massacre of the poor English Protestants began to break out in the country, which was by the all-seeing providence of God prevented in the city of Dublin, where we were. We were forced upon the alarum to leave our house and fly into the castle that night with all my mother's family and what goods she could. From thence we

* May the King, the Queen, and their supporters all flourish.

were forced into the city, continuing for fourteen days and nights in great fears, frights, and hideous distractions and disturbances from the alarums and outcries given in Dublin each night by the rebels. These frights, fastings, and pains about packing the goods, and wanting sleep, times of eating, or refreshment, wrought so much upon my young body, that I fell into a desperate flux, called the Irish disease, being nigh unto death, while I stayed in Dublin, as also in the ship coming for England.

After our coming to Chester when we fled out of the Irish rebellion, it pleased God to move the gentry of the city to be exceeding courteous and civil to my dear mother and myself, assisting her with what necessaries she wanted in a strange place. The wars falling out hot at the time, being we were beleaguered in Chester by Sir William Brereton's forces for the Parliament, there happened a strange accident which raised that siege, July 19th, 1643. As I was informed, there was three granadoes shot into the town, but, through Providence, hurt nobody. The first, being shot into the sconce [earthwork] of our soldiers within, two men of the Captain Manwaring, but having an ox's hide ready, clapped it thereon, and it smothering away in shells did not spread but went out. The second light short of the city, in a ditch within a pasture amongst a company of women milking, but was quenched without doing them harm at all, praised be the Lord our God. The last fell amongst their own horse, short of the town, slaying many of them, and by that means the siege was raised.

I had in this time of the siege a grand deliverance. Standing in a turret in my mother's house, having been at prayer in the first morning, we were beset in the town; and not hearing of it before, as I looked out at a window towards St Mary's Church, a cannon bullet flew so nigh the place where I stood that the window suddenly shut with such a force the whole turret shook. It pleased God I escaped without more harm, save that the waft took my breath from me for that present, and caused a great fear and trembling, not knowing from whence it came.

My brother, John Wandesford, was preserved from death in the smallpox, he having taken them of one of my cousin

William Wandesford's sons, living then at Chester. Great was my mother's fear for him, and care and pains she took about him, and at last he, through mercy, was recovered, although he was very much disfigured, having been a very beautiful child, and of a sweet complexion. In the time of his sickness I was forbidden to come to him lest I should get the smallpox and endanger my own life, and so observed my mother's command in that. But my love for him could not contain itself from sending in letters to him, by a way found out of my foolish invention, tying them about a little dog's neck, which, being taken into his bed, brought the infection of the disease upon myself, as also the sight of him after his recovery; being struck with fear seeing him so sadly used and all over very red, I immediately fell very ill . . .

From Chester my dear mother removed, with her three younger children, Alice, Christopher, and John [in August 1643]. With these and several servants and tenants, though with much difficulty, by reason of the interchange of the king's armies and the Parliament's, she was brought into the town of Warrington towards coming into Yorkshire: she finding more favour by reason of the captain's civility, and by a pass from Colonel Shuttleworth [of Gawthorpe Hall], than usual. Seeing nothing but a weak company for her person, and having lost all in Ireland, only two trunks of wearing linen, they gave her leave to pass, and about ten o'clock at night we came weary into the town of Warrington. After a while we were entertained with alarums, as was pretended, from the king's party in Chester; this was but to awaken their diligency the more, but there was no cause, for the poor town [Chester] had work enough to defend itself from its enemies. From Warrington we went to Wigan the next day, being a town zealous for their king and church. We found it sorely demolished, and all the windows broken; many sad complaints of the poor inhabitants. At our first coming they were scared, lest we should have been of the Parliament party. Their cries were the greater in respect they were enforced to see the burning of 500 of their own Bibles publicly at the Cross by the soldiers, which they plundered under pretence of being popery in their service-books, and reviling them with the name of papists' dogs.

The next day we passed from thence towards Yorkshire, with many prayers from this people, and when we came to the borders of Lancashire, at a place called Downham [near Clitheroe], we were not permitted to pass, but with harsh language and abuse by a Parliament corporal and his gang. They would not believe our pass, but took us down, swearing and threatening we should be stripped; so my dear mother and all of us was forced to come into a pitiful house for shelter, and lie there all night, with heavy hearts, lest we should have been used barbarously, as they continued in threatening against my father's widow and children. That night two of themselves, with my mother's servant, went to Colonel Shuttleworth, ten miles off, who, upon the sight of his own pass, did declare his grand displeasure for their rudenesses to my mother and children, causing his son-in-law, Captain John Ashton, to punish those villains, and convey her safe as far as his quarters lay, wishing her a good journey.

2 September 1643: My mother was minded to go to Snape [near Bedale, Yorkshire], where my sister Danby [wife of Sir Thomas Danby, Kt] was, and being invited by her she went thither to live till she could better dispose of herself and us in those troublesome times. For it being in the heat of the wars, she could not live at Hipswell, her jointure, which was molested sometimes with the Parliament's, and then the king's forces amongst them, so that for a whole year we lived with great comfort and safety with my sweet sister Danby at Snape, where she was delivered of a gallant son. Even in the midst of troubles God gave her comfort, and my brother would have him called Charles, because of his engagement for the king's service.

Nottingham Attacked
1643-4

The attack of the Newark royalists on Nottingham in September *1643*, which Lucy Hutchinson describes next, established the pattern of raid and counter-raid between the two Trent towns. As she said, 'all the horse having been drawn out of Nottingham for the relief of Gainsborough', the former was left in a vulnerable state. In spite of the vigilance of Colonel Hutchinson the disobedience of the towns-people nearly resulted in the fall of the castle.

As an interlude from war, there follows a self-portrait of the Duchess of Newcastle, that least bellicose of beings: 'Nay, the shoot-ing of a gun, although but a pot-gun, will make me start, and stop my hearing, much less have I courage to discharge one.' It ends with her appointment as maid-of-honour to Queen Henrietta Maria, newly arrived in Oxford after her march from York, in the autumn of *1643*.

The next passages from Lucy Hutchinson contain some of her most vivid descriptions of fighting in Nottinghamshire. First, in the bitter winter weather in January *1644*, an attack led by the Duchess of Newcastle's brother, Sir Charles Lucas, was repulsed after an initial display of cowardice by the Nottingham forces. Then a covert operation against the vital Trent bridges was discovered, before the parliamentarians went on the offensive against Shelford and Newark. This sequence was brought to an end by Prince Rupert who, in one of his most brilliant actions, relieved Newark in March *1644*.

Lucy Hutchinson

Sir John Meldrum, in marching forth to the relief of Gainsborough, left Nottingham to be guarded by few more than the very townsmen. There had been large works made about it, which would have required at least 3000 men to man and defend well, and upon these works there were about fourteen guns which the governor, when the forces were marching away, before they went, drew up to the castle, whereupon the townsmen, especially those that were ill-affected to the Parliament, made a great mutiny, threatening they would pull the castle down, but they would have their ordnance again upon their works, and wishing it on fire, and not one stone upon another. Hereupon the governor sent Alderman Drury, with fourteen more, who were heads of this mutiny, prisoners to Derby, whither Major Ireton convoyed them with his troop.

And now it was time for them at Nottingham to expect my Lord Newcastle [after his capture of Gainsborough], which the governor made provision for with all the diligence that it was possible under so many difficulties and obstacles, which would to anyone else have been discouragements; but he had so high a resolution that nothing conquered it. The townsmen, though discontent at the drawing out of the forces, whereby their houses, families, and estates were exposed, began to envy, then to hate the castle, as grieved that anything should be preserved when all could not; and indeed those who were more concerned in private interests than in the cause itself, had some reason, because the neighbourhood of the castle, when it was too weak to defend them, would endanger them.

The governor, perceiving this defection, set some of the most zealous honest men to find out how many there were in the town who, neglecting all private interests, would cheerfully and freely come in and venture all with him; intending, if he could not have found enough to defend the place, that he would have sent to other neighbouring garrisons to have borrowed some. Upon this enquiry, it was found that many of Colonel Pierrepont's own company were desirous to come in, but first wished to know their colonel's resolution as to how he would dispose of them; whereupon a hall was called, and the danger of the place declared to the whole town, that they might have time to provide for their goods and persons before the enemy came upon them. The colonel being present, his company asked him what he would advise them to do; to whom his answer was, 'You have but three ways to choose, either leave the town and secure yourselves in some other Parliament garrisons, or list into the castle, or stand on the works and have your throats cut.' Notwithstanding this public resolution in the hall to his company, he told them, and many others in private, that he preferred the interest of the town above that of his life, and would expose his life for the good of it, and stand on the works of the town as long as they could be defended, and when they could no longer be kept, he would retire to some other Parliament garrison. Others he told, he scorned that his colours should serve in the castle. At length, out of all the four companies and the whole town, about 300 men enlisted into the castle.

The governor had procured forty barrels of powder, and 2000-weight of match from London, and had increased the store of provision as much as the present poverty of their condition would permit him. Then the committee of Nottingham, so many of them as were remaining in the town, and all the ministers of the Parliament's party there, came up to the castle, and, with the officers of the garrison, ate at the governor's, to his very great charge. He was so far from receiving pay at that time, that all the money he could procure of his own credit, or take up with others, he was forced to expend for the several necessities of the soldiers and garrison. Yet were the soldiers then, and a long time after, kept together as long as they could live, without any pay, and afterwards paid part in victuals, and the rest run on in arrears.

The townsmen who came into the castle disposed their families into several villages in the country; and at length a trumpet was sent, for a safe conduct for a gentleman, from my Lord Newcastle; and having it, Major Cartwright came from him, with a summons for the delivery of the town and castle, to which the committee for the town, and the governor for the castle, returned a civil defiance in writing, about the 10th day of August. Cartwright, having received it, and being treated with wine by the governor and the rest of the officers, grew bold in the exercise of an abusive wit he had, and told both the Mr Hutchinsons that they were sprightly young men, but when my lord should come with his army, he would find them in other terms, beseeching my lord to spare them, as misled young men, and to suffer them to march away with a cudgel. 'And then', said he, 'shall I stand behind my lord's chair and laugh.' At which the governor, being angry, told him he was much mistaken, for he scorned ever to yield on any terms, to a papistical army led by an atheistical general. Mr George Hutchinson told him, 'If my lord would have that poor castle he must wade to it in blood.' Which words they say he told his general.

After these summonses were received, the governor drew all his soldiers into the castle, and committed the guard of the town to the aldermen, who were to set guards of fifty in a night, according to their wards. Then calling together his soldiers, he once again represented to them their condition, and told them, that being religious and honest men, he could be assured no extremity would make them fail in what they found themselves strong enough to undertake; and therefore he should not fear to let them freely understand their danger, which yet they had power to shun, and therefore whatever misery might be the issue of their undertaking, they could not justly impute it to him, it being their own election. For after this summons they must expect the enemy, and to be reduced to the utmost extremity by them, that thought could reach. It must not move them to see their houses flaming, and, if need were, themselves firing them for the public advantage, or to see the pieces of their families cruelly abused and consumed before them; they must resolve upon hard duty, fierce assaults, poor and sparing diet, perhaps famine, and the want of all comfortable accommodations. Nor was there very apparent hope of relief at last, but more than common hazard of losing their lives, either in defence of their fort or of the place; which, for want of good fortifications, and through disadvantage of a neighbouring mount and building, was not, in human probability, tenable against such an army as threatened it. All which, for his own part, he was resolved on; and if any of them found their courage failing, he only desired they would provide for their safety in time elsewhere, and not prejudice him and the public interest so highly, as they would do, to take upon them the defence of the castle, except they could be content to lay down their lives and all their interests in it.

The soldiers were none of them terrified at the dangers which threatened their undertaking; but at the latter end of August took, upon the solemn fast-day, the national covenant,* and besides it, a particular mutual covenant between them and the governor, to be faithful to each other, and to hold out the place to the death, without entertaining any parley, or accepting any terms from the enemy. This the governor was forced to do to confirm them, for he had his experience not only of the ungodly and ill-affected, but even of the godly themselves, who thought it scarcely possible for any one to continue a gentleman, and firm to a godly interest, and therefore repaid all his vigilancy and labours for them with a very unjust jealousy. The Governor of Newark was his cousin-german, to whom he was forced, against his nature, to be more uncivil than to any others that were governors in that place. Whether it was that the dissension of brethren is always most spitefully pursued, or that Sir Richard Byron, as it was reported, suffered under the same suspicions on his side, it is true they were to each other the most uncivil enemies that can be imagined.

After this summons, my Lord Newcastle came not, according to their bravadoes, but diverted his army to Hull, to besiege my Lord Fairfax there; they of Newark having gotten him to send this summons upon confidence, knowing the condition of the place, that it would have been yielded to a piece of paper. The governor immediately set upon the fortification of his castle, made a work behind it, another on the Leen side, turned the dovecote into a platform, and made a court of guard in Mortimer's Hole.

The poor soldiers had such short pay that they were, for the

* A formal oath to support the cause of Parliament.

most part, thirty weeks and more behind; and when they marched out at any time, the governor would not suffer them to take a cup of drink, unpaid for, in the country, but always, wherever they took any refreshment in their marches, paid it himself. He gave them besides much from his own house, especially when any of them were sick or wounded, and lent money to those who were most necessitous. All this ran him into a great private debt, besides many thousands of pounds, which he engaged himself in with other gentlemen, and took up for the supply of the garrison and carrying on of the public service. Although the allowance for his table was much envied by those mean fellows, that never knew what the expense of a table was, and although it was to him some ease, yet it did not defray the third part of his expense in the service, being but ten pounds a week allowed by the state. His expenses all that time, in the public service only, and not at all in any particular of his own family, were, as it was kept upon account, above £1500 a year.

As soon as his father was dead [August 1643], and rents became due to him, the enemies, in the midst of whom his estate lay, fetched in his tenants and imprisoned them, and took his rents; his estate was begged and promised by the king; those who lived not upon the place, flung up his grounds, and they lay unoccupied, while the enemy prevailed in the country. He was not so cruel as others were to their tenants, who made them pay over again those rents with which the enemy forced them to redeem themselves out of prison, but lost the most part of his rents, all the while the country was under the adverse power. He had some small stock of his own plundered, and his house, by the perpetual haunting of the enemy, defaced, and for want of inhabitation, rendered almost uninhabitable. For these things he never received one penny of recompense; and his arrears of pay, which he received after all the war was done, did not half pay the debts of those services contracted. He might have made many advantages by the spoil of his enemies, which was often brought in, and by other encroachments upon the country, which almost all the governors, on both sides, exacted everywhere else, but his heart abhorred it. The soldiers had all the prizes, and he never shared with them; all the malignants' goods the committee disposed of; and it ever grieved his heart to see the spoil of his neighbours, how justly soever they deserved it. He chose all loss, rather than to make up himself by violence and rapine.

And now Colonel Thornhagh brought back his troop from Lincoln, and quartered in the town. This being a bait to invite the enemy, the governor gave charge to all that belonged to the castle, being about 300 men, that they should not upon any pretence whatever be out of their quarters; but they having, many of them, wives and better accommodations in the town, by stealth disobeyed his commands, and seldom left any more in the castle than what were upon the guard.

The townsmen were every night out upon the guard of the town, according to the wards of the aldermen; but the most of them being disaffected, the governor, fearing treachery, had determined to quarter the horse in those lanes which were next to the castle, and to block up the lanes for the better securing them. Just the night before these lanes should have been blocked up, Alderman Toplady, a great malignant, having the watch, the enemy was, by treachery, let into the town, and no alarm given to the castle. Though there were two muskets at the gate where they entered, both of them were surrendered without one shot to give notice; and all the horse and about two parts of the castle soldiers were betrayed, surprised, and seized on in their beds. There were not above fourscore of the castle foot taken; the rest hid themselves, and privately stole away, some into the country, and some by night came up to the castle and got in, in disguises, by the river side. But the cavaliers were possessed of the town, and no notice at all given to the castle.

When, at the beating of reveille, some of the soldiers, that had been on the watch all night, were going down into the town to refresh themselves, they were no sooner out of the castle gates but some of the enemy's musketeers discharged upon them, and they hasting back, got in with such care that the enemy was prevented of their design of falling in with them. They brought a strong alarm into the castle, when the governor coming forth, was exceedingly vexed to find that his men were, so many of them, contrary to his command, wanting in their quarters. But it was no time to be angry, but to apply himself to do what was possible to preserve the place. He immediately despatched messengers by a private sally-port, to Leicester and Derby, to desire their assistance, either to come and help to beat the enemy out of the town, or to lend him some foot to help keep the castle, in which there were but fourscore men, and never a lieutenant nor any head officer but his brother, nor so much as a surgeon among them.

As soon as the governor had despatched his messengers he went up to the towers, and from thence played his ordnance into the town, which seldom failed of execution upon the enemy; but there was an old church, called St Nicholas Church, whose steeple so commanded the platform that the men could not play the ordnance without woolpacks before them. From this church the bullets played so thick into the outward castle yard, that they could not pass from one gate to the other, nor relieve the guards, but with very great hazard. One weak old man was shot the first day, who, for want of a surgeon, bled to death before they could carry him up to the governor's wife, who at that time supplied that want as well as she could; but at night the governor and his men dug a trench between the two gates, through which they afterwards better secured their passage. In the meantime the cavaliers that came from Newark, being about 600, fell to ransack and plunder all the honest men's houses in the town, and the cavaliers of the town, who had called them in, helped them in this work. Their prisoners they at first put into the sheep-pens in the market-place, whereupon an honest townsman, seeing four or five commanders go into his own house, procured a cunning boy that came with him, while the enemy regarded more their plunder than their prisoners, to run privately up to the castle and give them notice, who presently sent a cannon bullet into the house. The cavaliers called in all the country as soon as they were in the town, and made a fort at the Trent bridges, and thither they carried down all their considerable plunder and prisoners.

The next day after Sir Richard Byron had surprised the town, Mr Hastings, since made Lord of Loughborough, then Governor of Ashby-de-la-Zouch, came with a body of about

400 men; but being displeased that the plunder was begun before he came, he returned again and left the Newark gentlemen to themselves. As they made a fort at the bridges, they threw down the half moons* and bulwarks that had been raised about the town. They stayed five days, but very unquietly, for the cannon and muskets from the castle failed not of execution daily upon many of them, and they durst not in all that time go to bed. The third day Major Cartwright sent a letter, desiring the governor or his brother to come and meet him in St Nicholas Church, and promised them safe passage and return; but the governor read the letter to his soldiers, and commanded a red flag to be set upon the tower to bid them defiance, and shot three pieces of cannon at the steeple in answer to his desired parley.

Five days the enemy stayed in the town, and all that time the governor and his soldiers were none of them off from the guard, but if they slept, which they never did in the night, it was by the side of them that watched. At length, on Saturday, September 23rd, in the afternoon, the governor saw a great many goods and persons going over the Leen bridge, and not knowing what it meant, sent some cannon bullets after them. On the other side of the town he discerned a body of men, whom he knew not at first, whether to be friends or foes. Having at that time about eightscore men in the castle, for in that five days' space fourscore were come in by stealth, he caused them all to be drawn out in the castle yard, and perceiving that those he last saw were friends, he sent out his brother, Major Hutchinson, with all the musketeers that could be spared, to help drive the enemy out of the town. They having effected what they came for, in fortifying the bridges, had nothing more to do but to get safe off, which they endeavoured with more haste and disorder than became good and stout soldiers.

When Major Hutchinson came into the town with his men, they, greedy of knowing what was become of their wives and houses, dropped so fast from behind him to make the enquiry, that they had left him at the head of only sixteen men, when Sir Richard Byron, with Captain Hacker, followed by a whole

* Crescent-shaped earthworks.

troop of horse and a company of foot, came upon him. The major commanded his men to charge them, which they did, but shot over; yet falling in with them pell-mell, they had gotten Sir Richard Byron down, and they had his hat, but he escaped, though his horse was so wounded that it fell dead in the next street.

These men that came to the governor's relief were Captain White with his troop, who were quartered at Leicester, on his return from Lincolnshire, from whence he was coming back to Nottingham. At Leicester he met the messenger the governor had sent for assistance, which he prosecuted so well, that from the two garrisons of Leicester and Derby, with his own troop, he brought about 400 men. As soon as they were come into the town, Sir John Gell's [Derby] men, seeing the cavaliers had a mind to be gone, interrupted them not, but being as dextrous at plunder as at fight, they presently went to Toplady's house, who had betrayed the town, and plundered it and some others, while the governor's soldiers were busy in clearing the town of the enemy. When they had done this, the governor did what he could to restrain the plunder; but the truth is, Gell's men were nimble youths at that work, yet there was not very much mischief done by them. Toplady's house fared the worst, but his neighbours saved much of his goods; he himself, with several other townsmen and countrymen, who had been very active against the well-affected, at this time were brought up prisoners to the castle. There were not above five-and-twenty of the Newark soldiers taken; how many were slain at their going off, and during the time of their stay, we could not certainly tell, because they had means of carrying them off by the bridge, where they left Captain Hacker* governor of their new fort with fourscore men. Their prisoners and plunder they sent

---

* The brother of the parliamentarian Colonel Hacker, who was tried, condemned, and executed in 1660 for attending the execution of Charles I. This brother, who served the king during the whole war with great zeal, could not obtain the pardon of Colonel Hacker, nor prevent the confiscation of his family estate, which was granted to the Duke of York, Charles II's brother, from whom he was obliged to ransom it at a high rate. It lay at Colston Bassett, next to Owthorpe.

away in boats to Newark; many of the townsmen went with them, carrying away not only their own but their neighbours' goods; and much more had been carried away, but that the unexpected sally from the castle prevented them.

As soon as the enemy was driven out of the town, the governor brought down two pieces of ordnance to the market-place, and entreated the soldiers that were come from Leicester and Derby to march with him immediately, to assault them in their fort at the bridges, before they had time to put themselves in order, and re-collect their confused souls, after their chase. But the Mayor of Derby, an old dull-headed Dutchman, said 10,000 men could not do it, and could by no means be entreated to go on, nor to stay one day longer. The governor, much discontented that he could not effect his desire, drew back his ordnance into the castle. Here his women, while the men were all otherwise employed, had provided him as large a supper as the time and present condition would permit, at which he entertained all the strangers, and his own officers and gentlemen.

There was a large room, which was the chapel, in the castle: this they had filled full of prisoners, besides a very bad prison, which was no better than a dungeon, called the Lion's Den; and the new Captain Palmer [a 'vainglorious' minister], and another minister, having nothing else to do, walked up and down the castle-yard, insulting and beating the poor prisoners as they were brought up. In the encounter, one of the Derby captains was slain, and five of our men hurt, who for want of another surgeon, were brought to the governor's wife, and she having some excellent balsams and plasters in her closet, with the assistance of a gentleman that had some skill, dressed all their wounds, whereof some were dangerous, being all shots, with such good success, that they were all well cured in convenient time. After our wounded men were dressed, as she stood at her chamber door, seeing three of the prisoners sorely cut, and carried down bleeding into the Lion's Den, she desired the marshal to bring them in to her, and bound up and dressed their wounds also. While she was so doing, Captain Palmer came in and told her his soul abhorred to see this favour to the enemies of God; she replied, she had done nothing but what she thought was her duty, in humanity to them, as fellow-creatures, not as enemies. But he was very ill satisfied with her, and with the governor presently after, when he came into a very large room where a very great supper was prepared, and more room and meat than guests; to fill up which the governor had sent for one Mr Mason, one of the prisoners, a man of good fashion, who had married a relation of his, and was brought up [to the castle] more in fury, than for any proof of guilt in him. Captain Palmer bellowed loudly against him, as a favourer of malignants and cavaliers. But the governor took no notice of it, though he set the very soldiers a-muttering against himself and his wife, for these poor humanities.

The governor broke up the Leen Bridge to prevent the cavaliers coming suddenly by that way into the town; then he blocked up the lanes next the castle, and cut up all the hedges that were dangerous to make approaches to the castle; and having the experience of the mischief of it, pulled down St Nicholas's Church by the advice of the committee. Presently after the cavaliers were gone out of town, some naughty people, set on by them, fired the town, but it was quenched without burning above two or three houses. Yet for a fortnight together it was perpetually attempted, fire being laid to hay-barns and other combustible places, insomuch that the women were forced to walk nightly by fifties to prevent the burning. The committee, perceiving this to be attempted by the instigation of the Newark gentlemen, wrote them word, that if they forbade not their instruments, if so much as one house were fired, they would fire all the cavaliers' houses near them. The gentlemen returned them a scornful letter, full of taunts and disdain, but after that no more houses were attempted with fire.

The governor resolved he would set upon the cavaliers at the bridges alone, whenever it was seasonable; and watching an opportunity, he soon took it, at a time when intelligence was brought him that all the forces Newark could send forth, were gone upon a design into Lincolnshire. Then, on the Lord's day, under colour of hearing a sermon at the great church in the town, he went thither, and after sermon, from the steeple, took a view of the fort at the bridges; no one perceiving his design, but his engineer, who was with him, and took a full survey of Hacker's works. After supper, he called the committee together, and communicated his intentions to them, which they approved of. So all that night he spent in preparations against the next morning; he sent away orders to the horse and foot that lay at Broxtowe to come to him in the morning by eight o'clock, with all the pioneers they could gather up in the country; he sent into the town, and caused all the pioneers there to be brought up. Under pretence of making a breastwork before the castle gates, he caused all the cannon-baskets to be filled, which he intended for rolling trenches. All things, betimes in the morning, were gotten into perfect readiness, and so discreetly ordered, that the enemy had no notice from any of their friends in town, nor knew anything of the design, till it was ready. The governor's own company marched through the meadows, and gave the alarm to the enemy's foot, while Mr George Hutchinson's company went through the lanes, to gain a nook, which was very advantageous for the approaches of our men, and of which they easily possessed themselves. Then advancing, they planted their colours within musket-shot of the fort. Although they planted so many colours, the governor had but eightscore foot, and a hundred horse, in all that went with him out of the castle, but he set the pioneers fairly among them to make the better show.

When the colours were thus planted, the pioneers were set at work to cast up a breastwork; and being left in a safe posture with the inferior officers, the governor and his brother went up to the castle, to order the drawing down of the ordnance. Meanwhile the cavaliers sallied out of their fort to gain the colours, at whose approach all the pioneers ran away from their works; but the soldiers kept their ground and their colours, and beat back the enemy into their own fort, killing some of them, whereof two were left dead before our men, whom they thought it not safe to carry off. Our horse meeting the flying pioneers, brought them back again to their works, which they continued all that day, and the cavaliers attempted no more sallies. At evening the ordnance were brought down and planted within musket-shot of the fort, and then the governor despatched a messenger to Derby to tell Sir John Gell, if he pleased to send any of his men, they might come and see the fort taken. Accordingly, on Tuesday the Dutch major came, with about sixscore foot and dragoons.

Hard by the fort at the bridges, and at that side which our men approached, there were two houses full of coals, into which, if the cavaliers had put any men, they might have done much mischief to the assailants. Therefore the governor sent two or three soldiers, who very boldly went almost under their works and fired them both, by the light of which, they burning all night, the governor's men wrought all that night in their trenches, and cut a trench in the meadows, some of them calling to the cavaliers in the fort, and keeping them in abusive replies, one upon another, while the pioneers carried on their works. The governor and his brother, and all the other officers, continuing all night in the trenches with them, they behaved themselves so cheerfully that the governor gave them the next morning twenty pounds. They had very good drink and provisions brought them out of the garrison, which much encouraged them, but the governor's presence and alacrity among them much more.

When the Derby men came on Tuesday, the Dutch major came down to the trenches, and told the governor that he wondered he would attempt the fort, for it was impregnable, and therefore much dissuaded him from going on, and said that he and his men would return. The governor told him that he and the soldiers with him were resolved to leave their lives rather than their attempt; and if they failed for want of seconding by that force which was sent with him to their assistance let the blame lie on him. When the Derby officers saw him so resolute to persist, they, after much dissuasion and dispute, determined to stay, and the officers went up with the governor to supper in the castle, and the soldiers to quarters provided for them in the town: but after supper, the governor went down again, and stayed all night in the trenches with his men, and left them not as long as they stayed there, but only to fetch down what was necessary for them. He, his brother, and all the officers, were every night with them, and made them continue their custom of railing at each other in the dark, while they carried on their approaches.

There was in the Trent, a little piece of ground of which, by damming up the water, the cavaliers had made an island; and while some of the soldiers held them in talk, others on Wednesday night cut the sluice, and by break of day on Thursday morning had pitched two colours in the island, within carbine-shot of the fort, and the governor's company had as much advanced their approach on the other side. When they in the fort saw, in the morning, how the assailants had advanced, while they were kept secure in talk all the night, they were extremely mad, and swore like devils, which made the governor and his men great sport. Then it was believed they in the fort began to think of flight; which the besiegers not expecting, still continued their approaches, and that day got forty yards nearer to the island and also to the other side. Although Sir John Gell's men came but on Tuesday, on Thursday the second messenger came from him, to call them back. The governor entreated them to stay that night and keep the trenches, while his men refreshed themselves: which they did, but his men would not go out of their trenches, but slept there to fit themselves for the assault, which the governor had resolved on for the morning. For that purpose, after he had left them with all things provided in their trenches, he went to the castle to see the fire-balls and other necessaries for the assault brought down.

At three in the morning he came back to them, when the soldiers told him the cavaliers in the fort had for two hours left off shooting. He sent some soldiers then to the work sides to discover what this meant; but they, perceiving the place empty, went in and found that all the garrison had stolen away, and had left behind them fourscore sheep, a hundred loads of coals, twenty quarters of oats, much hay, a great deal of plundered lead, and a fort so strong, that if they had had such courage as became men of their profession, they would never have quitted it. They left all their works standing, and only broke up two arches of the Trent bridges, to hinder the governor's men from following them. Their flight was by that means secured, the river being so out that the horse could not ford over. Mr George Hutchinson and his company were appointed to possess and keep the fort at the bridges, which he did; and the next week the garrison kept a day of solemn thanksgiving to God, for this success and the mercy in it, whereby all their men were preserved, notwithstanding their very bold adventures, so that not one of them was slain, and but four of them wounded, whereof three were so slightly hurt, that they returned again next day into the field. To increase their thanks to God, news was brought them that the same week the forces that went out from Newark, joined with Henderson's, had received a great overthrow by Cromwell;* and that my Lord Newcastle had been forced to raise his siege of Hull with great loss and dishonour.

The Duchess of Newcastle

My letters seem rather as a ragged rout, than a well armed body, for the brain being quicker in creating than the hand in writing, or the memory in retaining, many fancies are lost, by reason they oft-times outrun the pen. That little wit I have, it delights me to scribble it out, and disperse it about, I being addicted from my childhood to contemplation rather than conversation, to solitariness rather than society, to melancholy rather than mirth, to write with the pen than to work with a needle, passing my time with harmless fancies, their company being pleasing, their conversation innocent, in which I take such pleasure, as I neglect my health. It is as great a grief to leave their society, as a joy to be in their company; my only trouble is, lest my brain should grow barren, or that the root of my fancies should become insipid, withering into a dull stupidity for want of maturing subjects to write on. For I am of a lazy nature, and not of an active disposition, as some are that love to journey from town to town, from place to place, from house to house, delighting in variety of company. For revelling I am of too dull a nature,

* At Winceby Fight on 11 October 1643, in Lincolnshire. Sir John Henderson, a professional Scottish soldier, was the royalist Governor of Newark.

to make one in a merry society; as for feasting, it would neither agree with my humour or constitution, for my diet is for the most part sparing, as a little boiled chicken, or the like, my drink most commonly water.

I exercise little, only walking a slow pace in my chamber, whilst my thoughts run apace in my brain, so that the motions of my mind hinder the active exercises of my body: for should I dance or run, or walk apace, I should dance my thoughts out of measure, run my fancies out of breath, and tread out the feet of my numbers. But I hold necessary sometimes to appear abroad, besides I do find, that several objects do bring new material for my thoughts and fancies to build upon, yet I must say this in the behalf of my thoughts, that I never found them idle; for if the senses bring no work in, they will work of themselves, like silk-worms that spin out of their own bowels.

I was from my childhood given to contemplation, being more taken or delighted with thoughts than in conversation with a society, in so much as I would walk two or three hours, and never rest, in a musing, considering, contemplating manner, reasoning with myself of everything my senses did present. I never took delight in closets, or cabinets of toys, but in the variety of fine clothes, and such toys as only were to adorn my person: likewise I had a natural stupidity towards the learning of any other language than my native tongue. My brothers and sisters were for the most part serious, and staid in their actions, not given to sport or play, or to dance about, whose company I keeping, made me so too: but I observed, that although their actions were staid, yet they would be very merry amongst themselves, delighting in each other's company. As for my study of books it was little, yet I chose rather to read, than to employ my time in any other work, or practise, and when I read what I understood not, I would ask my brother, the Lord Lucas, he being learned, the sense or meaning thereof. My serious study could not be much, by reason I took great delight in attiring, fine dressing, and fashions, especially such fashions as I did invent myself, not taking that pleasure in such fashions as was invented by others. Also I did dislike any should follow my fashions, for I always took delight in a singularity.

As for my disposition, it is more inclining to be melancholy than merry, but not crabbed or peevishly melancholy, but soft, melting, solitary, and contemplating melancholy. I am so vain, as to be so self-conceited, or so naturally partial, to think my friends have as much reason to love me as another, since none can love more sincerely than I, and it were an injustice to prefer a fainter affection. I fear my ambition inclines to vainglory, for I am very ambitious; yet 'tis neither for beauty, wit, titles, wealth, or power, but as they are steps to raise me to Fame's Tower, which is to live by remembrance in after-ages. Likewise I am, that the vulgar calls, proud, not out of a self-conceit, or to slight or condemn any, but scorning to do a base or mean act, and disdaining rude or unworthy persons. Also in some cases I am naturally a coward, and in other cases very valiant; as for example, if any of my nearest friends were in danger; but in a danger where my friends, or my honour is not concerned, or engaged, but only my life to be unprofitably lost, I am the veriest coward in nature, as upon the sea, or any dangerous places, or of thieves, or fire, or the like. Nay, the shooting of a gun, although but a pot-gun, will make me start, and stop my hearing, much less have I courage to discharge one; or if a sword should be held against me, although but in jest, I am afraid.

When the queen was in Oxford [July 1643], I had a great desire to be one of her maids-of-honour, hearing the queen had not the same number she was used to have, whereupon I wooed and won my mother to let me go. But my brothers and sisters seemed not very well pleased, by reason I had never been from home, nor seldom out of their sight. Though they knew I would not behave myself to their, or my own dishonour, yet they thought I might to my disadvantage, being unexperienced in the world, which indeed I did. I was so bashful when I was out of my mother's, brothers', and sisters' sight, whose presence used to give me confidence, thinking I could not do amiss whilst any one of them were by, for I knew they would gently reform me if I did. Besides, I was ambitious they should approve of my actions and behaviour, that when I was gone from them, I was like one that had no foundation to stand, or guide to direct me, which made me afraid, lest I should wander with ignorance out of the ways of honour, so that I knew not how to behave myself. I had heard that the world was apt to lay aspersions even on the innocent, for which I durst neither look up with my eyes, nor speak, nor be any way sociable, insomuch as I was thought a natural fool; indeed I had not much wit, yet I was not an idiot. My wit was according to my years; and though I might have learnt more wit and advanced my understanding by living in a court, yet being dull, fearful, and bashful, I neither heeded what was said or practised, but just what belonged to my loyal duty, and my own honest reputation.

In truth, my bashfulness and fears made me repent my going from home to see the world abroad, and much I did desire to return to my mother again. But my mother said it would be a disgrace for me to return out of the court so soon after I was placed.

Lucy Hutchinson

The governor not growing secure by his successes, was but stirred up to more active preparations for the defence of the place he had undertaken; and having a very ingenious person, Mr Hooper, who was his engineer, and one that understood all kind of operations, in almost all things imaginable, they procured some saltpetre men and other necessary labourers, and set up the making of powder and match in the castle, both of which they made very good; they also cast mortar pieces in the town, and finished many other inventions for the defence of the place. The governor also caused a mount near the castle to be bulwarked, and made a platform for ordnance, and raised a new work before the castle gates, to keep off approaches, and made a new in-work in the fort at the bridges.

Sir Thomas Fairfax came with those horse that were left him [after Winceby] into the Vale of Belvoir, and so visited Nottingham Castle. He and the commanders that were with him, considering of what advantage it was to the Parliament to keep that place, by reason of the commodious situation of it, and the pass which might be there maintained, between the north and south, and the happy retreat it might afford to their northern forces, very much pressed the governor and the committee to raise all the force they could, offering arms and commissions for them. Especially he pressed the governor to complete a regiment for himself, which at that time he would not accept, because Colonel Pierrepont had not yet declared what he would do with his regiment. The colonel was then at Derby, whither some of his officers going to him, to know what they should do, he dismissed them; yet coming to the town, he gave out strange envious whispers, and behaved himself so disingenuously to the governor, that he had just cause to have no more regard for him; and being again importuned by Sir Thomas Fairfax, he received a commission to raise a regiment of 1200. He presently recruited his own companies, and began to raise more: Mr George Hutchinson was his lieutenant-colonel, and one Mr Widmerpoole his major.*

An order of Parliament, dated 20th November 1643, was sent to Nottingham, for Colonel Hutchinson to be governor both of the town and castle, with an acknowledgement of the good service he had done in preserving the place. Letters directed to the governor from Sir Thomas Fairfax, enclosed a commission from his father [Lord Fairfax], then general of all the north, for the government of both the town and castle.

Now was my Lord Newcastle's army come into Derbyshire, and having taken some places there, nothing was expected at Derby and Nottingham but a siege. His forces came and quartered almost at the town side, and in all the near towns, and Henry Hastings took this opportunity to make a garrison at Wilden Ferry. The regiments that were quartered the nearest to Nottingham were Sir Marmaduke Langdale's and Colonel Dacre's, who had been a familiar acquaintance of Colonel

---

* Possibly the ancestor of Kenneth Widmerpool in Anthony Powell's sequence of novels, *A Dance To The Music of Time*; though elsewhere in her *Memoir* Lucy Hutchinson describes the major as having 'a perfect honest heart to God, his country, and his friend', and being 'so humble as to be content to come in the rear of all', which makes this unlikely.

Hutchinson's when he was in the north, and they loved each other as well as if they had been brothers. Colonel Dacre sent a trumpet to desire Colonel Hutchinson to send him a safe convoy, that he might come and see him. [The two met, and a few days later Captain Poulton from the castle made a return visit to Colonel Dacre, who propositioned him:] If Colonel Hutchinson would deliver up the bridges he should have £3000, and what command he would ask in the army; and offered Captain Poulton £2000 to effect this. The captain told him, for his own part, nothing should buy him to such a villainy, and he believed the same of the governor and his brother, and made no question but they had before been attempted. Colonel Dacre told him he did not this without authority, and thereupon pulled a paper out of his pocket wherein were words to this effect: 'These are to authorise Colonel Dacre to treat with Colonel Hutchinson and Lieutenant-Colonel Hutchinson for the delivery of Nottingham Castle and the bridges, and to make them large promises, which shall be performed by W. Newcastle.' Captain Poulton told the governor and his brother, and they told the committee, and showed them what very disdainful refusals they all had written to the colonel, and sent him by a drum.

After this, the weather being pretty fair, and the moon shining at that time, the governor sent out a foot company to beat up their quarters, and gave them a fierce alarm throughout, and took twelve horses out of one of their stables, which they sent home. On their return, meeting a great body of horse, they all at once discharged upon them, and killed some eight of them, as we were told in the morning. After this charge the horse immediately retreated and would not stand another, and the next day removed their quarters further from the garrison. Then the governor and committee sent for the Nottingham horse back from Leicester, and appointed them to bring 500 muskets which were come to Leicester for the governor. He called a committee and council of war, where it was put to the question and voted that the town should be fortified.

The town being well satisfied, or at least seeming so (for he treated them with that dexterity that they could not for shame openly oppose him, though he was not ignorant that the cavalier party cursed him in their hearts, as the only obstacle in their greater desire of having declared themselves on the other side), with general outward cheerfulness, in Christmas week the works were begun. About this time Sir Thomas Fairfax having to march into Staffordshire, sent for some arms he had left in Nottingham Castle; and by the same convoy that went with them the governor got his 500 muskets brought home from Leicester. Sir Thomas sent orders to the governor to send him all the horse in the garrison; but when the governor acquainted them with it, they would none of them obey him and go, though Sir Thomas sent twice very earnestly for them, but they stayed in Nottingham, where they would obey no order of the governor's; and by doing things that concerned the garrison without and against his orders, they made a sad confusion and thwarting of powers. Although the horse would not obey Sir Thomas Fairfax, it was not out of cowardice, for the men were very stout and cheerful in the service, but only had the general fault of all the Parliament party, that they were not very obedient to commands, except they knew and approved their employment. The governor's men encountering a party where Colonel Frecheville and Sir Henry Humlack were in person, fought them, killed many of their men, and took Frecheville prisoner; but his Captain-Lieutenant Jammot came to his rescue and freed him, though he himself was taken in his stead and brought to Nottingham. Here, after he had been some time kept, he corrupted a soldier, who disguised and led him out, and went away with him. The man being a Frenchman and a proper black man, some would needs report him to be Prince Rupert, and thereupon raised a great clamour at the governor.

But before his escape, upon the 15th of January, intelligence was brought that all the forces in Newark were marching on a design upon Sleaford in Lincolnshire. The governor, not trusting that pretence, commanded all the soldiers and townsmen to sit up that night and expect them. The next morning two of his intelligencers came and brought him word very early that the design was against Nottingham. After them the horse scouts came in with the news of their approach, the enemy's scouts and they having fired upon each other. Hereupon a strong alarm was given throughout the garrison, and a foot company sent down from the castle to the works, and the horse were there set with them, to dispute the enemy's entrance into the town; but the horse perceiving the enemy's body to be a great one, retreated to the castle, and the foot seeing them gone, and none of the townsmen come forth to their assistance, made also an orderly retreat back to the castle, in which there was not a man lost nor wounded. The works being imperfect and quitted, were easily entered, though the cannon that played upon them from the castle took off wholly the second file of musketeers that entered the gates. The first was led up by Lieutenant-Colonel Cartwright, who two days before had sent to the governor for a protection to come in and lay down his arms. The enemy being entered, possessed themselves of St Peter's Church and certain houses near the castle, from whence they shot into the castle yard and wounded one man and killed another, which was all the hurt that was done our men that day.

The governor was very angry with the horse for coming up so suddenly, and stirred them up to such a generous shame, that they dismounted, and all took muskets to serve as foot, with which they did such very good service, that they exceedingly well regained their reputations. Having taken foot arms, the governor sent one of his own companies with part of them, and they beat the cavaliers out of the nearest lanes and houses, which they had possessed, and so made a safe way for the rest to sally out and retreat, as there should be occasion.

When this was done, which was about noon, the governor sent out all the rest of the horse and foot, to beat the enemy out of the town. Sir Charles Lucas, who was the chief commander of all the forces there, had prepared a letter to send up to the governor to demand of him the castle; or if he would not deliver it, that then he should send down the mayor and aldermen, threatening, that if they came not immediately, he would sack and burn the town. There were, at that time, above 1000 cavaliers in the town, and as many in a body without the town, to have beaten off the Derby and Leicester forces, if they should have made any attempt to come in to the assistance of their

friends in Nottingham. On the other side the Trent, were all
the forces Mr Hastings could bring out, from his own garrison
and Belvoir and Wiverton, to force the bridges. All the cavalier
forces that were about the town, were about 3000.

When Sir Charles Lucas had written his letter, he could find
none that would undertake to carry it to the castle, whereupon
they took the mayor's wife, and with threats, compelled her to
undertake it. But just as she went out of the house from them,
she heard an outcry, that 'the roundheads were sallying forth',
whereupon she flung down their letter and ran away; and they
ran as fast, from 400 soldiers, who came furiously upon them
out of the castle, and surprised them; while they were secure
the castle would not have made so bold an attempt. But the
governor's men chased them from street to street, till they had
cleared the town of them, who ran away confusedly. The first
that went out shot their pistols into the thatched houses to have
fired them, but by the mercy of God neither that, nor other
endeavours they showed to have fired the town, as they were
commanded, took effect. Between thirty and forty of them were
killed in the streets, fourscore were taken prisoners, and abundance of arms were gathered up, which the men flung away in
haste, as they ran. They put some fire into a hay barn and hay
mows, and all other combustible things they could discern in
their haste, but by God's mercy, the town, notwithstanding,
was preserved from burning.

While their foot marched away, their horse faced the town
in a valley where their reserve stood, till towards evening, and
then they all drew off. Many of them died on their return, and
were found dead in the woods and in the towns they passed
through. Many of them, discouraged by this service, ran away,
and many of their horses were quite spoiled. For two miles they
left a great track of blood, which froze as it fell upon the snow,
for it was such bitter weather that the foot had waded almost to
the middle in snow as they came, and were so numbed with
cold when they came into the town, that they were fain to be
rubbed to get life into them, and in that condition were more
eager for fires and warm meat than for plunder. This, together
with their feeling of security, saved many men's goods; as they

did not believe that an enemy, who had unhandsomely, to speak truth, suffered them to enter the town without any dispute, would have dared, at such great odds, to have set upon driving them out.

Indeed, no one can believe, but those that saw that day, what a strange ebb and flow of courage and cowardice there was in both parties on that day. The cavaliers marched in with such terror to the garrison, and such gallantry, that they startled not when one of their leading files fell before them all at once, but marched boldly over the dead bodies of their friends, under their enemy's cannon, and carried such valiant dreadfulness about them, as made very courageous stout men recoil. Our horse, who ran away frighted at the sight of their foes, when they had breastworks before them, and the advantage of freshness to beat back assailants already vanquished with the sharpness of the cold and a killing march, within three or four hours, as men that thought nothing too great for them, returned fiercely upon the same men, after their refreshment, when they were entered into defensible houses. If it were a romance, one should say, after the success, that the heroes did it out of excess of gallantry, that they might the better signalise their valour upon a foe who was not vanquished to their hands by the inclemency of the season: but we are relating wonders of Providence, and must record this as one not to be conceived of, but by those who saw and shared in it. It was indeed a great instruction, that the best and highest courages are but the beams of the Almighty; and when he withholds his influence, the brave turn cowards, fear unnerves the most mighty, makes the most generous base, and great men to do those things they blush to think on. When God again inspires, the fearful and the feeble see no dangers, believe no difficulties, and carry on attempts whose very thoughts would, at another time, shiver their joints like agues.

The governor would not let his men pursue the rear, but thought they might, in the night, have completed their day's work, if they had fallen upon the enemy's quarters, which he gave orders to the horse to do; but Colonel Thornhagh would not obey them, because they came from him, and so lost a great opportunity, and contented himself with praising God for the great deliverance of the day, wherein there was not one townsman that came in to the assistance of the soldiers. The governor went on again successfully in his employment, and began to endear himself to all the town as well as to the soldiery; which awakening White's sleeping envy, he cast new plots to disturb him.

Lucy Hutchinson here goes on to describe the first major row between her husband the governor and the committee of Nottingham town, over the governor's powers. Captain Charles White, whom she names as the main instigator, is someone in whom she sees no redeeming features, '. . . of mean birth and low fortunes, yet had kept company with the underling gentry of his neighbourhood. This man had the most factious, envious, and malicious nature imaginable. Knowing himself to be inferior to all gentlemen, he put on a vizard of godliness and humility, and courted the common people with all plausibility and flattery that could be practised. He gave large contributions to puritan preachers, who had the art to stop people's mouths from speaking ill of their benefactors.'

Upon the 11th of February, Cornet Palmer, who had been prisoner at Newark, came home and told the governor that he had discovered in his prison a design intended about this time to surprise the bridge by Hacker's soldiers, who were to come in the habit of market people on the next Saturday. This intelligence was seconded, whereupon the governor sent his officers to command all the bridge soldiers to keep in their quarters that day. He commanded also all the horse in the town to be ready to go out upon the first sound of the trumpet, and gave orders for all the drums in the garrison to beat betimes in the morning; the lieutenant-colonel set a guard beyond the bridge, with charge strictly to examine all passengers. About eleven o'clock on Saturday, the 17th of February, they took twelve of Hacker's soldiers upon the bridge, disguised like market men and women, with pistols, long knives, hatchets, daggers, and great pieces of iron about them. They sent and acquainted the governor, who being himself on horseback at the works, went immediately down to the bridge, and commanded all the horse to come away and pursue them; but the horse commanders, being always slow in obeying his commands, came not till the enemy's foot beyond the bridge, perceiving their fellows were taken upon the bridge, retired and got safe off. Only nine, who were to have assassinated those at the bridge, and had advanced fowarder than the rest for that purpose, were overtaken, and with their captain leaped into the Trent to have saved themselves, of whom our men plucked four out of the water, five were drowned, and the captain swam to shore on the other side. The governor was in doubt whether these men, taken in disguises, were to be released as prisoners of war, or executed as spies and assassins by martial law; but though he would not have cared if the bridge-soldiers had turned them into the Trent when they took them, he afterwards released them all upon exchange, except one Slater, a soldier of his own that had run away to the enemy. He was taken coming into the town, with a montero* pulled close about his face, but denied that he was of the design; yet after, upon trial at a court martial, he was condemned and executed.

The governor had sent out some horse and foot, to drive the grounds at the enemy's garrison at Shelford, which they did, and from under the very works from which the enemy shot at them, brought away many beasts and horses, that belonged to the garrison, and brought them up into the castle yard. The governor being then in the committee chamber, told them it was fit the soldiers should have a reward, whereupon it was ordered to give them six pounds, and the governor told the soldiers the committee had assigned them a reward. But when they came to receive it, Salisbury, the treasurer, tithed it out, and gave the soldiers a groat apiece, and sixpence apiece to the officers, which in all came but to forty shillings and odd money. The soldiers, being mad, flung back his money and desired a council of war to do them right, which the governor assented to. The next day the business being heard at a full council of all the officers of the garrison, it was determined by the unanimous vote of all but Mr Salisbury, that as the enemy shot at

* A kind of cap.

them, when they took the booty, it did of right belong to the soldiers that fought for it, and so they had it. Whereupon Salisbury flung himself away from the board in a great huff and muttering, for which the governor rebuked him, and told him such carriage ought not to be suffered in him, who, as an officer, ought to have more respect for the place and those that sat there.

After this, about eighteen of the lieutenant-colonel's men went out and met twenty-five men in arms; between them there was a brook. The bridge-men called to them, and asked of what side they were, and perceiving they were cavaliers, told them, after some little defies between them, that though the number was unequal, they would fight with them; and passing over the brook, charged them, put them to flight, killed two of them, took eight prisoners, and twelve of their horses. Upon examination they were found to be northern gentlemen, who having enlisted themselves in the prince's own troop, after the death of Sir Thomas Byron that commanded under the prince, were assigned to my Lord Wentworth, at which being discontented, they were now returning into their own country, being almost all of them gentlemen. Sir Richard Byron, for his brother's memory, exchanged them for prisoners of Nottingham, taken when the town was first surprised.

Sir John Meldrum was now come, with about 7000 men, and had laid siege to Newark. The governor went down to the leaguer,* at Newark, where Sir John Meldrum had made all things ready for a general assault on the town; but at a council of war that was called in the field, it was determined that it should not then be, whereupon the Governor of Nottingham returned to his garrison. Coming to take his leave of Sir John Meldrum, Sir John entreated him that he would return again and be among them as much as he could, making a sad complaint of the envyings, heart-burnings, and dissensions that were among the several commanders, so that he had much ado to hold them together. The forces were gathered out of several associated counties, and the commanders were so emulous of one another, and so refractory to commands, and so piquing in

* The camp of a besieging army.

all punctilios of superiority, that it galled the poor old gentleman to the heart.

Prince Rupert was expected to come to raise the siege and
the Governor of Nottingham kept out spies upon the enemy's
motions, and sent word to the leaguer, but the gentlemen there
were so over-confident, they would not believe any force could
come to raise their siege. At length, the Governor of Nottingham being there himself, word was brought that Prince Rupert
was come to Ashby; wherefore he, fearing some attempt upon
his garrison, to divert the forces at the siege, returned home
with his brother to look to their charge. It was late upon
Wednesday night when the governor came home, and was
certainly informed that Prince Rupert had, that afternoon,
marched by to raise the siege with about 6000 men. Immediately the governor sent two men, excellently well mounted
upon his own horses, to carry the alarm to Sir John Meldrum,
who by two o'clock on Thursday morning delivered him their
letters, and he presently prepared to fight with the prince, who
came about nine or ten o'clock.

Sir John had drawn all his ordnance within the walls of a
ruined house, called the spittle, and the horse were the first to
charge the enemy. Colonel Thornhagh and Major Rossiter
gave them a very brave charge, routed those whom they first
encountered, and took prisoners Major-General Gerrard and
others, and had they been seconded by the rest of the horse,
had utterly defeated the prince's army. But the Lincolnshire
troops fled away before ever they charged, and left Colonel
Thornhagh engaged, with only his own horse, with the prince's
whole body. They say he charged the prince himself, and made
his way and passed very gallantly through the whole army, with
a great deal of honour, and two desperate wounds, one in the
arm, the other in the belly. After the Lincolnshire horse were
run away, Sir John Meldrum sent the Derby horse and the
Nottingham foot, with two companies of Colonel King's, to
keep Muskham bridge,* and Molanus, the Derbyshire major,
to be their commander. Colonel Thornhagh was sent home in
a wagon to Nottingham. Sir John himself, with the few horse

* Across the northern arm of the Trent outside Newark.

and dragoons that were left from Nottingham and Derby, being about 500, went into the spittle to his foot.

The prince lost more than Sir John in the skirmish, but as soon as ever Sir John had betaken himself to the spittle, the prince sent horse and foot between him and Muskham bridge. The horse that were left there to guard the foot ran every man away, so that they had not a horse left to fetch them any provision. The major that commanded them told them that he would go to the next town to buy them some bread, and with that pretence came away and never saw them more. The enemy was endeavouring to make a passage over the river, to come on the other side of them and encompass them. When they saw this they considered that they had no order what to do, nor bread for one meal, nor bullet more than their muskets were loaded withal, and that it was impossible for them to come off if they stayed till the enemy enclosed them. Further discovering that their friends in the spittle were in parley, they conceived it their best way to come home, which they plotted so to do that the enemy might not perceive it till they were out of their reach; so leaving lighted matches and squibs laid at certain distances, to deceive the enemy, they came safe home. But within less than half an hour after they were gone the enemy came on the other side, and not missing them till morning, by reason of the squibs, they pursued them not, by which means they came safe to Nottingham. This was a very seasonable mercy, for had they stayed the choicest arms in the garrison had been lost, and the best and most confiding soldiers disarmed. For Sir John had agreed upon articles with the prince, to deliver up the spittle wherein he lay, with all the muskets, ordnance, and ammunition in it;* the foot soldiers to march away with colours flying, swords and pikes, the horsemen with their horses and swords, and all the commanders with their pistols; but the prince broke all these conditions, and pillaged them to their shirts, and sent many captains quite naked away.

The committee of Nottingham now began again to mutter

* One of the surrendered guns was a basilisk, a 32-pounder, four yards long, called Sweet Lips after a notorious whore of Hull in the sixteenth century.

at the governor, but he would not take notice of it, but applied himself to take care for the securing of his town, where the enemy now daily threatened to come. So he floated [flooded] the meadows on the Leen side, where there was no fortification, and raised a fort in the midst of the meadows to preserve the float, and fortified the Trent bridges more strongly; and, expecting the enemy every hour, was forced to let the work go on during the Lord's day. When, calling the captains together to consult on the best way of preparing for their defence, Mason, the new town captain, took this time to revive the old mutiny, and said the townsmen would not stand to their works except the ordnance were drawn down from the castle to the town works; the governor rebuked him for this unseasonable insolence, as he and his men were, all the time of this great exigency, so backward that they were rather an obstruction than assistance, and there was much ado to get them either to the works or to the guards. The wives, children, and servants of such as were in the enemy's garrisons and armies, he thought it not safe to suffer any longer to be in the town in such a time of danger, and therefore commanded them all to depart, not sparing even some of his own relations. Prince Rupert was advanced within three miles of Nottingham, when it pleased God to divert him from coming against the town by letters which were brought him from Oxford, which occasioned his hasty return into the south.

Marston Moor
1644

After his success against the Fairfaxes at Adwalton Moor in June 1643, and in taking first Gainsborough then the rest of Lincolnshire in July and August, the tide turned against Newcastle. The defeat of the Newark royalists at Winceby Fight in Lincolnshire in October forced him to abandon the siege of the Fairfaxes in Hull, but the worst blow was the arrival of the Scottish army over the border in January 1644 to fight for Parliament. The duke retired south towards Durham in good order, inflicting reverses on the Scots, but then Lord Bellasis, whom he had left as Governor of York, was routed at Selby by his cousins the Fairfaxes. We take up the duchess's account at this point.

It is held that Charles was in error, demanding Rupert leave Lancashire in June 1644 in order to relieve Newcastle in York before the expected Irish reinforcements had arrived or he had collected enough Welsh recruits. In turn, Rupert is criticised for regarding it as a point of honour that he fight, and for failing to liaise better with Newcastle, who could have told him of disaffection between the Scots and roundheads; and Newcastle is blamed for being over-cautious and standing on his dignity. The parliamentary forces were 30,000 strong against the 20,000 royalists, and the Battle of Marston Moor was decided in an hour. Of Newcastle's sailing to the Continent afterwards, Clarendon in his History of the Rebellion *has this to say: 'The strange manner of the prince's [Rupert's] coming, and undeliberated throwing himself and all the king's hopes into that sudden and unnecessary engagement, by which all the force the marquis [Newcastle] had raised, and with so many difficulties preserved, was in a moment cast away and destroyed, so transported him with passion and despair, that he could not compose himself to think of beginning the work again, and involving himself in the same undelightful condition, from which he might now be free. He hoped his past meritorious actions might outweigh his present abandoning the thought of future action; and so, without further consideration, he transported himself out of the kingdom.'*

Alice Thornton provides a vivid vignette of one of her brothers preventing another from straying innocently on to the battlefield, and then describes the unwelcome attentions she herself received from the billeted Scottish soldiery in the aftermath of the campaign.

In this same year Anne Halkett was also receiving attentions which, dutiful daughter that she was, she felt bound to turn away. Her admirer was Thomas Howard, eldest son of Lord Howard of Escrick. To Anne's account of this frustrated affair it need only be added that Thomas Howard returned to England in 1646 and in March sent a message to Anne that he 'had resolved for a time to forbear all converse with me and to make love to all that came his way, and then he might with the less suspicion prosecute his design, which was never to marry any but me'. At the end of July Anne heard that he had in fact married Lady Elizabeth Mordaunt the week before.

The Duchess of Newcastle

My lord took a resolution not to stay between the two armies of the enemies, *viz.* the Scots and the English, that had prevailed in Yorkshire; but immediately to march into Yorkshire with his army, to preserve (if possible) the city of York out of the enemy's hands. The retreat was ordered so well, and with such excellent conduct, that though the army of the Scots marched close upon their rear, and fought them every day of their retreat, yet they gained several passes for their security, and entered safe and well into the city of York, in April 1644.

My lord, finding three armies against him, *viz.* the army of the Scots, the army of the English that gave the defeat to the Governor of York, and an army that was raised out of associate counties,* and but little ammunition and provision in the town, was forced to send his horse away to quarter in several counties, *viz.* Derbyshire, Nottinghamshire, Leicestershire, for their subsistance, under the conduct of his lieutenant-general of the horse, my dear brother Sir Charles Lucas, himself remaining at York, with his foot and train, for the defence of that city.

In the meantime, the enemy having closely besieged the city on all sides, came to the very gates thereof, and pulled out the earth at one end, as those in the city put it in at the other end; they planted their great cannons against it, and threw in granadoes at pleasure. But those in the city made several sallies upon them with good success. At last, the general of the associate army of the enemy, having closely beleaguered the north side of the town, sprung a mine under the wall of the Manor yard, and blew part of it up. Having beaten back the town forces (although they behaved themselves very gallantly) he entered the Manor house with a great number of their men, which as soon as my lord perceived, he went away in all haste, even to the amazement of all that were by, not knowing what he intended to do. He drew eighty of his own regiment of foot, called the Whitecoats, all stout and valiant men, to that post, who fell pell-mell with the butt-ends of their muskets upon them and fought the enemy with that courage, that within a little time they killed and took 1500 of them. My lord gave present order to make up the breach which they had made in the wall; whereupon the enemy remained without any other attempt in that kind, so long, till almost all provision for the support of the soldiery in the city was spent, which nevertheless was so well ordered by my lord's prudence, that no famine or great extremity of want ensued.

My lord, having held out in that manner above two months and withstood the strength of three armies, seeing that his lieutenant-general of the horse whom he had sent for relief to

* The army of the Eastern Association counties under the Earl of Manchester and Cromwell.

His Majesty, could not so soon obtain it (although he used his best endeavour), for to gain yet some little time he began to treat with the enemy; ordering in the meanwhile, and upon the treaty, to double and treble his guards. At last after three months' time from the beginning of the siege, His Majesty was pleased to send an army, which joining with my lord's horse that were sent to quarter in the aforesaid countries, came to relieve the city, under the conduct of the most gallant and heroic Prince Rupert, his nephew. Upon his approach near York, the enemy drew from before the city, into an entire body, and marched away on the west side of the River Ouse, that runs through the city, His Majesty's forces being then of the east side of that river.

My lord immediately sent some persons of quality to attend His Highness, and to invite him into the city to consult with him about that important affair, and to gain so much time as to open a port to march forth with his cannon and foot which were in the town, to join with His Highness's forces. He went himself the next day in person to wait on His Highness. After some conferences, he declared his mind to the prince, desiring His Highness not to attempt anything as yet upon the enemy; for he had intelligence that there was some discontent between them, and that they were resolved to divide themselves, and so to raise the siege without fighting. Besides, my lord expected within two days, Colonel Clavering, with above 3000 men out of the north, and 2000 drawn out of several garrisons (who also came at the same time, though it was then too late). But His Highness answered my lord, that he had a letter from His Majesty (then at Oxford) with a positive and absolute command to fight the enemy; which in obedience, and according to his duty he was bound to perform. My lord replied that he was ready and willing for his part, to obey His Highness in all things, no otherwise than if His Majesty was there in person himself. Though several of my lord's friends advised him not to engage in battle, because the command (as they said) was taken from him, yet my lord answered them that, happen what would, he would not shun to fight, for he had no other ambition but to live and die a loyal subject to His Majesty.

Then the prince and my lord conferred with several of their officers, amongst whom there were several disputes concerning the advantages which the enemy had of sun, wind and ground. The horse of His Majesty's forces was drawn up in both wings upon that fatal moor called Hessom Moor [Marston Moor]. My lord asked His Highness what service he would be pleased to command him; who returned this answer, that he would begin no action upon the enemy, till early in the morning, desiring my lord to repose himself till then. Which my lord did, and went to rest in his own coach that was close by in the field, until the time appointed.*

Not long had my lord been there, but he heard a great noise and thunder of shooting, which gave him notice of the armies being engaged. He immediately put on his arms, and was no sooner got on horseback, but he beheld a dismal sight of the horse of His Majesty's right wing, which out of a panic fear had left the field, and run away with all the speed they could; and though my lord made them stand once, yet they immediately betook themselves to their heels again, and killed even those of their own party that endeavoured to stop them. The left wing in the meantime, commanded by those two valiant persons, the Lord Goring, and Sir Charles Lucas, had the better of the enemy's right wing, which they beat back most valiantly three times, and made their general retreat, in so much that they sounded victory.

In this confusion my lord (accompanied only with his brother Sir Charles Cavendish, Major Scot, Captain Mazine, and his page) hastening to see in what posture his own regiment was, met with a troop of gentlemen-volunteers, who formerly had chosen him their captain, notwithstanding he was general of an army. To whom my lord spake after this manner: 'Gentleman, you have done me the honour to choose me your captain, and now is the fittest time that I may do you service; wherefore if you'll follow me, I shall lead you on the best I can, and show you the way to your own honour.' They being as glad of my lord's proffer, as my lord was of their readiness, went on with the greatest courage; and passing through two bodies of

* He is said to have smoked a pipe in his coach.

foot, engaged with each other not at forty yards' distance, received not the least hurt, although they fired quick upon each other. They marched towards a Scots regiment of foot, which they charged and routed; in which encounter my lord himself killed three with his page's half-leaden sword,* for he had no other left him, and though all the gentlemen in particular offered him their swords, yet my lord refused to take a sword of any of them. At last, after they had passed through this regiment of foot, a pikeman made a stand to the whole troop; and though my lord charged him twice or thrice, yet he could not enter him; but the troop despatched him soon. In all these encounters my lord got not the least hurt, though several were slain about him; and his Whitecoats showed such an extraordinary valour and courage in that action, that they were killed in rank and file.

My lord being the last in the field, and seeing that all was lost, and that every one of His Majesty's party made their escapes in the best manner they could; he being moreover enquired after by several of his friends, who had all a great love and respect for my lord (especially by the then Earl of Crawford who loved my lord so well that he gave 20s. to one that assured him of his being alive and safe, telling him, that that was all he had) went towards York late at night, accompanied only with his brother, and one or two of his servants. Coming near the town, he met His Highness Prince Rupert, with the lieutenant-general of the army, the Lord Ethyn. His Highness asked my lord how the business went? To whom he answered, that all was lost and gone on their side.

That night my lord remained in York. He had nothing left in his power to do His Majesty any further service in that kind; for he had neither ammunition, nor money to raise more forces, to keep either York, or any other towns that were yet in His Majesty's devotion. Well knowing that those which were left could not hold out long, and being also loath to have aspersions cast upon him, that he did sell them to the enemy, in case he could not keep them, he took a resolution, and that justly and

* Presumably a dress-sword meant for show and not made out of true steel.

honourably, to forsake the kingdom. He went the next morning to the prince, and acquainted him with his design, desiring His Highness would be pleased to give this true and just report of him to His Majesty, that he had behaved himself like an honest man, a gentleman, and a loyal subject. Which request the prince having granted, my lord took his leave; and being conducted by a troop of horse and a troop of dragoons to Scarborough, went to sea, and took shipping for Hamburg. The gentry of the country also came to take their leaves of my lord, being much troubled at his departure, and speaking very honourably of him, as surely they had no reason to the contrary.

Alice Thornton

My mother and family came to Kirklington, where she stayed at Mr Daggett's, the minister, being most kindly entertained and received till the hall was made fit to dwell in. In that time, after she came thither, in the year 1644, was the Battle of Marston Moor, and the taking of York, and she was much concerned for my brother Christopher Wandesford, being then at York for cure and at school. But it pleased God in providence so to order it unexpectedly, [that] my brother George was newly come out of France and wanting supplies in the war's time was forced to come toward his estate about Richmond, at that time when the armies was in battle, and was surrounded in his passage to York. When he perceived that the day was lost from the king, he rode to fetch my brother Kit from thence. As he happily met him riding out of the town toward the moor, with other boys in their simplicity, to see the fight, he took him up behind him, and brought him safe to Kirklington that night. My poor brother George durst not stay at Kirklington the next day, by reason that a party of horse was despatched to seize on him, supposing him a commander in arms for the king. He was forced to fly for his life, and secure himself where he could, the Lord still preserving him from his unjust enemies, being an innocent person, and never engaged in either party, and who was but newly returned into his country; and this was his first salutation and welcome into it.

After this when the Scots had helped to overthrow the king's army at York, these Scotch rebels quartered themselves all over the country, especially in and about Richmond, forcing all people to take the Covenant, how contrary soever it was to their duty of allegiance or conscience. Those who would not, were forced to flee, or were imprisoned and ruined. My mother went to live at Hipswell and there she was troubled with the Scots one while, and the Parliament forces another while tormented us, getting all our provisions of meat and drink, let us want all necessaries, that their domineering and insulting voluptuousness must be supplied. My mother was charged for eighteen or twenty months together with £25 a month in moneys to the soldiers, besides the quartering of a troop of Scots on free quarter, which was treble the value of her estate, and at that time she borrowed moneys to maintain all her four children, which she paid afterwards.

At length there came one Captain Innis, which was over that troop we had in town. He coming on a surprise into the house, I could not hide myself from them as I used to do; but coming boldly into my mother's chamber, where I was with her, he began to be much more earnest and violent to have stayed in the house. He said he would stay in his quarters, but we so ordered the matter that we got him out, by all the fair means could be, to get quit of him, who was so wild a bloody-looked man, that I trembled all the time he was in the house. After which time this man impudently told my Aunt Norton that he would give all he was worth if she could procure me to be his wife, and offered three or four thousand pounds, and Lord Adair should come and speak for him. She said it was all in vain; he must not presume to look that way, for I was not to be obtained. And she was sure he might not have any encouragement, for I was resolved not to marry, and put him off the best she could; but writ me private word that my Lord of Adair and he would come to speak to me and my mother about it, and wished me to get out of his way. It was not to further that desire in me, who did perfectly hate him and them all like a tod [fox] in such a kind. Immediately I acquainted my dear mother, which was surprised and troubled, for she feared they would burn her house and destroy all. She wished me to go whither I would to secure myself; and I did so forthwith. I ran into the town, and hid myself privately in great fear and a fright with a good old woman, one of her tenants, where, I bless God, I continued safely till the visit was over, and at night came home. We was all joyful to escape so, for my dear mother was forced to give them the best treat she could, and said, indeed, she did not know where I was, and sent out [servants?] a little to seek me, but I was safe from them.

After which time this villain captain did study to be revenged of my dear mother, and threatened cruelly what he would do to her because she hid me, though that was not true, for I hid myself. About the time that the Scots was to march into Scotland this Scot in a boasting manner sent for his pay, and she sent all she ought to him, which he would not take from her, but demanded double money, which she would nor could not do. So on Sunday morning he brought the company, and threatened to break the house and doors, and was most vile and cruel in his oaths and swearing against her and me. He went to drive all her goods in her ground, she having this delicate cattle of her own breed. I went up to the leads [roof] to see whether he did drive them away, and he looked up and thought it had been my dear mother, cursed me bitterly, and wished the Deale blaw [Devil blow] me blind and into the air, and I had been a thorn in his heel, but he would be a thorn in my side, and drove the cattle away to Richmond, where General Leslie was. So my dear mother was forced to take the pay he was to have, and carried it to the general and acquainted him how that captain had abused her and wronged her; which, by mercy of God to her, this General Leslie did take notice of, and took her money, and bid her not trouble herself, for he would make him take it, or punish him for his rudeness.

This was a great deliverance at last from this beast, from being destroyed and deflowered by him, for which I have reason to praise the great and mighty God of mercy to me. There was one of his men that I had cured of his hand, being cut of it, and lame; so that fellow did me a signal return of gratitude for it. Thus it was sometimes a refreshment to me after I had sat up much with my dear weak mother in her illness, or writing of letters for her, that she did bid me walk out to Lowes with her maids to rest myself, so I used this sometimes. But this man whom I cured, came to me one day, saying, 'Dear mistress, I pray do not think much if I desire you, for God's sake, not to go out with the maids to Lowes.' I said, 'Why?' He said again, he was bound to tell me that his captain did curse and swear that he would watch for me, and that very night he had designed with a great many of his comrades to catch me at Lowes, and force me on horseback away with them, and God knows what end he would make of me. I said, 'I hope God would deliver me from all such wickedness,' and so I gave the man many thanks, who was so honest to preserve me from these plots, rewarding him for his pains, and did never go abroad out of the house again, but forced to keep like a prisoner while they was here.

Anne Halkett

Until the year 1644 I may truly say all my converse was so innocent that my own heart cannot challenge me with any immodesty, either in thought or behaviour, or an act of disobedience to my mother, to whom I was so observant that as long as she lived I do not remember that I made a visit to the nearest neighbour or went anywhere without her liberty. And so scrupulous I was of giving any occasion to speak of me, as I know they did of others, that though I loved well to see plays and to walk in the Spring Garden sometimes (before it grew something scandalous by the abuse of some), yet I cannot remember three times that ever I went with any man besides my brothers; and if I did, my sisters or others better than myself was with me. I was the first that proposed and practised it, for three or four of us going together without any man, and everyone paying for themselves by giving the money to the footman who waited on us, and he gave it in the playhouse. This I did first upon hearing some gentlemen telling what ladies they had waited on to plays and how much it had cost them, upon which I resolved none should say the same of me.

In the year 1644 I confess I was guilty of an act of disobedience, for I gave way to the address of a person whom my mother, at the first time that ever he had occasion to be conversant with me, had absolutely discharged me ever to allow of. Before ever I saw him several did tell me that there would be something more than ordinary betwixt him and me (which I believe they fadged from the great friendship betwixt his sister and me). He was half a year in my company before I discovered anything of a particular inclination for me more than another. Having never any opportunity of being alone with me to speak himself, he employed a young gentleman to tell me how much he had endeavoured all this time to smother his passion which he said began the first time that ever he saw me, and now was come to that height that if I did not give him some hopes of favour he was resolved to go back again into France (from whence he had come when I first saw him) and turn Capuchin [become a monk].

Knowing that his father had sent for him out of France with an intention to marry him to some rich match that might improve his fortune, it would be high ingratitude in me to do anything to hinder such a design, since his father had been so obliging to my mother and sister as to use his lordship's interest with the Parliament to prevent the ruin of my brother's house and kin. But when all I could say to him by his friend could not prevail, but that he grew so ill and discontented that all the house took notice, I did yield so far to comply with his desire as to give him liberty one day when I was walking in the gallery to come there and speak to me. What he said was handsome and short, but much disordered, for he looked pale as death, and his hand trembled when he took mine to lead me, and with a great sigh said, 'If I loved you less I could say more.' I told him I was two or three years older than he, and were there no other objection, yet that was of such weight with me as would never let me allow his further address.

After that, he sought, and I shunned, all opportunities of private discourse with him; but one day in the garden his friend took his sister by the hand and led her into another walk and left him and I together. And he with very much seriousness began to tell me that if I would not give him hopes of marrying him, he was resolved to put himself out of a capacity of marrying any other and go immediately into a convent, and that he had taken order to have post horses ready against the next day. I looked on this as a violent passion which would not last long and perhaps might grow the more by being resisted, when as a seeming complaisance might lessen it. I told him that I would not marry till I saw him first married. But I deceived myself by thinking this was the way to moderate his passion, for now he gave way to it without any restraint. He resolved to acquaint my sister with it and to employ her to speak of it to his father and my mother.

My mother was so passionately offended with the proposal that, whereas his father might have been brought to have given his consent (having ever had a good opinion of me and very civil), she did so exasperate him against it that nothing could satisfy her, but presently to put it to Mr H.'s choice either presently to marry a rich citizen's daughter that his father had designed for him, or else to leave England. The reason I believe that made my mother the more incensed was, first, that it was what in the beginning of our acquaintance she had absolutely discharged my having a thought of allowing such an address; and though in some respect his quality was above mine and therefore better than any she could expect for me, yet my Lord H.'s fortune was such as had need of a more considerable portion than my mother could give me, or else it must ruin his younger children. And therefore my mother would not consent to it, though my Lord H. did offer to do the utmost his condition would allow him if she would let me take my hazard with his son.

Finding both by my mother and my Lord H. that they intended nothing but to part us so as never to meet again, except it was as strangers, Mr H. was very importunate to have an opportunity to speak with me that night, which I gave. [During the meeting] he fell down in a chair that was behind him, but as one without all sense, which I must confess did so much move me that, laying aside all former distance I had kept him at, I sat down upon his knee, and laying my head near his I suffered him to kiss me, which was a liberty I never gave before. 'No,' says he, 'since they will not allow me to converse with you, France will be more agreeable to me than England, nor will I go there except I have liberty to come here again and take my leave of you.' To that I could not disagree if they thought fit to allow it.

The next morning early my Lord H. went away, and took with him his son and daughter, and left me to the severities of my offended mother, whom nothing could pacify. After she had called for me and said as many bitter things as passion could dictate upon such a subject, she discharged me to see him and did solemnly vow that if she should hear I did see Mr H. she would turn me out of her doors and never own me again. All I said to that part was that it should be against my will if ever she heard of it. My chamber and liberty of lying alone was taken from me, and my sister's woman was to be my guardian, who watched sufficiently so that I had not the least opportunity either day or night to be without her. Having got liberty to walk in the hall, my mother sent a child of my sister's and bid him walk with me and keep me company. I had not been there a quarter of an hour but my maid Miriam came to me and told me she was walking at the back gate and Mr H. came to her and sent her to desire me to come there and speak but two or three words with him, for he had sworn not to go away without seeing me. He had left London that morning very early and had rode up and down that part of the country only till it was the gloom of the evening to have the more privacy in coming to see me. I bid her go back and tell him I durst not see him because of my mother's oath and her discharge. While she was pressing me to run to the gate and I was near to take the start, the child cried out, 'Oh, my aunt is going,' which stopped me, and I sent her [Miriam] away to tell the reason why I could not come.

I still stayed walking in the hall till she returned, wondering she stayed so long. When she came she was hardly able to speak and with great disorder said, 'I believe you are the most unfortunate person living, for I think Mr H. is killed.'

Anyone that hath ever known what gratitude was may imagine how these words disordered me, but impatient to know how (I was resolved to hazard my mother's displeasure rather than not see him), she told me that while she was telling him my answer, there came a fellow with a great club behind him and struck him down dead, and others had seized upon Mr T. (who formerly had been his governor and was now entrusted to see him safe on shipboard) and his man. The reason of this was from what there was too many sad examples of at that time, when the division was betwixt the king and Parliament, for to betray a master or a friend was looked upon as doing God good service.

My brother-in-law Sir Henry Newton had been long from home in attendance on the king, for whose service he had raised a troop of horse upon his own expense and had upon all occasions testified his loyalty. For which his estate was sequestered, and with much difficulty my sister got liberty to live in her own house and had the fifth part to live upon, which was obtained with importunity. There was one of my brother's tenants called Musgrove, who was a very great rogue, who farmed my brother's land [as a tenant] of the Parliament and was employed by them as a spy to discover any of the cavaliers that should come within his knowledge. He, observing three gentlemen upon good horses scouting about all day and keeping at a distance from the highway, apprehends it was my brother who had come privately home to see my sister. He resolves to watch when he came near the house, and had followed so close as to come behind and give Mr H. that stroke, thinking it had been my brother Newton, and seized upon his governor and servant (the post boy being left at some distance with the horses).

In the midst of this disorder Moses [a servant] came there, and Miriam having told what the occasion of it was, he told Musgrove it was my Lord H.'s son he had used so, upon which he and his accomplices went immediately away. Moses and Mr H.'s man carried him into an alehouse hard by and laid him on a bed, where he lay some time before he came to himself. So, hearing all was quiet again and that he had no hurt, only stunned with the blow, I went into the room where I had left my mother and sister, which being at a good distance from the back gate they had heard nothing of the tumult that had been there.

My mother now believing Mr H. gone, I was not as former nights sent to my bed, and the guard upon me that was usual, but I stayed in my mother's chamber till she and my sister (who lay together) were abed. In the meantime Mr H. had sent for Moses and told him whatever misfortune he might suffer by his stay there, he was fully determined not to go away without seeing me, and desired I would come to the banqueting house in the garden and he would come to the window and speak to me; which he told me. I sent him word when my mother was abed I would contrive some way to satisfy him, but not where he proposed, because it was within the view of my mother's chamber window.

After I had left my mother and sister in their bed, I went alone in the dark through my brother's closet to the chamber where I lay, and as I entered the room I laid my hand upon my eyes and with a sad sigh said, 'Was ever creature so unfortunate and put to such a sad difficulty'. My hand being still upon my eyes, it presently came in my mind that if I blindfolded my eyes that would secure me from seeing him, and so I did not transgress against my mother. And he might that way satisfy himself by speaking with me. I had as much joy in finding out this means to yield to him without disquiet to myself as if it had been of more considerable consequence. Immediately I sent Moses to tell him upon what conditions I would speak with him: first, that he must allow me to have my eyes covered, and that he should bring Mr T. with him, and if thus he were satisfied I ordered him to bring them in the back way into the cellar where I with Miriam would meet them the other way; which they did.

As soon as Mr H. saw me he much importuned the taking away the cover from my eyes; which I not suffering, he left disputing that, to employ the little time he had in regretting my not yielding to his importunity to marry him. I told him I was sorry for being the occasion of his discontent, but I ever looked upon marrying without consent of parents as the highest act of ingratitude and disobedience that children could commit, and I resolved never to be guilty of it. It is unnecessary to repeat the solemn oaths he made never to love nor marry any other. I called for a bottle of wine, and giving Mr T. thanks for his civility and care, drunk to him, wishing a good and happy journey to Mr H. So taking a farewell of them both, I went up the way I came and left them to Moses' care to conduct them out quietly as he led them in. (This was upon Thursday night, the 10th of October, 1644.)

I was in hopes, after some time that Mr H. was gone, my mother would have received me into her favour again, but the longer time she had to consider of my fault the more she did aggravate it. And though my Lord H. (who returned shortly after with his daughter) and my sister did use all the arguments imaginable to persuade her to be reconciled to me, yet nothing would prevail except I would solemnly promise never to think more of Mr H. and that I would marry another whom she thought fit to propose. To which I begged her pardon, for till Mr H. was first married I was fully determined to marry no person living. She asked me if I was such a fool as to believe he would be constant. I said I did, but if he were not, it should be his fault, not mine, for I resolved not to make him guilty by example.

My mother's anger against me increased to that height that for fourteen months she never gave me her blessing, nor never spoke to me but when it was to reproach me, and one day said with much bitterness she did hate to see me. That word I confess struck deeply to my heart and put me to my thoughts what way to dispose of myself to free my mother from such an object.

8

Nottingham, Oxford
and the West
1644-5

Lucy Hutchinson tells a story of 'a sad confusion and thwarting of
powers' early in 1645, when her husband, the governor, was frus-
trated by a clique within the town committee of Nottingham who
were prepared to carry their intrigues to the northern area com-
mander, Lord Fairfax, and to Parliament itself. Reading between
the lines, Colonel Hutchinson sounds an aloof figure inclined to stand
on the dignity of his social class and position. As Lucy puts it, 'having
a certain spirit of government, in an extraordinary manner ...
carrying an awe in his presence'. He was without the common touch
of his brother, a man 'of the most humble familiar deportment in the
world'. But it is also clear that the colonel was pitted against some
unscrupulous and unsavoury characters in a situation where the
chain of command had been left woefully undefined by Parliament.
   John Aubrey, in his Brief Lives, *gives a wonderful snapshot of*
a Mistress Fanshawe in royalist Oxford in his piece on Ralph
Kettell, the old President of Trinity College there. It is too good to
miss, even though Kettell's claim that her husband was at Trinity
casts a doubt on whether this is Ann Fanshawe, since her husband
was at Jesus College, Cambridge. 'I remember one time my Lady
Isabella Thynne and fine Mistress Fanshawe (her great and intim-
ate friend who lay at our college) would have a frolic to make a

visit to the president. The old doctor quickly perceived that they came to abuse him; he addressed his discourse to Mistress Fanshawe, saying, "Madam, your husband and father I bred up here, and I knew your grandfather; I know you to be a gentlewoman, I will not say you are a whore; but get you gone for a very woman." Mistress Fanshawe was wont, and my Lady Thynne, to come to our chapel, mornings, half-dressed, like angels [loose women].' Lady Thynne was the daughter of the Earl of Holland, whose career veering between the two sides in the Civil War ended with his execution in 1649. She was the wife of Sir James Thynne of Longleat.

In May 1645 Ann Fanshawe set out on her wanderings, which were to continue through France, Ireland, Spain and England, until the final ending of the wars after the Battle of Worcester in September 1651.

Lucy Hutchinson

The governor sent to the general [Lord Fairfax] about his cannoneers, whom some days before he had been forced to confine as prisoners to their chamber till the general's pleasure could be known concerning them. At the instigation of Captain Palmer, all the ministers in town, and, to make the cry the louder, certain loose malignant priests, which they had gotten to join with them, had most violently urged, in a petition to the committee, that these men might be turned out of the town for being separatists, separating from the public worship and keeping little conventicles in their own chambers. The governor was forced, against his will, to confine them to prevent mutiny, though they were otherwise honest, obedient, and peaceful.

The general, upon the governor's letters, sent down a letter to the governor to release the cannoneers; which he accordingly did, to the satisfaction of his own conscience, which was not satisfied in keeping men prisoners for their consciences, so long as they lived honestly and inoffensively.

The governor and the rest of the committee had required Mr Salisbury, their treasurer, to give his accounts, which he being either unwilling or unable to do, he bent his utmost endeavours to raise a high mutiny and faction against the governor. Captain White, the Devil's exquisite solicitor, never being backward in any mischief, made a close confederacy and called home Colonel James Chadwick to their assistance. Chadwick was at first a boy that scraped trenchers in the house of one of the poorest justices in the county, from whom this boy picked such ends of law, that he became first the justice's then a lawyer's clerk. He then, I know not how, got to be a parcel-judge* in Ireland, and came over to his own country swelled with the reputation of it. Having an insinuating wit and tongue, he procured himself to be deputy recorder of Nottingham. Among other villainies which he secretly practised, he was a libidinous goat, for which his wife, they say, paid him with making him a cuckold; yet there were not two persons to be found that pretended more sanctity than these two. He naturally delighted in mischief and treachery, and was so exquisite a villain that he destroyed those designs he might have thriven by, with overlaying them with fresh knaveries.

After York was taken [after Marston Moor], the Earl of Manchester marched into our parts, upon whose coming Bolsover and Tickhill castles were delivered up to him, and Welbeck, the Earl of Newcastle's house, which was given into Colonel Thornhagh's command, and much of the enemy's wealth, by that means, brought into Nottingham. Winkfield Manor, a strong garrison in Derbyshire, was taken upon composition, and by this means a rich and large side of the country was laid open to help to maintain the garrison at Nottingham, and more hoped for by these gentlemen, who were now as greedy to catch at the rewards of another's labours, as unable to merit anything themselves. But when the hopes of the harvest of the whole country had tempted them to begin their wicked plots, God, seeming angry at their ill use of mercy, caused the Earl of Manchester to be called back into the south, when he was going to have besieged Newark, and so that town, with the petty garrisons at Wiverton, Shelford, and Belvoir, were still left for further exercise to Nottingham.

* 'Some sort of' judge.

The conspirators, as I may more justly term them, than the committee, had sent Captain White to York, to my Lord Fairfax, to get the governor's power defined; which the governor understanding, the next day went thither himself. When my lord gave them a hearing together, he asked whether the governor had done anything of consequence without consulting the committee, which White could not say he had; then he asked White if he had any other misgovernment to accuse him of, which when White could not allege against him, the governor before his face told my lord all the business, whereupon White was dismissed with reproof and laughter, and letters were written to the committee, to justify the governor's power, and to entreat them to forbear disturbing him in his command, and to Mr Millington,* to desire him to come over to York to my lord, both which the governor delivered. Mr Millington would not go over, but, on the contrary, continued to foment and raise up the factions in the town against the governor, and by his countenance the committee every day meditated and practised new provocations, to stir up the governor to rage, or at least to weary him in his employment. The horse, without his knowledge, they frequently sent abroad; protections, tickets, and passes, they gave out; and, encroaching upon his office in all things whatsoever, wrought such a confusion in the garrison, that while all men were distracted and amazed, in doubt whose orders to obey, and who were their commanders, they obeyed none, but every man did what he listed; and by that means the public service was in all things obstructed and prejudiced.

The governor went to the committee and after much debate it was on all hands agreed that they should not at all intermeddle with anything belonging to the soldiery, nor interrupt the governor in his command until the House of Parliament should decide it, and that the governor and Captain White should both go to London to procure a speedy determination of the powers in a fair and open way. When the governor came to London, the committee of both kingdoms appointed a sub-committee to

* The MP for Nottingham, and in league with the conspirators.

hear his business.* As they were statesmen, so they were not so ready to relieve him as they ought to have been, because they could not do it without a high reflection upon one of their own members [Mr Millington], who encouraged all those little men in their wicked persecution of him. They were such exquisite rogues, that all the while some of them betrayed one another to the governor, and told him, under pretence of honesty and conscience, the bottom of their whole designs, showed the foul original drafts of their articles, in the men's own hands that contrived them; and told him how, not so much dislike of him, as covetousness and ambition to advance themselves upon his ruins, had engaged them thus against him, and made them contrive that villainy to accuse him and his brother of treachery, and to have seized their garrisons, under that pretence, and gotten them to be made prisoners; and then Mr Millington undertook to have so lodged their petitions in the Parliament, that they should never have been heard and relieved.

Lamentable it was to behold how those wretched men fell away under this temptation, not only from public spiritedness, but from sobriety and honest, moral conversation; not only conniving at and permitting the wickedness of others, but themselves conversing in taverns and brothels. At last Millington and White were so ensnared that they married a couple of alehouse wenches, to their open shame and the conviction of the whole country of the vain lives they led, and some reflection on the Parliament itself, as much as the miscarriage of a member could cast on it, when Millington, a man of sixty, professing religion, and having but lately buried a religious matronly gentlewoman, should go to an alehouse to take a flirtish girl of sixteen.

At London, the governor being grown into acquaintance with the gentlemen of the sub-committee that were to hear his business; and they perceiving with how much wicked malice he was prosecuted, Sir Henry Vane was so honourable as to give him advice to put his business in such a way, as might take

* Colonel Pierrepont's brother William and Sir Harry Vane, later the leading republican within the House of Commons, were on this sub-committee, see p. 241.

away all colour from his enemies. Forthwith the whole business was determined at the committee of both kingdoms, and the governor sent back to his charge, with instructions drawn up for all parties, and letters written to the officers and soldiers, both of horse and foot, to be obedient; and likewise letters to the mayor of the town and to the committee.

Shortly after the governor returned to Nottingham Colonel Thornhagh charged the enemy's quarters at Muskham Bridge with the town's horse and took eighty horse, two horse colours, a major and some other officers. The [Trent] bridge troop also met with Colonel Stanhope, Governor of Shelford, who had two parties, each as many as they. His party where he himself was, routed, and he ran away, while the other party charged them [the bridge troop] in the rear, upon whom they turned, routed, and chased them out of the field, took Lieutenant-Colonel Stanhope* and his ensign, and many other prisoners, with many horse and arms. In the absence of the governor and his brother, the committee had done all they could to discourage and dissipate this troop, and would neither give them money nor provisions; yet, upon hopes of their captain's return, they kept themselves together, and when the governor came home he recruited them.

The committee of both kingdoms had sent down at this time [December 1644] an order for all the horse of Nottingham and Derbyshire to join with three regiments of Yorkshire, and quarter about Newark, to straiten the enemy there; and accordingly they rendezvoused at Mansfield, and from thence marched to Thurgarton, where Sir Roger Cooper had fortified his house, and lined the hedges with musketeers, who, as the troops passed by, shot and killed one Captain Heywood. Hereupon Colonel Thornhagh sent to the governor, and desired to borrow some foot to take the house. The governor accordingly lent him three companies, who took the house, with Sir Roger Cooper and his brother, and forty men in it who were sent prisoners to Nottingham. Sir Roger Cooper was in great dread of being put into the governor's hands, whom he had provoked

* Ferdinando Stanhope, who died presumably as a result of wounds received in this action.

before upon a private occasion, yet he received such a civil treatment from him, that he seemed to be much moved and melted with it. The foot had done all the service, and run all the hazard, in taking the house, yet the booty was all given to the horse; this they had very just reason to resent, but notwithstanding, they marched along with them to Southwell, and there were most sadly neglected, and put upon keeping out-guards for the horse, and had no provisions, so that the governor was forced to send them some out of his garrison, or else they had been left to horrible distress. Hereupon they sent to the governor to desire they might come home, but upon Colonel Thornhagh's entreaty and engagement that they should be better used, the governor was content to let them stay a little longer, till more horse came up, which were sent for out of Yorkshire. In the meantime, those who were there already did nothing but harass the poor country; and the horse officers were so negligent of their own duty, and so remiss in the government of their soldiers, that the service was infinitely prejudiced, and the poor country miserably distressed. The Nottingham horse, being in their own country, and having their families in and about Nottingham, were more guilty of straggling than any of the rest; and Captain White's whole troop having presumed to be away one night when they should have been upon the guard, the Newarkers beat up our quarters, and took almost two whole troops of that regiment. White's lieutenant, without any leave from the colonel, thereupon posted up to London, and contrived a complaint against the governor, to make him appear guilty of this disorder; but soon after Newark gave them another alarm, and the Parliament horse made so slender an appearance that the officers, thereupon consulting in a council of war, concluded that the design could not be prosecuted without more force, and for the present broke up their quarters.

The committee men that ran away when the governor returned [from London to Nottingham] had taken the treasurer away with them, and left neither any money, nor so much as the rent rolls whereby the governor could be instructed where to fetch in any [from forfeited estates]; but by the prudence and interest of himself and his friends, he procured a month's pay for the foot, and twenty shillings a man for the horse, as soon as he came home. He recruited all the stores, which the committee had purposely wasted in his absence, and fetched in a small stock of powder they had laid in at Salisbury's house. While he was thus industriously setting the things in order which they had confounded, they at London were as maliciously active to make more confusion. They contrived many false and frivolous articles and petitions against him, and proceeded to that degree of impudence in desiring alterations, and casting reflections upon the sub-committee itself, that they grew weary of them.

The conspirators quitting all modesty, and pressing the committee with false affirmations and forgeries, that all men would lay down their arms if the governor were not removed, at length prevailed, that he should be the second time sent for to London to justify himself against them. The committee at London could never finish the business by reason of the impertinent clamours of the governor's enemies, therefore at length, wearied with the continual endless papers they had daily brought in, they made an order, wherein they assigned a certain day for the determination of their power, and in the meantime commanded all matter of crimination on both sides should be forborne. They ordered that the governor should return and pursue his first instructions, till he received new ones, and that the business should be reported to the House. The governor sent his brother down to take care of the garrison, and stayed himself to receive the final determination of the House, where Mr Millington, through his interest, kept off the report, by several tricks and unjust delays, for about three or four months.

When the lieutenant-colonel came down, the captains were wonderfully obedient, and all things pretty quiet, but the governor's officers were discouraged at the countenance which was given to his enemies, and the impunity of all the crimes of that faction. He having a certain spirit of government, in an extraordinary manner, which was not given to others, carrying an awe in his presence that his enemies could not withstand, the garrison was much disordered by his absence, and in daily peril;

although the lieutenant-colonel was as faithful and industrious in managing that charge as any person could be, and as excellent a person, but in a different way from his brother. Firmness and zeal to the cause, and personal valour he had equally, but that vigour of soul which made him invincible against all assaults, and overcoming all difficulties he met in his way, was proper to himself alone. The lieutenant-colonel was a man of the kindest heart and the most humble familiar deportment in the world, and lived with all his soldiers as if they had been his brothers; dispensing with that reverence which was due to him, and living cheerful and merry, and familiar with them, in such a manner that they celebrated him, and professed the highest love for him in the world, and would magnify his humility and kindness, and him for it, in a high degree above his brother. But with all this they grew so presumptuous that, when any obedience was exacted beyond their humours or apprehensions, they would often dare to fail in their duty; whereas the governor, still keeping a greater distance, though with no more pride, preserved an awe that made him to be equally feared and loved. Though they secretly repined at their subjection, yet they durst not refuse it; and, when they came to render it on great occasions, they found such wisdom and such advantage in all his dictates that, their reason being convinced of the benefit of his government, they delighted in it, and accounted it a happiness to be under his command.

As the governor's absence was the occasion of many neglects in the government, not by his brother's fault, but the soldiers' who, wanting their pay, were therefore discontented, and through that, careless of their duty; so, on the other side, the cavaliers, who were not ignorant of the dissensions in the garrison, took the advantage, and surprised the lieutenant-colonel's fort at the Trent bridges, while he was employed in keeping the castle. His soldiers in his absence lying out of their quarters, had not left above thirty men upon the guard, who were most of them killed, the ensign fighting it out very stoutly, after their entrance, till he died. The lieutenant-colonel was exceedingly afflicted with this loss, but presently applied himself to secure what remained. The whole town was in a sad uproar, and this happening upon a Lord's day in the morning, in May, 1645, all the people were in such a consternation that they could keep no sabbath that day. Then the lieutenant-colonel had an experiment of vulgar spirits, for even his own soldiers, who were guilty of the loss of the place by being out of their quarters, began to exclaim against him for a thousand causeless things.

As soon as the news came to the governor at London, he thought it time to throw off that patience with which he had hitherto waited at great expense, and went to the Parliament House before the House sat, and there acquainted the Speaker what had befallen at Nottingham, desiring he might be called to make a relation of it in the open House, or else he told the Speaker, though he died for it, he would press in and let them know how much the cause suffered by the indirect practices, which were partially connived at by some of their members. The Speaker seeing him so resolved, procured him, when the House was set, to be called in. There he told them how their fort was lost, and, for aught he knew, the garrison, by that time; which was no more than what he had long expected, through the countenance that was, by one of their members, given to a malignant faction, that obstructed all the public service, disturbed all the honest soldiers and officers in their duty, and spent the public treasury, to carry on their private malice. He further told them, how dishonourable, as well as destructive to their cause, it was, that their members should be protected in such unjust prosecutions, and should make the privilege of the House their shelter, to oppress the most active and faithful of their servants. Many of the guilty members had a mind to have committed him, but he spoke with such truth and convincing reason, that all those of more generous spirits, were much moved by it, and angry that he had been so injuriously treated, and desired him to take post down and to use all means to regain the place, and gave him full orders to execute his charge without disturbance. From that time Mr Millington so lost his credit, that he never recovered the esteem he formerly had among them; and after that time, the governor's enemies perceiving they were not able to mate him, made no more public attempts, though they continued that private malice.

Almost all the Parliament garrisons were infested and disturbed with like factious little people, insomuch that many worthy gentlemen were wearied out of their commands, and oppressed by a certain mean sort of people in the House, whom to distinguish from the more honourable gentlemen, they called *Worsted-Stocking Men*. Some as violently curbed their committees, as the committees factiously molested them. Nor were there factions only in particular garrisons, but the Parliament House itself began to fall into the two great oppositions of Presbytery and Independency: and, as if discord had infected the whole English air with an epidemical heart-burning and dissension in all places, even the king's councils and garrisons were as factiously divided. The king's commissioners and the governor at Newark fell into such high discontents, that Sir Richard Byron, the governor, was changed, and Sir Richard Willis put into his place.

The governor being dismissed from the Parliament, immediately took post, and arrived safe about three days after the loss of the bridges, and was welcomed as if safety and victory, and all desirable blessings, had come in his train. His presence reinforced the drooping garrison, and he immediately consulted how to go about regaining the fort. To this purpose, and to hinder the enemy from having an inlet into the town by the bridges, he made a little fort on the next bridge, and put a lieutenant and thirty men into it, thereby enclosing those in the fort the enemy had surprised, whom he resolved to assault on the town side, having thus provided that their friends should not come from the other side* to help them. But those of Newark understanding this, came as strong as they could one morning, and assaulted the little new fort, where Lieutenant Hall, failing of that courage which he had professed when he begged the honour of keeping it, gave it up. The governor seeing this from the other side, was exceedingly vexed, and marched up to the bridge to assault them in that fort; but he found that they had only stormed the other little fort to make their own

---

* Approaching Nottingham from the south there is a very wide valley, through which the Trent and the Leen ran in several branches, over which were bridges united by a causeway.

way to be gone, and that they had made shift to get to their friends upon the ribs of two broken arches, which, when they had served to help their passage, they pulled up, to hinder pursuit after them. Thus in a month's space God restored to the governor the fort which was lost in his absence; and he newly fortified the place and repaired the bridges, whereby the great market out of the vale was again brought into the town, to their exceeding joy and benefit.

Ann Fanshawe

Having buried my dear brother, William Harrison, in Exeter College Chapel, I then married your dear father in 1644 in Wolvercote Church, two miles from Oxford, upon the 18th day of May. None was at our wedding but my dear father, who, at my mother's desire, gave me her wedding ring, with which I was married, and my sister Margaret, and my brother and sister Boteler, Sir Edward Hyde, afterwards Lord Chancellor [Lord Clarendon], and Sir Geoffrey Palmer, the King's Attorney. Before I was married, my husband was sworn Secretary of War to the prince, now our king [Charles II], with a promise from Charles I to be preferred as soon as occasion offered it. Both his fortune and my promised portion, which was made £10,000, were both at that time in expectation, and we might truly be called merchant adventurers, for the stock we set up our trading with did not amount to £20 betwixt us. However, it was to us as a little piece of armour is against a bullet, which if it be right placed, though no bigger than a shilling, serves as well as a whole suit of armour. So our stock bought pen, ink, and paper, which was your father's trade, and by it, I assure you, we lived better than those that were born to £2000 a year as long as he had his liberty.

As faith is the evidence of things not seen, so we, upon so righteous a cause, cheerfully resolved to suffer what that would drive us to, which afflictions were neither few nor small, as you will find. The king would have had my husband then to have been sworn His Highness's [the Prince of Wales] secretary; but the queen, who was then no friend to my husband, because he had formerly made Secretary Windebank appear in his colours [as a Catholic], who was one of Her Majesty's favourites, wholly obstructed that then, and placed with the prince Sir Robert Long, for whom she had a great kindness; but the consequence will show the man.

The beginning of March, 1645, your father went to Bristol with his new master, and this was his first journey. I then lying-in of my first son, Harrison Fanshawe, who was born on the 22nd of February, he left me behind him: as for that, it was the first time we had parted a day since we married. He was extremely afflicted, even to tears, though passion was against his nature; but the sense of leaving me with a dying child, which did die two days after, in a garrison town, extremely weak, and very poor, were such circumstances as he could not bear with, only the argument of necessity. For my own part, it cost me so dear, that I was ten weeks before I could go alone. He, by all opportunities, wrote to me to fortify myself, and to comfort me in the company of my father and sister, who were both with me, and that as soon as the lords of the [Prince of Wales's] council had their wives come to them I should come to him, and that I should receive the first money he got, and hoped it would be suddenly. By the help of God, with these cordials I recovered my former strength by little and little, nor did I in my distressed condition lack the conversation of many of my relations then in Oxford, and kindnesses of very many of the nobility and gentry, both for goodness' sake, and because your father being there in good employment, they found him serviceable to themselves or friends, which friendships none better distinguished between his place and person than your father.

It was in May, 1645, the first time I went out of my chamber and to church, where, after service, Sir William Parcoust, a very honest gentleman, came to me, and said he had a letter for me from your father, and fifty pieces of gold, and was coming to bring them me. I opened first my letter, and read those inexpressible joys that almost overcame me, for he told me I should the Thursday following come to him, and to that purpose he had sent me that money, and would send two of his men with horses, and all accommodation both for myself, my father, and sister, and that Lady Capel and Lady Bradford would meet me on the way; but that gold your father sent me when I was ready to perish, did not so much revive me as his summons. I went immediately to walk, or at least to sit in the air, being very weak, in the garden of St John's College, and there, with my good father, communicated my joy, who took great pleasure to hear of my husband's good success and likewise of his journey to him. We, all of my household being present, heard drums beat in the highway, under the garden wall. My father asked me if I would go up upon the mount to see the soldiers march, for it was Sir Charles Lee's company of foot, an acquaintance of ours; I said yes, and went up, leaning my back to a tree that grew on the mount. The commander seeing us there, in compliment gave us a volley of shot, and one of their muskets being loaded, shot a brace of bullets not two inches above my head as I leaned to the tree, for which mercy and deliverance I praise God.

Next week we were all on our journey for Bristol very merry, and I thought that now all things would mend, and the worst of my misfortunes past, but little thought I to leap into the sea that would toss me until it had racked me. We were to ride all night by agreement, for fear of the enemy surprising us as we passed, they quartering in the way. About nightfall, having travelled about twenty miles, we discovered a troop of horse coming towards us, which proved to be Sir Marmaduke Roydon, a worthy commander, and my countryman. He told me, that hearing I was to pass by his garrison he was come out to conduct me, he hoped as far as was danger, which was about twelve miles. With many thanks we parted, and having refreshed ourselves and horses, we set forth for Bristol, where we arrived on the 20th of May.

My husband had provided very good lodgings for us, and as soon as he could come home from the council, where he was at my arrival, he with all expressions of joy received me in his arms, and gave me a hundred pieces of gold, saying, 'I know thou that keeps my heart so well, will keep my fortune, which from this time I will ever put into thy hands as God shall bless me with increase.' Now I thought myself a perfect queen, and my husband so glorious a crown, that I more valued myself to be called by his name than born a princess, for I knew him very wise and very good, and his soul doted on me, upon which confidence I will tell you what happened.

My Lady Rivers, a brave woman, and one that had suffered many thousand pounds' loss for the king, and whom I had a great reverence for, and she a kindness for me as a kinswoman, in discourse she tacitly commended the knowledge of state affairs.* Some women were very happy in a good understanding thereof, as my Lady Aubigny, Lady Isabel Thynne, and divers others, and yet none was at first more capable than I. In the night, she knew, there came a post from Paris from the queen; and she would be extremely glad to hear what the queen commanded the king in order to his affairs; saying, if I would ask my husband privately, he would tell me what he found in the packet, and I might tell her. I that was young and innocent, and to that day had never in my mouth what news, began to think there was more in enquiring into public affairs than I thought of, and that it being a fashionable thing would make me more beloved of my husband, if that had been possible, than I was. When my husband returned home from council, after welcoming him, as his custom ever was, he went with his hand-ful of papers into his study for an hour or more. I followed him; he turned hastily, and said, 'What wouldst thou have, my life?' I told him, I heard the prince had received a packet from the queen, and I guessed it was that in his hand, and I desired to know what was in it; he smilingly replied, 'My love, I will immediately come to thee, pray thee go, for I am very busy.' When he came out of his closet I revived my suit; he kissed me, and talked of other things. At supper I would eat nothing; he as usual sat by me, and drank often to me which was his custom, and was full of discourse to company that was at table. Going to bed I asked again, and said I could not believe he loved me if he refused to tell me all he knew, but he answered

* Two of her houses, St Osyth's Priory in Essex and Melford Hall in Suffolk, were sacked in 1642.

nothing, but stopped my mouth with kisses. So we went to bed, I cried, and he went to sleep.

Next morning early as his custom was, he called to rise, but began to discourse with me first, to which I made no reply; he rose, came on the other side of the bed and kissed me, and drew the curtains softly and went to court. When he came home to dinner he presently came to me as was usual, and when I had him by the hand, I said, 'Thou dost not care to see me troubled.' To which he, taking me in his arms, answered, 'My dearest soul, nothing upon earth can afflict me like that, and when you asked me of my business, it was wholly out of my power to satisfy thee, for my life and fortune shall be thine, and every thought of my heart, but my honour is my own, which I cannot preserve if I communicate the prince's affairs; and pray thee with this answer rest satisfied.' So great was his reason and goodness, that upon consideration it made my folly appear to me so vile, that from that day until the day of his death I never thought fit to ask him any business, but what he communicated freely to me in order to his estate or family.

My husband grew much in the prince's favour, and Mr Long was not suffered to execute the business of his place, as the council suspected that he held private intelligence with the Earl of Essex. When Mr Long perceived this he went into the enemy's quarters, and so to London, and then into France, full of complaints of the prince's council to the queen-mother, and when he was gone your father supplied his place.

About July, 1645, the plague increased so fast in Bristol, that the prince and all his retinue went to Barnstaple, which is one of the finest towns in England; and your father and I went two days after the prince. During all the time I was in the court I never journeyed, but either before him, or when he was gone, nor ever saw him but at church, for it was not in those days the fashion for honest women, except they had business, to visit a man's court. I saw there at Mr Palmer's, where we lay, who was a merchant, a parrot above a hundred years old. They have, near this town, a fruit called a massard, like a cherry, but different in taste, and makes the best pies with their sort of cream I ever ate. My Lady Capel here left us, and with a pass from the Earl of Essex, went to London with her eldest daughter, now Marchioness of Worcester. Sir Allen Apsley* was governor of the town, and we had all sorts of good provision and accommodation, but the prince's affairs calling him from that place, we went to Launceston, in Cornwall, and thither came very many gentlemen of that county to do their duties to His Highness. They were generally loyal to the crown and hospitable to their neighbours, but they are of a crafty and censorious nature, as most are so far from London. That country hath great plenty, especially of fish and fowl, but nothing near so fat and sweet as within forty miles of London. We were quartered at Truro, twenty miles beyond Launceston, in which place I had like to have been robbed. One night having with me but seven or eight persons, my husband being then at Launceston with his master, somebody had discovered that my husband had a little trunk of the prince's in keeping, in which were some jewels that tempted them to us assay. But, praised be God, I defended, with the few servants I had, the house so long that help came from the town to my rescue, which was not above a flight shot from the place where I dwelt. The next day upon my notice my husband sent me a guard by His Highness's command.

From thence the court removed to Pendennis Castle, some time commanded by Sir Nicholas Slanning, who lost his life bravely in the king's service, and left an excellent name behind him. In this place came Sir John Grenville into His Highness's service, and was made a gentleman of his bed-chamber. His father [Sir Bevil] was a very honest gentleman, and lost his life in the king's service; and his uncle, Sir Richard, was a good commander, but a little too severe.† I was at Penzance with my father, and in the same town was my brother Fanshawe and his lady and children. My father and that family embarked for Morlaix, in Brittany, with my father's new wife.

---

* Lucy Hutchinson's brother.
† Sir Bevil was killed at the Battle of Lansdown in 1643. Sir Richard was in fact a deplorable figure, guilty of many outrages in the West Country. Slanning had been killed at the siege of Bristol in 1643.

War's End
1645-8

The high point in Lucy Hutchinson's description of her husband's part in the closing stages of the First Civil War after the Battle of Naseby in June 1645 is the storming of Shelford Manor, one of the outstations of the Newark cavaliers, in November that year. She also covers the final siege of Newark and its dramatic conclusion with the arrival of Charles, having ridden from Oxford in disguise, to surrender to the Scottish contingent among the besieging forces, in May 1646. There are then telling examples of this steadfast couple's determination to go their own way through these troubled times— the colonel's reluctance to join the Independent faction within the House of Commons, although labelled as one of them by the Presbyterian group; their sudden conviction that infant baptism was wrong; his strenuous efforts to secure justice for his cavalier brother-in-law.

The Duchess of Newcastle left Oxford for the West Country in April 1644 as part of the entourage of Queen Henrietta Maria. In July, shortly after the Battle of Marston Moor, the queen set sail from Falmouth, only to be attacked by some parliamentary ships off the Devon coast. The queen threw her maids-of-honour into panic by ordering that the ship's magazine was to be exploded if they were captured. Eventually they made the French port of Brest, the start of the duchess's long exile. In 1645 she was wooed and married by the Duke of Newcastle in Paris. It was only in 1652 that she returned to London in an attempt to raise money. Her husband was

branded a delinquent by Parliament and therefore exempted from
the general pardon, so could not come back himself. Her brother Sir
Charles Lucas, to whose death she refers and whom we have already
encountered attacking Nottingham in January 1644, met his end in
a particularly bitter manner. He was one of the ringleaders in the
Second Civil War, which began in February 1648, and was taken
prisoner at the end of the siege of Colchester (his own home town)
in August. He and Sir George Lisle were executed by firing squad
on the orders of Thomas Fairfax, prompted it is said by Henry
Ireton. Fairfax's excuse was that Lucas had broken parole. It was
reported that the besieging forces desecrated the tomb of Lucas's
mother, who had died the previous year, scattering the limbs and
putting locks of her hair in their hats.

Ann Fanshawe came on a similar money-raising errand in 1647,
but she was also able to arrange for her husband to come over from
France and compound—that is, buy his pardon—for £300. The rate
for so compounding was two years'-worth of annual income from
one's estates. Her narrative is punctuated with great regularity by
the births of her children.

Lucy Hutchinson

This summer there was a much greater progress made in the
war than had been before, and the new Parliament [New
Model] army prosecuted it so much in earnest, that they made
a show to block up the king in his main garrison at Oxford, but
he broke out and, joining Prince Rupert's horse, came, after
several attempts elsewhere, to Leicester, which he took by
storm. The loss of this town was a great affliction and terror to
all the neighbouring garrisons and counties, whereupon Fairfax,
closely attending the king's motions, came within a few days
and fought with the king, and overcame him in that memor-
able battle at Naseby [14 June 1645]. His coach and cabinet
of letters were taken; which letters being carried to London
were printed, and manifested his falsehood, how that, contrary
to his professions, he had endeavoured to bring in Danes and

Lorrainers, and Irish rebels, to subdue the good people here, and had given himself up to be governed by the queen in all affairs both of state and religion. After this fight Fairfax took again the town of Leicester, and went into the west, relieved Taunton, took Bristol, and many other garrisons. Chester also, and other places were taken that way. Meanwhile, the king, having coasted about the countries, came at last to Newark [October 1645], and there, his commanders falling out among themselves, he changed the governor, and put the Lord Bellasis into the place, and went himself to Oxford, where he was at last blocked up.

When Sir Thomas Fairfax was made chief general, Poyntz was made major-general of the northern counties, and a committee of war was set up at York, whereof Colonel Pierrepont, by his brother's* procurement, was appointed one, and was pretty well satisfied, as thinking himself again set above Colonel Hutchinson, because all the northern garrisons were to receive orders from that committee: but the governor heeding not other men's exaltations or depressions, only attended to his own duty. About the latter end of this summer, Poyntz came to Nottingham with all the horse that could be gathered in the neighbouring counties. He had before marched with them and the Nottingham regiment into Cheshire, and brought several gentlemen prisoners into the garrison of Nottingham, who had been taken in divers encounters.

By reason of the rout at Naseby, and the surrender of Carlisle and several other garrisons to the Scots, the broken forces of the cavaliers had all repaired to Newark, and that was now become the strongest and best fortified garrison the king had, and Poyntz was ordered to quarter his horse about it, till the Scots should come on the other side and besiege it. At that time also the king himself was there. The governor having informed Poyntz how prejudicial it would be to his design to suffer those little garrisons in the Vale at Shelford and Wiverton to remain, it was agreed that all the forces should take them in their way. But the governor having obtained permission of Poyntz, through a respect he had to the family, sent a letter to Colonel

---

* William Pierrepont MP.

Philip Stanhope,* Governor of Shelford, to persuade him to surrender the place he could not hold, and to offer to obtain honourable terms for him, if he would hearken to propositions. Stanhope returned a very scornful, huffing reply, in which one of his expressions was, that he should lay Nottingham Castle as flat as a pancake, and such other bravadoes, which had been less amiss, if he had done anything to make them good.

Hereupon the whole force marched against the place, and the several posts were assigned to the several colonels. The governor, according to his own desire, had that which seemed most difficult assigned to him, and his quarters that night were appointed in Shelford town. When he came thither, a few of the Shelford soldiers were gotten into the steeple of the church, and from thence so played upon the governor's men that they could not quietly take up their quarters. There was a trap door that led into the belfry, and they had made it fast, and drawn up the ladder and the bell-ropes, and regarded not the governor's threatening them to have no quarter if they came not down, so that he was forced to send for straw and fire it, and smother them out. Hereupon they came down, and among them there was a boy who had marched out with the governor's company, when he went first against Newark, and carried himself so stoutly, that Captain Wray begged him for a foot-boy, and when his troop was once taken by the enemy, this boy, being taken among them, became one of their soldiers. The governor making him believe he should be hanged immediately for changing his party, and for holding out to their disturbance, where he could not hope for relief, the boy begged he might be spared, and offered to lead them on to the only place where they could enter, where the palisade was unfinished. The governor, without trusting to him, considered the probability of his information, kept him under guard, and set him in the front of his men, and he accordingly proved to have told them the truth in all that he had said, and did excellent good service, behaving himself most stoutly.

The governor being armed, and ready to begin the assault, when the rest were also ready, Captain White came to him, and,

* Colonel Hutchinson's step-mother was Colonel Stanhope's aunt.

notwithstanding all his former malicious prosecutions, now
pretended the most tender care and love that could be declared,
with all imaginable flattery; and persuaded the governor not to
hazard himself in so dangerous an attempt, but to consider his
wife and children, and stand by among the horse, but by no
means to storm the place in his own person. Notwithstanding
all his false insinuations, the governor, perceiving his envy at
that honour which his valour was ready to reap in this encounter, was exceedingly angry with him, and went on upon the
place. This being seated on a flat, was encompassed with a very
strong bulwark, and a great ditch without, in most places wet
at the bottom, so that they within were very confident of being
able to hold it out, there being no cannon brought against them;
because also a broken regiment of the queen's, who were all
papists, were come in to their assistance. A regiment of Londoners was appointed to storm on the other side, and the
governor at the same time began the assault at his post.

His men found many more difficulties than they expected,
for after they had filled up the ditches with faggots and pitched
the scaling ladders, they were twenty staves too short, and the
enemy, from the top of the works, threw down logs of wood,
which would sweep off a whole ladderful of men at once: the
lieutenant-colonel himself was once or twice so beaten down.
The governor had ordered other musketeers to beat off those
men that stood upon the top of the works, which they failed to
do by shooting without good aim. But the governor directed
them better, and the Nottingham horse dismounting, and assail-
ing with their pistols, and headpieces, helped the foot to beat
them all down from the top of the works, except one stout man,
who stood alone, and did wonders in beating down the assailants. The governor being angry at this, fetched two of his own
musketeers and made them shoot, and he immediately fell, to
the great discouragement of his fellows.

Then the governor himself first entered, and the rest of his
men came in as fast as they could. But while this regiment was
entering on this side, the Londoners were beaten off on the
other side, and the main force of the garrison turned upon him.
The cavaliers had half moons within, which were as good a

defence to them as their first works. Into these the soldiers that were of the queen's regiment were gotten, and they in the house shot from out of all the windows. The governor's men, as soon as they got in, took the stables and all their horses, but the governor himself was fighting with the captain of the papists and some others, who, by advantage of the half moon and the house, might have prevailed to cut him off and those that were with him, which were not many. The enemy being strengthened by the addition of those who had beaten off the assailants on the other side, were now trying their utmost to vanquish those that were within. The lieutenant-colonel, seeing his brother in hazard, made haste to open the drawbridge, that Poyntz might come in with his horse; which he did, but not before the governor had killed that gentleman who was fighting with him, at whose fall his men gave way.

Poyntz, seeing them shoot from the house, and apprehending the king might come to their relief, when he came in, ordered that no quarter should be given. And here the governor was in greater danger than before, for the strangers hearing him called governor, were advancing to have killed him, but that the lieutenant-colonel, who was very watchful to preserve him all that day, came in to his rescue. He scarcely could persuade them that it was the Governor of Nottingham; because he, at the beginning of the storm, had put off a very good suit of armour that he had, which being musket-proof, was so heavy that it heated him, and so would not be persuaded by his friends to wear anything but his buff coat. The governor's men, eager to complete their victory, were forcing their entrance into the house. Meanwhile Rossiter's* men came and took away all their horses, which they had taken away when they first entered the works and won the stables, and left in the guard of two or three, while they were pursuing their work.

The Governor of Shelford, after all his bravadoes, came but meanly off; it is said he sat in his chamber, wrapped up in his cloak, and came not forth that day; but that availed him not, for how, or by whom, it is not known, but he was wounded and stripped, and flung upon a dunghill. The lieutenant-colonel,

* A parliamentary cavalry commander.

after the house was mastered, seeing the disorder by which our men were ready to murder one another, upon the command Poyntz had issued to give no quarter, desired Poyntz to cause the slaughter to cease, which was presently obeyed, and about sevenscore prisoners were saved. While he was thus busied, enquiring what was become of the governor, he was shown him naked upon the dunghill; whereupon the lieutenant-colonel called for his own cloak and cast it over him, and sent him to a bed in his own quarters, and procured him a surgeon. Upon his desire he had a little priest, who had been his father's chaplain, and was one of the [Nottingham] committee faction; but the man was such a pitiful comforter, that the governor [Colonel Hutchinson], who was come to visit him, was forced to undertake that office. Though he had all the supplies they could every way give him, he died the next day.

The house, which belonged to his father, the Earl of Chesterfield, was that night burned, none certainly knowing by what means, whether by accident or on purpose; but there was most ground to believe that the country people, who had been sorely infested by that garrison, to prevent the keeping it by those who had taken it, purposely set it on fire. If the queen's regiment had mounted their horses and stood ready upon them when our men entered, they had undoubtedly cut them all off; but they standing to the works, it pleased God to lead them into that path he had ordained for their destruction, who being papists, would not receive quarter, nor were they much offered it, being killed in the heat of the contest, so that not a man of them escaped.

The next day our party went to Wiverton, a house of the Lord Chaworth's, which, terrified with the example of the other, yielded upon terms, and was by order pulled down and rendered incapable of being any more a garrison.

Poyntz now quartered all his horse in the towns about Newark, and since he had no peculiar regiment of his own, the governor's regiment served him for his guards. The Scots also came and quartered on the other side of the town towards the north.

All that winter the governor lay at the leaguer, and about Christmas time writs were sent down for new elections to fill up the Parliament. There being a burgess-ship* void at Nottingham, the town would needs, in a compliment, make the governor free [a freeman], in order to elect him to the Parliament. Mr Francis Pierrepont hearing this, wrote to the governor to desire that he would rather come into his father's place in the county, and give him his assistance in this, as he should engage his own and all his friends' interest for him in the county. The governor, who was ever ready to requite injuries with benefits, employed his interest in the town to satisfy the gentleman's desire, and having very many in his regiment that had votes, he sent for them all home the night before the day of election; which had like to have been a very sad one, but that by the mercy of God, and the courage of Poyntz and the lieutenant-colonel and Captain Poulton, it had not so bad an event.

The Newarkers, hearing that so many of the regiment were away, fell upon their quarters, and most of the men being surprised, were rather endeavouring flight than resistance. The lieutenant-colonel and Captain Poulton rallied all they could find, lined some pales with musketeers, and beat the enemy again out of their quarters, and Poyntz, mounting with as many horse as were about him, which was very few, followed them in the night up to the very works of Newark. Some loss there was in the quarters, but nothing considerable; some soldiers ran away home, and brought the governor word they were all cut off, but his brother sent a messenger to acquaint him with the contrary. Hereupon, immediately after the election, he returned back again with his men.

Not long after, the elections were made for the county, who all pitched upon the governor, in his father's room. White, whose envy never died, used all the endeavours he could to have hindered it; but when he saw he could do no harm, with a sad heart, under a false face, he came and took his part of a noble dinner the new knights had provided for the gentlemen of the country.

Poyntz drew a line about the town [of Newark], and made a very regular entrenchment and approaches, in such a soldier-like manner as none of them who had attempted the place before

* A seat for the town of Nottingham.

had done. Most of that winter they lay in the field, and the governor, carried on by the vigour and greatness of his mind, felt no distemper then by that service, which all his captains and the soldiers themselves endured worse than he. Besides daily and hourly providences, by which they were preserved from the enemy's cannons and sallies, there were some remarkable ones, by which God kept the governor's life in this leaguer. Once as Poyntz and he, and another captain, were riding to view some quarter of the town, a cannon bullet came whizzing by them, as they were riding all abreast, and the captain, without any touch of it, said he was killed. Poyntz bid him get off, but he was then sliding down from his horse, slain by the wind of the bullet; they held him up till they got off from the place, but the man immediately turned black all over. Another time the governor was in his tent, and was by chance called out; when he was scarcely out of it, a cannon bullet came and tore up the whole tent, and killed the sentinel at the door. But the greatest peril wherein all on the English side were, was the treachery of the Scots, which they had very good reason to apprehend might have been the cutting off of all that force.

Sir Thomas Fairfax had now besieged Oxford, and the king was stolen out of the town and gone in disguise, no man knew whither, but at length he came into the Scots' army. They had before behaved themselves very oddly to the English, and been taking sundry occasions to pick quarrels, when at the last certain news was brought to the English quarters that the king was come to the Scots, and by them received at Southwell [5 May 1646]. The English could then expect nothing but that the Scots, joining with those that were in Newark, would fall upon them, who were far inferior in number to the other, and therefore they all prepared themselves, as well as they could, to defend themselves in their trenches. The governor had then very fine horses at the leaguer, which he sent home to the garrison. While they were in expectation of being thus fallen upon, the king had more mind to be gone; and because the Scots knew not how to break up their quarters while the town was not taken, the king sent to my Lord Bellasis, the Governor of Newark, to surrender up the place immediately. This he did upon pretty handsome terms, but was much discontented that the king should have no more regard for them who had been so constant to his service.

The governor with his regiment was appointed to receive the town and the arms, and to quarter in it; where he now went and had the greatest danger of all, for the town was all over sadly infected with the plague; yet it so pleased God that neither he nor any of the fresh men caught the infection, which was so raging there that it almost desolated the place.

Whether the king's ill council or his destiny led him, he was very failing in this action; for had he gone straight up to the Parliament and cast himself upon them, as he did upon the Scots, he had in all probability ruined them, who were highly divided between the Presbyterian and Independent factions. But in putting himself into the hands of the mercenary Scotch army, rather than the Parliament of England, he showed such an embittered hate to the English nation, that it turned many hearts against him. The Scots in this business were very false both to the Parliament and to the king. For them to receive and carry away the king's person with them, when they were but a hired army, without either the consent or knowledge of the Parliament, was a very false carriage in them; but besides that, we had certain evidences that they were prepared, and had an intent to have cut off the English army which beleaguered Newark, but that God changed their counsels and made them take another course, which was to carry the king to Newcastle, where they again sold him to the Parliament for a sum of money.

The country being now cleared of all the enemy's garrisons, Colonel Hutchinson went up to London to attend his duty there, and to serve his country as faithfully, in the capacity of a senator, as he had before in that of a soldier. When he came there he found a very bitter spirit of discord and envy raging, and the Presbyterian faction (of which were most of those lords and others that had been laid aside by the self-denying ordinance)* were endeavouring a violent persecution, upon the

* Passed in April 1645, this ensured that command of the New Model Army went to Thomas Fairfax and Cromwell, and excluded discredited commanders like Essex and Manchester.

account of conscience, against those who had in so short a time accomplished, by God's blessing, that victory which he was not pleased to bestow upon them. Their directory of worship was at length sent forth for a three years' trial, and such as could not conform to it, marked out with an evil eye, hated and persecuted under the name of separatists. Colonel Hutchinson, who abhorred that malicious zeal and imposing spirit which appeared in them, was soon taken notice of for one of the independent faction, whose heads were accounted William Pierrepont, Sir Harry Vane, and Oliver St John, and some few other grandees, being men that excelled in wisdom and utterance. Though, to speak the truth, they very little knew Colonel Hutchinson that could say he was of any faction; for he had a strength of judgement able to consider things himself and propound them to his conscience, which was so upright that the veneration of no man's person alive, nor the love of the dearest friend in the world, could make him do the least thing, without a full persuasion that it was his duty so to act.

His attendance in the Parliament House changing his custom of life into a sedentary employment, less suitable to his active spirit, and more prejudicial to his health, he fell into a long and painful sickness, which many times brought him near the grave, and was not perfectly cured in four years. The doctors could not find a name for it; but at length resolved upon the running gout, and a cure, proper for that disease, being practised upon him, took effect.

During this time Sir Thomas Fairfax himself lay at Nottingham, and the governor was sick in the castle.* The general's lady was come along with him, having followed his camp to the siege of Oxford, and lain at his quarters all the while he abode there. She was exceeding kind to her husband's chaplains, independent ministers, till the army returned to be nearer London, and then the Presbyterian ministers quite changed the lady into such a bitter aversion against them, that they could not endure to come into the general's presence while she was there. The general had an unquiet, unpleasant life with her,

---

* Sir Thomas became Lord Fairfax in 1647, on the death of his father.

who drove away from him many of those friends, in whose conversation he had found such sweetness. At Nottingham they had gotten a very able minister into the great church, but a bitter Presbyterian; him and his brethren my Lady Fairfax caressed with so much kindness, that they grew impudent enough to preach up their faction openly in the pulpit, and to revile the others, and at length would not suffer any of the army chaplains to preach in the town. They then coming to the governor and complaining of their unkind usage, he invited them to come and preach in his house, which when it was known they did, a great concourse of people came thither to them; and the Presbyterians, when they heard of it, were mad with rage, not only against them, but against the governor, who accidentally gave them another occasion about the same time, a little before the general came.

When formerly the Presbyterian ministers had forced him, for quietness' sake, to go and break up a private meeting in the cannoneers' chamber, there were found some notes concerning paedobaptism,* which were brought into the governor's lodgings. His wife having then more leisure to read than he, having perused them and compared them with the Scriptures, found not what to say against the truths they asserted, concerning the misapplication of that ordinance to infants; but being then young and modest, she thought it a kind of virtue to submit to the judgment and practice of most churches, rather than to defend a singular opinion of her own, she not being then enlightened in that great mistake of the national churches. But in this year she, happening to be with child, communicated her doubts to her husband, and desired him to endeavour her satisfaction; which while he did, he himself became as unsatisfied, or rather satisfied against it. First, therefore, he diligently searched the Scriptures alone, and could find in them no ground at all for that practice; then he bought and read all the eminent treatises on both sides, which at that time came thick from the presses, and was still more satisfied of the error of the paedobaptists. After this, his wife being brought to bed, that he might, if possible, give the religious party no offence, he invited all the

* The baptism of infants.

ministers to dinner, and propounded his doubt, and the ground thereof to them. None of them could defend their practice with any satisfactory reason, but the tradition of the church, from the primitive times, and their main buckler of federal holiness. He and his wife then, professing themselves unsatisfied in the practice, desired their opinions, what they ought to do. Most answered, to conform to the general practice of other Christians, how dark soever it were to themselves; but Mr Foxcraft, one of the assembly, said, that except they were convinced of the warrant of that practice from the Word, they sinned in doing it: whereupon that infant was not baptised. And now the governor and his wife, notwithstanding that they forsook not their assemblies, nor retracted their benevolences and civilities from them, yet were they reviled by them, called fanatics and anabaptists, and often glanced at in their public sermons.

This year [1647] Sir Allen Apsley, Governor of Barnstaple for the king, after the surrender of that garrison, came and retired to the governor's house, till his composition with the Parliament was completed, the governor's wife being his sister, and the governor's brother having married the other sister; and this was another occasion of opening the mouths of the malignants, who were ready to seize upon anyone to his prejudice.

Sir Allen Apsley had articles* at the surrender of Barnstaple, and contrary to these he was put to vast expense and horrible vexation by several persons, but especially by one wicked woman, who had the worst and the smoothest tongue that ever her sex made use of to mischief. She was handsome in her youth, and had very pretty girls for her daughters, whom, when they grew up, she prostituted for her revenge and malice against Sir Allen Apsley, which was so venomous and devilish, that she stuck not at inventing false accusations, and hiring witnesses to swear to them, and a thousand other practices as enormous. In those days there was a committee set up, for relief of such as had any violation of their articles, and of this Bradshaw was president;† into whose easy faith this woman, pretending herself religious, and of the Parliament's party, had so insinuated

* Terms granted to him.
† Later president of the court that tried Charles I.

herself, that Sir Allen's way of relief was obstructed. Colonel Hutchinson, labouring mightily in his protection, and often foiling this vile woman, and bringing to light her devilish practices, turned the woman's spite into as violent a tumult against himself.

At last it was manifest how much they were mistaken who would have assisted this woman upon a score of her being on the Parliament's side, for she was all this while a spy for the king, and after his return [in 1660], Sir Allen Apsley met her in the king's chamber waiting for recompense for that service. The thing she sued Sir Allen Apsley for, was for a house of hers in the garrison of Barnstaple, which was pulled down to fortify the town for the king, before he was governor of the place. Yet would she have had his articles violated to make her a recompense out of his estate, treble and more than the value of the house; pretending she was of the Parliament's party, and that Sir Allen, in malice thereunto, had without necessity pulled down her house.

The Duchess of Newcastle

I continued almost two years [at the court of Queen Henrietta Maria], until such time as I was married from thence. My lord the Marquis of Newcastle did approve of those bashful fears which many condemned, and would choose such a wife as he might bring to his own humours, and not such an one as was wedded to self-conceit, or one that had been tempered to the humours of another; for which he wooed me for his wife. Though I did dread marriage, and shunned men's companies as much as I could, yet I could not, nor had not the power to refuse him, by reason my affections were fixed on him, and he was the only person I ever was in love with. Neither was I ashamed to own it, but gloried therein, for it was not amorous love, I never was infected therewith. It is a disease, or a passion, or both, I only know by relation, not by experience. Neither could title, wealth, power, or person entice me to love; but my love was honest and honourable, being placed upon merit. I was joyed at the fame of his worth, pleased with delight in his wit, proud of the respects he used to me, and triumphing in the affections he professed for me, which he hath confirmed to me by a deed of time, sealed by constancy, and assigned by an unalterable decree of his promise.

But not only the family I am linked to is ruined, but the family from which I sprung, by these unhappy wars; which ruin my mother lived to see, and then died. They plundered her and my brothers of all their goods, plate, jewels, money, corn, cattle, and the like, cut down their woods, pulled down their houses, and sequestered them from their lands and livings. This unnatural war came like a whirlwind, which felled down their houses, where some in the wars were crushed to death, as my youngest brother Sir Charles Lucas, and my brother Sir Thomas Lucas; though he died not immediately of his wounds, yet a wound he received on his head in Ireland shortened his life.

After I was married some two or three years, my lord travelled out of France, from the city of Paris, and went into Holland, to a town called Rotterdam, in which place he stayed some six months. From thence he returned to Brabant, unto the city of Antwerp. In that city my lord settled himself and family, choosing it for the most pleasantest, and quietest place to retire himself and ruined fortunes in [1648]. After we had remained some time therein, we grew extremely necessitated, tradesmen being there not so rich as to trust my lord for so much, or so long, as those of France; yet they were so civil, kind and charitable, as to trust him, for as much as they were able. At last necessity enforced me to return into England to seek for relief [1652]; for I hearing my lord's estate, amongst the rest of many more estates, was to be sold, and that the wives of the owners should have an allowance therefrom, it gave me hopes I should receive a benefit thereby. Accompanied with my lord's only brother Sir Charles Cavendish, who was commanded to return to live therein, or to lose his estate (which estate he was forced to buy with a great composition before he could enjoy any part thereof), over I went. When I came there I found their hearts as hard as my fortunes, and their natures as cruel as my miseries, for they sold all my lord's estate, which was a very great one, and gave me not any part thereof, or any allowance thereout which few or no other was so hardly dealt withal. Indeed, I did not stand as a beggar at the Parliament door, for I never was at the Parliament House as a petitioner, neither did I haunt the committees, but one in my life, which was called at Goldsmith's Hall. But I received neither gold nor silver from them, only an absolute refusal. My brother, the Lord Lucas, did claim in my behalf such a part of my lord's estate as wives had allowed them, but they told him, that by reason I was married since my lord was made a delinquent, I could have nothing, nor should have anything, he being the greatest traitor to the State. I whisperingly spoke to my brother to conduct me out of that ungentlemanly place, so without speaking to them one word good or bad, I returned to my lodgings.

I had a firm faith, or strong opinion, that the pains was more than the gains, and being unpractised in public employments, unlearned in their uncouth ways, ignorant of the humours and dispositions of those persons to whom I was to address my suit, and not knowing where the power lay, and being not a good flatterer, I did not trouble myself or petition my enemies; besides I am naturally bashful. I find my bashfulness riseth not so often in blushes, as contracts my spirits to a chill paleness, but the best of it is, most commonly it soon vanisheth away, and many times before it can be perceived. The more foolish, or unworthy, I conceive the company to be, the worse I am, and the best remedy I ever found is to persuade myself that all those persons I meet are wise and virtuous. Naturally I have such an aversion to ill-bred creatures, as I am afraid to meet them, as children are afraid of spirits, or those that are afraid to see or meet devils; which makes me think that natural defect in me, if it be a defect, is rather a fear than a bashfulness.

I was in England a year and a half, in which time I gave some half a score visits, and went with my lord's brother to hear music in one Mr Lawes* his house, three or four times, as also some three or four times to Hyde Park with my sisters, to take the

* Henry Lawes was a celebrated composer, the friend of Milton.

air, else I never stirred out of my lodgings, unless to see my brothers and sisters. Nor seldom did I dress myself, as taking no delight to adorn myself, since he I only desired to please was absent, although report did dress me in a hundred several fashions. Then I resolved to return, although I was grieved to leave Sir Charles, my lord's brother, he being sick of an ague, of which sickness he died: for though his ague was cured, his life was decayed.

Heaven hitherto hath kept us, and though Fortune hath been cross, yet we do submit, and are both content with what is, and cannot be mended. However our fortunes are, we are both content, spending our time harmlessly, for my lord pleaseth himself with the management of some few horses, and exercises himself with the use of the sword; which two arts he hath brought by his studious thoughts, rational experience, and industrious practice, to an absolute perfection. Also he recreates himself with his pen, writing what his wit dictates to him. I pass my time rather with scribbling than writing, with words than wit, not that I speak much, because I am addicted to contemplation, unless I am with my lord, yet then I rather attentively listen to what he says, than impertinently speak.

Ann Fanshawe

In April 1646 the prince and all his council embarked themselves in a ship called the *Phoenix*, for the Isles of Scilly. They went from the Land's End, and so did we. We left our house and furniture with Captain Bluett, who promised to keep them until such a time as we could dispose of them; but when we sent, he said he had been plundered of them, notwithstanding it was well known he lost nothing of his own. At that time this loss went deep with us, for we lost to the value of £200 and more, but as the proverb saith, an evil chance seldom comes alone. We having put all our present estate into two trunks, and carried them aboard with us in a ship commanded by Sir Nicholas Crispe, whose skill and honesty the master and seamen

had no opinion of, my husband was forced to appease their
mutiny which his miscarriage caused, taking out money to
pay the seamen. That night following they broke open one of
our trunks, and took out a bag of £60 and a quantity of gold
lace, with our best clothes and linen, with all my combs, gloves,
and ribbons, which amounted to near £300 more. The next
day, after having been pillaged, and extremely sick and big
with child, I was set on shore almost dead in the Island of
Scilly. When we had got to our quarters near the castle, where
the prince lay, I went immediately to bed, which was so vile,
that my footman ever lay in a better, and we had but three in
the whole house, which consisted of four rooms, or rather parti-
tions: two low rooms and two little lofts, with a ladder to go up.
In one of these they kept dried fish, which was his trade, and in
this my husband's two clerks lay; one there was for my sister,
and one for myself, and one amongst the rest of the servants.
When I waked in the morning, I was so cold I knew not what
to do, but the daylight discovered that my bed was near swim-
ming with the sea, which the owner told us afterwards it never
did so but at spring tide. With this we were destitute of clothes,
and meat, and fuel, and truly we begged our daily bread of God,
for we thought every meal our last. The council sent for provisions to France, which served us, but they were bad, and a little
of them.

After three weeks and odd days, we set sail for the Isle of
Jersey, where we safely arrived, praised be God, beyond the
belief of all the beholders from that island. The pilot, not knowing the way into the harbour, sailed over the rocks, but being
spring tide, and by chance high water, His Highness and all of
us came safe ashore through so great a danger. Sir George
Carteret was lieutenant governor of the island. There are in this
island many gentlemen's houses, at which we were entertained:
they have fine walks along to their doors, double elms or oaks,
which is extremely pleasant, and their ordinary highways are
good walks, by reason of the shadow. The whole place is grass,
except some small parcels where corn is grown; the chiefest
employment is knitting; they neither speak English nor good
French; they are a cheerful, good-natured people, and truly

subject to the present government. We quartered at a widow's house in the market-place, Madame de Pommes, a stocking merchant; here I was delivered of my second child, a daughter, christened Anne. And now it was resolved by His Highness to go to Paris, upon which Lord Capel, Lord Hopton, and the chancellor, stayed at Jersey, and with them my husband, whose employment ceased when his master went out of his father's kingdom. Your father and I remained fifteen days in Jersey, and resolved that he would remain with his brother in Caen, whilst he sent me into England, whither my father was gone a month before, to see if I could procure a sum of money. The beginning of August we took our leave of the governor's family, and left our child with a nurse under the care of the Lady Carteret, and in four days we came to Caen, and myself, sister, and maid, went aboard a small merchantman that lay in the river.

Upon the 30th of August, I arrived in the Cowes, near Southampton, to which place I went that night, and came to London two days after. This was the first time I had taken a journey without your father, and the first manage of business he ever put into my hands, in which I thank God I had good success. Lodging in Fleet Street, at Mr Eates, the Watchmaker, with my sister Boteler, I procured by the means of Colonel Copley, a great Parliament man, whose wife had formerly been obliged to our family, a pass for your father to come and compound for £300, which was a part of my fortune, but it was only a pretence, for your grandfather was obliged to compound for it, and deliver it us free. When your father was come, he was very private in London, for he was in daily fears to be imprisoned before he could raise money to go back again to his master, who was not then in a condition to maintain him. Thus upon thorns he stayed until October, 1647. This year my sister Boteler married Sir Philip Warwick,* her second husband, for her first, Sir William Boteler, was killed at Cropredy Bridge, commanding a part of the king's army: he was a most gallant, worthy, honest gentleman. The 30th of July 1647 I

---

* Author of one of the best contemporary books on the Civil War.

was delivered of a son, called Henry, in lodgings in Portugal Row, Lincoln's Inn Fields.

During the king's stay at Hampton Court, my husband was with him, to whom he was pleased to talk much of his concerns, and gave him there credentials for Spain, with private instructions, and letters for his service; but God for our sins disposed His Majesty's affairs otherwise. I went three times to pay my duty to him, both as I was the daughter of his servant, and wife of his servant. The last time I ever saw him, when I took my leave, I could not refrain weeping: when he had saluted me, I prayed to God to preserve His Majesty with long life and happy years; he stroked me on the cheek, and said, 'Child, if God pleaseth it shall be so, but both you and I must submit to God's will, and you know in what hands I am in.' Then turning to your father, he said, 'Be sure, Dick, to tell my son all that I have said, and deliver those letters to my wife; pray God bless her! I hope I shall do well.' Taking him in his arms, he said, 'Thou hast ever been an honest man, and I hope God will bless thee, and make thee a happy servant to my son, whom I have charged in my letter to continue his love, and trust to you,' adding, 'I do promise you that if ever I am restored to my dignity I will bountifully reward you both for your service and sufferings.' Thus did we part from that glorious sun, that within a few months after was murdered, to the grief of all Christians that were not forsaken by God.

In October 1647, my husband and I went into France, by the way of Portsmouth, where, walking by the seaside about a mile from our lodgings, two ships of the Dutch, then in war with England, shot bullets at us so near that we heard them whiz by us. I called to my husband to make haste back and began to run, but he altered not his pace, saying, 'If we must be killed it were as good to be killed walking as running.' We embarked the next day, and that journey fetched home our girl we had left in Jersey.

In about April 1648, my husband was forced to come out of France to Hammerton, in Huntingdonshire, to my sister Bedell's, to the wedding of his nephew, the last Lord Thomas Fanshawe, who then married the daughter of Ferrers. About two months after this, in June, I was delivered of a son on the 8th day, 1648. The latter end of July I went to London, leaving my little boy Richard at nurse with his brother at Hattenford-bury. It happened to be the very day after that the Lord Holland was taken prisoner at St Neots, and Lord Francis Villiers was killed; and as we passed through the town, we saw Colonel Montagu, afterwards Earl of Sandwich, spoiling the town for the Parliament and himself.*

* This was an episode during the Second Civil War. Sandwich was later the patron of Samuel Pepys and succeeded Sir Richard Fanshawe as Ambassador to Madrid in 1666 (see p. 221). Lord Holland was later to be executed together with Lord Capel. In fact Lord Francis Villiers, younger son of the Duke of Buckingham, had been killed at Kingston-on-Thames a little earlier.

The Second Civil War
1648

In one respect the pattern of the Second Civil War was the same for John Hutchinson as the First—the Byron family remained at the head of the Nottinghamshire cavaliers. But the major new element was his disenchantment with his own side, as his suspicion of the ambitions of Cromwell 'and his idolaters' grew.

The gentleman, 'Colonel B', who replaced the inconstant Thomas Howard in Anne Halkett's affections, was Colonel Joseph Bampfield. He seems to have been one of those characters made familiar by twentieth-century spy fiction. At this time a royalist soldier and secret agent, by the 1650s he was working under cover for Cromwell, and in the 1660s he was in the pay of the Dutch when they were at war with England. Deception was obviously second nature to him and carried over into his relations with Anne Halkett, who believed he was a widower, when his wife was still very much alive. Anne's brother-in-law, Sir Henry Newton, was to meet Bampfield on a ship going to Holland some time after the rescue of the fourteen-year-old Duke of York described here, and fought a duel over Anne's honour, in the process getting badly wounded in the hand. Bampfield was nothing if not plausible and persistent; as late as 1653 Anne was still unconvinced that his wife was alive. Her last meeting with him was in December 1654.

Lucy Hutchinson

In 1647 Colonel Hutchinson came down to his garrison at Nottingham, which, the war being ended, was reduced only to the castle; the works at the town and the bridges being slighted [destroyed]; the companies of the governor's regiment, all but two, disbanded, and he thinking, now in a time when there was no opposition, the command not worthy of himself or his brother, gave it over to his kinsman, Captain Poulton. With the assistance of his fellow Parliament men he procured an order from the Parliament for £5000, that had been levied for the Scotch army, but which they, departing with too much haste, had not received, to be distributed among the officers and soldiers of his regiment that were at this time disbanded, in part of their arrears; and, that it might go the farther amongst them, he himself had none of it.

The garrison at Nottingham being reduced, Colonel Hutchinson removed his family back to his own house at Owthorpe, but found that, having stood uninhabited, and been robbed of everything which the neighbouring garrisons of Shelford and Wiverton could carry from it, it was so ruined that it could not be repaired, to make a convenient habitation, without as much charge as would almost build another. By reason of the debt his public employment had run him into, and not being able to do this at present while all his arrears were unpaid, he made a bad shift with it for that year. At this time his distemper of rheum was very sore upon him, and he was so afflicted with pains in his head, which fell down also with violent torture upon all his joints, that he was not able to go for many weeks out of his chamber.

While he was thus distempered at home, Major-General Ireton sent him a letter, with a new commission in it, for the resuming his government of Nottingham Castle: for the principal officers of the army, foreseeing an approaching storm, desired to place it in his hands, by whom it had before been so prosperously and faithfully preserved. But the colonel sent them word, that as he should not have put his kinsman into the place, although [unless] he was assured of his fidelity, so he would never join with those who were so forgetful of the merits of men that had behaved themselves well, as to discourage them without a cause. Colonel Gilbert Byron, a brother of Lord Byron's, meeting Captain Poulton, began to insinuate into him, and tempt him to betray Nottingham Castle; which proposition he thought fit not utterly to reject, lest the castle being then in a weak condition, and the soldiers discontented, some of his under officers might be more ready to embrace it and betray both the place and him. He therefore took a little time to consider of it, and came to Colonel Hutchinson and acquainted him with it. He advised him to hold his cousin Byron on in the treaty, till he himself could go to London and provide for the better securing of the place, which, his distemper of health a little abating, he did. When the place was well provided, Captain Poulton, who was too gentle-hearted to cut off Mr Byron under a pretence of assenting to him, sent to him to shift for himself, which Mr Byron accordingly did; and now the insurrection began everywhere to break out [February 1648].

Colonel Gilbert Byron rose, with other gentlemen of Nottinghamshire and Lincolnshire, and got together about 500 horse; wherewith they intended to go and join themselves with others that were up in other countries. This was so suddenly and secretly done, that they were upon their march before the rising was suspected. The Governor of Nottingham had not time enough to send a messenger to be with Colonel Hutchinson at his house before them, and therefore shot off a piece of cannon; which Colonel Hutchinson hearing as he sat at dinner, and believing some extraordinary thing to be in it, commanded horses to be made ready, and went to Nottingham; but met the messenger who came to give him notice of the enemy's approach. The news being sent home in haste, his arms and writings, and other things of value, were put in a cart and sent away. This was not long gone before the enemy marched by the house, and keeping their body on a hill at the town's end, only sent a party to the house to fetch them what provisions of meat and drink they found there; besides which, they took nothing but a groom with two horses, who having ridden out to air them, fell into their mouths, because he could not be readily found when the rest of the horses were sent away. The reason why no more mischief was done by the cavaliers to his family, at that time, was, partly because Colonel Gilbert Byron had commanded not to disturb them, if he were not there, and partly because they were so closely pursued by the Lincolnshire troops, that they could not stay to take, nor would burden themselves with plunder, now they saw it unlikely to get off without fighting. This they did the next day at Willoughby within three miles of Owthorpe, and were there totally routed, killed, and taken by a party under Colonel Rossiter's command, by whom Colonel Byron was carried prisoner to Belvoir Castle. Being in distress there, although he was an enemy, and had dealt unhandsomely with Colonel Hutchinson, in endeavouring to corrupt one for whom he was engaged, yet the colonel sent him a sum of money for his present relief, and afterwards procured him a release and composition with the Parliament.

At London things were in a very sad posture, the two factions of Presbytery and Independency being so engaged to suppress each other, that they both ceased to regard the public interest; insomuch, that at that time a certain sort of public-spirited men stood up in the Parliament and the army, declaring against these factions and the ambition of the grandees of both, and the partiality that was in these days practised. These good-hearted people would have common justice equally to belong to the poorest as well as to the mighty; and for this and such other honest declarations, they were nicknamed Levellers. Indeed, as all virtues are mediums, and have their extremes, there rose up afterwards with that name a people, who endeavoured the levelling of all estates and qualities; which these sober Levellers were never guilty of desiring, but were men of just and sober principles, of honest and religious ends, and therefore hated by all the designing self-interested men of both factions. Colonel Hutchinson had a great intimacy with many of these; and so far as they acted according to the just, pious, and public spirit which they professed, he owned and protected them as far as he had power. These were they who first began to discover the ambition of Lieutenant-General Cromwell and his idolaters, and to suspect and dislike it.

When Cromwell came to Nottingham, Colonel Hutchinson went to see him, whom he embraced with all the expressions of kindness that one friend could make to another, and then retiring with him, pressed him to tell him what his friends, the Levellers, thought of him. The colonel, who was the freest man in the world from concealing truth from his friend, especially when it was required of him in love and plainness, not only told him what others thought of him, but what he himself conceived; and how much it would darken all his glories, if he should become a slave to his own ambition. Cromwell made mighty professions of a sincere heart to him, but it is certain that for this and suchlike plain dealing with him, he dreaded the colonel, and made it his particular business to keep him out of the army; but the colonel desiring command, not to serve himself but his country, would not use that art he detested in others, to procure himself any advantage.

Anne Halkett

This gentleman came to see me sometimes in the company of ladies who had been my mother's neighbours in St Martin's Lane, and sometimes alone. But whenever he came, his discourse was serious, handsome, and tending to impress the advantages of piety, loyalty, and virtue. At this time he had frequent letters from the king, who employed him in several affairs, but that of the greatest concern which he was employed in was to contrive the Duke of York's escape out of St James's (where His Highness and the Duke of Gloucester and the Princess Elizabeth lived under the care of the Earl of Northumberland and his lady). The difficulties of it were represented by Colonel B., but His Majesty still pressed it, and I remember this expression was in one of the letters: 'I believe it will be difficult, and if he miscarry in the attempt it will be the greatest affliction that can arrive to me, but I look upon James's escape as Charles's preservation, and nothing can content me more. Therefore be careful what you do.'*

This letter amongst others he showed me, and where the king approved of his choice of me to get the duke's clothes made and to dress him in his disguise. So now all C.B.'s care was how to manage this business of so important concern which could not be performed without several persons' concurrence in it. For he being generally known as one whose stay at London was in order to serve the king, few of those who were entrusted by the Parliament in public concerns durst own converse or hardly civility to him, lest they should have been suspect by their party, which made it difficult for him to get access to the duke. But (to be short) having communicated the design to a gentleman attending His Highness, who was full of honour and fidelity, by his means he had private access to the duke, to whom he presented the king's letter and order to His Highness for consenting to act what C.B. should contrive for his escape. This was so cheerfully entertained and so readily obeyed, that being once designed there was nothing more to do than to prepare all things for the execution.

I had desired him to take a ribbon with him and bring me the bigness of the duke's waist and his length to have clothes made fit for him. In the meantime C.B. was to provide money for all necessary expense, which was furnished by an honest citizen. When I gave the measure to my tailor to enquire how much mohair would serve to make a petticoat and waistcoat to a young gentlewoman of that bigness and stature, he considered it a long time and said he had made many gowns and suits, but he had never made any to such a person in his life. I thought he was in the right; but his meaning was, he had never seen any woman of so low a stature have so big a waist. However, he made it as exactly fit as if he had taken the measure himself. It was a mixed mohair of a light hair colour and black, and the under petticoat was scarlet.

All things being now ready, upon the 20th of April, 1648, in the evening, was the time resolved on for the duke's escape.

* There were rumours of a plan to depose the king, disinherit the Prince of Wales, and crown the Duke of York.

And in order to that, it was designed for a week before every night as soon as the duke had supped, he and those servants that attended His Highness (till the Earl of Northumberland and the rest of the house had supped) went to a play called hide and seek, and sometimes he would hide himself so well that in half an hour's time they could not find him. His Highness had so used them to this that when he went really away they thought he was but at the usual sport. A little before the duke went to supper that night, he called for the gardener (who only had a treble key, besides that which the duke had) and bid him give him that key till his own was mended, which he did. And after His Highness had supped, he immediately called to go to the play, and went down the privy stairs into the garden and opened the gate that goes into the park, treble locking all the doors behind him. At the garden gate C.B. waited for His Highness, and putting on a cloak and periwig, hurried him away to the park gate where a coach waited that carried them to the water side. Taking the boat that was appointed for that service, they rowed to the stairs next the bridge, where I and Miriam waited in a private house hard by that C.B. had prepared for dressing His Highness, where all things were in a readiness.

But I had many fears, for C.B. had desired me, if they came not there precisely by ten o'clock, to shift for myself, for then I might conclude they were discovered, and so my stay there could do no good, but prejudice myself. Yet this did not make me leave the house though ten o'clock did strike, and he that was entrusted, [who] often went to the landing-place and saw no boat coming, was much discouraged, and asked me what I would do. I told him I came there with a resolution to serve His Highness and I was fully determined not to leave that place till I was out of hopes of doing what I came there for, and would take my hazard. He left me to go again to the water side, and while I was fortifying myself against what might arrive to me, I heard a great noise of many as I thought coming up stairs, which I expected to be soldiers to take me; but it was a pleasing disappointment, for the first that came in was the duke, who with much joy I took in my arms and gave God thanks for his safe arrival. His Highness called, 'Quickly, quickly, dress me,' and putting off his clothes I dressed him in the woman's habit that was prepared, which fitted His Highness very well and was very pretty in it. After he had eaten something I made ready while I was idle, lest His Highness should be hungry, and having sent for a Woodstreet cake (which I knew he loved) to take in the barge, with as much haste as could be His Highness went across the bridge to the stairs where the barge lay, C.B. leading him. Immediately the boatmen plied the oars so well that they were soon out of sight, having both wind and tide with them. But I afterwards heard the wind changed and was so contrary that C.B. told me he was terribly afraid they should have been blown back again. And the duke said, 'Do anything with me rather than let me go back again,' which put C.B. to seek help where it was only to be had, and after he had most fervently supplicated assistance from God, presently the wind blew fair and they came safely to their intended landing place. But I heard there was some difficulty before they got to the ship at Gravesend, which had like to have discovered them had not Colonel Washington's lady assisted them.*

After the duke's barge was out of sight of the bridge, I and Miriam went where I appointed the coach to stay for me and made drive as fast as the coachman could to my brother's house, where I stayed. I met none in the way that gave me any apprehension that the design was discovered, nor was it noised abroad till the next day. For (as I related before) the duke having used to play at hide and seek, and to conceal himself a long time, when they missed him at the same play, thought he would have discovered himself as formerly when they had given over seeking him. But a much longer time being past than usually was spent in that divertisement, some began to apprehend that His Highness was gone in earnest past their finding, which made the Earl of Northumberland (to whose care he was committed), after strict search made in the house of St James and all there-

* Probably Elizabeth Washington, whose husband Henry was a distinguished royalist soldier. His first cousins, John and Lawrence Washington, emigrated to Virginia.

abouts to no purpose, to send and acquaint the Speaker of the House of Commons that the duke was gone, but how or by what means he knew not. He desired that there might be orders sent to the Cinque Ports for stopping all ships going out till the passengers were examined and search made in all suspected places where His Highness might be concealed.

Though this was gone about with all the vigilancy imaginable, yet it pleased God to disappoint them of their intention by so infatuating those several persons who were employed for writing orders that none of them were able to write one right, but ten or twelve of them were cast by before one was according to their mind. This account I had from Mr N., who was mace bearer to the Speaker at that time and a witness of it. This disorder of the clerks contributed much to the duke's safety, for he was at sea before any of the orders came to the ports and so was free from what was designed if they had taken His Highness.

Execution, Ireland, Scotland
1649-50

Colonel Hutchinson continued to display his independence of mind through the crisis of the king's trial. He thoroughly disapproved of the army's forcible exclusion of all those members from the House of Commons who were regarded as hostile, yet he was prepared to sign the king's death warrant. This, he felt, was the only way to avoid the 'blood and desolation' of further civil war, since it was impossible to negotiate with so untrustworthy a man. But, in spite of the king's death, the killing went on, first in Ireland in 1649 and then in Scotland in 1650. Ann Fanshawe followed her husband to Cork, Limerick and Galway, before sailing to Spain and then France once Cromwell got a firm grip on Ireland. In June 1650 Charles II landed in Scotland, only for his covenanting army to be defeated by Cromwell in September at Dunbar. Anne Halkett describes how she tended its sad remnants.

Lucy Hutchinson

About Michaelmas 1648, Colonel Hutchinson went to attend his duty at the Parliament, carrying his whole family with him, because his house had been so ruined by the war that he could no longer live in it, till it was either repaired or newly built. When he was well again to attend the House, he found the Presbyterian party so prevalent there, that the victories obtained by the army displeased them; and they had grown so hot in the zeal of their faction, that they from thenceforth resolved and endeavoured to close [ally] with the common enemy, that they might thereby compass the destruction of their Independent brethren.

Amidst these things, at last a treaty was sent to the king, by commissioners, who went from both Houses, to the Isle of Wight;* and although there were some honourable persons in this commission, yet it cannot be denied, but that they were carried away by the others, and concluded, upon most dangerous terms, an agreement with the king. He would not give up bishops, but only lease out their revenues; and upon the whole, such were the terms upon which the king was to be restored, that the whole cause was evidently given up to him. Only one thing he assented to, to acknowledge himself guilty of the blood spilt in the late war, with this proviso, that if the agreement were not ratified by the House, then this concession should be of no force against him. At length it was voted to accept his concessions. Colonel Hutchinson was that night among them, and being convinced in his conscience that both the cause, and all those who with an upright honest heart asserted and maintained it, were betrayed and sold for nothing, he told them that the king, after having been exasperated, vanquished, and captived, would be restored to that power which was inconsistent with the liberty of the people, who, for all their blood, treasure, and misery, would reap no fruit, but a confirmation of their bondage. It had been a thousand times better never to have

* Charles had been imprisoned there, after his escape from Hampton Court in November 1647 was swiftly followed by rearrest.

struck one stroke in the quarrel, than, after victory, to yield up a righteous cause; whereby they should not only betray the interest of their country and the trust reposed in them, and those zealous friends who had engaged to the death for them, but be false to the covenant of their God, which was to extirpate prelacy [the bishops], not to lease it. He and four more, therefore, entered into the House-book a protestation against that night's votes and proceedings.

By this violent proceeding of the Presbyterians they finished the destruction of him in whose restitution they were now so fiercely engaged, for this gave heart to the vanquished cavaliers, and such courage to the captive king that it hardened him and them to their ruin. On the other side, it so frightened all the honest people, that it made them as violent in their zeal to pull down, as the others were in their madness to restore, this kingly idol. The army, who were principally levelled and marked out as the sacrifice and peace-offering of this ungodly reconciliation, had some colour to pursue their late arrogant usurpations upon that authority which it was their duty rather to have obeyed than interrupted. The debates of that night, which produced such destructive votes to them and all their friends, being reported to them, they the next morning came and seized about forty of the members as they were going to the House, and carried them to a house hard by, where they were for the present kept prisoners.* Colonel Hutchinson was one of these who infinitely disliked this action of the army. Those who were suffered to remain, not at all approving thereof, sent out their mace to demand their members, but the soldiers would not obey. Yet the Parliament thought it better to sit still and go on in their duty than give up all, in so distempered a time, into the hands of the soldiery.

After the purgation of the House, upon the new debate of the treaty at the Isle of Wight, it was concluded dangerous to the realm and destructive to its better interest, and the trial of the king was determined. He was sent for to Westminster, and a commission was given forth to a court of high justice, whereof

* Pride's Purge, December 1648. Colonel Pride commanded the soldiers who carried out this action against Parliament.

Bradshaw, Serjeant-at-Law, was president, and divers honourable persons of the Parliament, city, and army, nominated commissioners. Among them Colonel Hutchinson was one, who,
very much against his own will, was put in; but looking upon
himself as called hereunto, durst not refuse it, as holding himself obliged by the covenant of God and the public trust of his
country reposed in him, although he was not ignorant of the
danger he ran as the condition of things then was.*

In January 1649, the court sat, the king was brought to his
trial, and a charge drawn up against him for levying war against
the Parliament and people of England, for betraying the public
trust reposed in him, and for being an implacable enemy to the
commonwealth. But the king refused to plead, disowning the
authority of the court, and after three several days persisting in
contempt thereof, he was sentenced to suffer death. One thing
was remarked in him by many of the court, that when the blood
spilt in many of the battles where he was in his own person, and
had caused it to be shed by his own command, was laid to his
charge, he heard it with disdainful smiles, and looks and ges-
tures which rather expressed sorrow that all the opposite party
to him were not cut off, than that any were. He stuck not to
declare in words, that no man's blood spilt in this quarrel
troubled him except one, meaning the Earl of Strafford. The
gentlemen that were appointed his judges, and divers others,
saw in him a disposition so bent on the ruin of all that opposed
him, and of all the righteous and just things they had contended
for, that it was upon the consciences of many of them, that if
they did not execute justice upon him, God would require at
their hands all the blood and desolation which should ensue by
their suffering him to escape, when God had brought him into
their hands.

As for Mr Hutchinson, finding no check, but a confirmation
in his conscience that it was his duty to act as he did, he, upon
serious debate, both privately and in his addresses to God, and
in conferences with conscientious, upright, unbiased persons,

---

* When the trial opened, the roll of commissioners was called over. On
Fairfax's name being reached, a masked lady in the gallery cried out, 'he
has more wit than to be here.' This was his wife Anne.

proceeded to sign the sentence against the king.

After the death of the king, Mr Hutchinson was chosen into the first Council of State, much against his own will; for, understanding that his cousin Ireton was one of the commissioners to nominate that council, he sent his wife to him, before he went to the House, that morning they were to be named, to desire him, upon all the scores of kindred and kindness that had been between them, that he might be left out, in regard that he had already wasted his time and his estate in the Parliament's service. These and other things he privately urged upon him; but he [Ireton], who was a man regardless of his own or of any man's private interest, wherever he thought the public service might be advantaged, instead of keeping him out got him in.

He did his duty faithfully, and employed his power to relieve the oppressed and dejected, freely becoming the advocate of those who had been his late enemies, in all things that were just and charitable. Among the rest one Sir John Owen may stand for a pillar of ingratitude. This man was wholly unknown to him, and with the Duke of Hamilton, the Earl of Holland, the Lord Capel, and the Lord Goring,* was condemned to death by a second high court of justice. Of this, though the colonel was nominated a commissioner, he would not sit, his unbloody nature desiring to spare the rest of the delinquents, after the highest had suffered, and not delighting in the death of men, when they could live without cruelty to better men. The Parliament also was willing to show mercy to some of these, and to execute others for example; whereupon the whole House was diversely engaged, some for one and some for another of these lords, and striving to cast away those they were not concerned in, that they might save their friends. While there was such mighty labour and endeavour for these lords, Colonel Hutchinson observed that no man spoke for this poor knight; sitting next to Colonel Ireton, he expressed himself to him, 'and so', said he, 'am I moved with compassion that, if you will second

---

* George Goring's father, Lord Norwich, who raised Kent for the king in the Second Civil War. Capel had been captured at Colchester (see p. 160). For Holland see pp. 18, and 143. Hamilton's Scottish army had been defeated at Preston by Cromwell in August 1648.

me, I am resolved to speak for him, who, I perceive, is a stranger and friendless.' He took the petition, delivered it, spoke for him so nobly, and was so effectually seconded by Ireton, that they carried his pardon clear. Yet he never was the man that so much as once came to give him thanks; nor was his fellow-prisoner Goring, for whom the colonel had also effectually solicited, more grateful.

Colonel Hutchinson's old opponents and enemies of the Nottingham committee had entered into the Presbyterian conspiracy [in late 1648] so deeply, that had they been brought to public trial, their lives would have been forfeited to the law, and this was discovered to him, and also that Colonel Pierrepont was the chief of them. He took care to have the business so managed, that Colonel Pierrepont was passed by in the information, and others so favourably accused, that they were only restrained from the mischief they intended, and kept prisoners till the danger was over, and afterwards, through his mediation released, without any further punishment on their persons and estates, though Chadwick's eldest son was one of these. For Colonel Pierrepont, he only privately admonished him, and endeavoured to reclaim him, which the man, being good-natured, was infinitely overcome with; insomuch, that ever after, to his dying day, all his envy ceased, and he professed all imaginable friendship and kindness to the colonel.

Some of the army, being very desirous to get amongst them a person of whose fidelity and integrity to the cause they had such good experience, had moved it to the general, my Lord Fairfax; who commanded to have it enquired in what way he would choose to be employed; and when he told them that, in regard of his family, which he would not willingly be much absent from, he should rather accept the government of some town than a field employment, four governments were brought to him, to select which he would have. He made choice of Hull, thinking they had not offered him anything but what had fairly fallen into their disposal. Soon after this, the Lieutenant-General, Cromwell, desired him to meet him one afternoon at a committee, where, when he came, a malicious accusation against the Governor of Hull was violently prosecuted by a fierce faction in that town. To this the governor had sent up a very fair and honest defence, yet most of the committee, more favouring the adverse faction, were labouring to cast out the governor. Colonel Hutchinson, though he knew him not, was very earnest in his defence, whereupon Cromwell drew him aside, and asked him what he meant by contending to keep in that governor? (it was Overton.) The colonel told him, because he saw nothing proved against him worthy of being ejected. 'But', said Cromwell, 'we like him not.' Then said the colonel, 'Do it upon that account, and blemish not a man that is innocent, upon false accusations, because you like him not.' 'But', said Cromwell, 'we would have him out, because the government is designed for you, and except you put him out you cannot have the place.' At this the colonel was very angry, and with great indignation told him, if there was no way to bring him into their army but by casting out others unjustly, he would rather fall naked before his enemies, than so seek to put himself into a posture of defence. Then returning to the table, he so eagerly undertook the injured governor's protection, that he foiled his enemies, and the governor was confirmed in his place.

Cromwell was moulding the army to his mind, weeding out the godly and upright-hearted men, both officers and soldiers, and filling up their rooms with rascally turn-coat cavaliers, and pitiful sottish beasts of his own alliance, and other such as would swallow all things, and make no questions for conscience' sake. All this while he carried to Colonel Hutchinson the most open face, and made the most obliging professions of friendship imaginable; but the colonel saw through him, and forebore not often to tell him what was suspected of his ambition.

In the meantime, the Scots having declared open war against the Parliament of England, it was concluded to send an army into Scotland, to prevent their intended advance hither. But when they were just marching out, my Lord Fairfax, persuaded by his wife and her chaplains, threw up his commission at such a time, when it could not have been done more spitefully and ruinously to the whole Parliament interest. Colonel Hutchinson and other Parliament men, hearing of his intentions the night before, and knowing that he would thus level the way to Cromwell's ambitious designs, went to him and laboured to dissuade him; which they would have effected, but that the Presbyterian ministers wrought with him to do it. He expressed his opinion that he believed God had laid him aside, as not being worthy of more, nor of that glory which was already given to him. This great man was then as immovable by his friends as [he was] pertinaceous in obeying his wife.*

Ann Fanshawe

In December [1648] my husband went to Paris on his master's business, and sent for me from London: I carried him £300 of his money. During our stay at Paris, I was highly obliged to the Queen Mother of England. My husband thought it convenient to send me into England again, there to try what sums I could raise, both for his subsistence abroad and mine at home. I took my leave with sad heart, and embarked myself in a hoy for Dover, with Mrs Waller [wife of the poet Edmund Waller] and my sister Margaret Harrison, and my little girl Nan; but a great storm arising, we had like to be cast away, the vessel being half full of water, and we forced to land at Deal, everyone carried upon men's backs, and we up to the middle in water, and very glad to escape so.

My husband went from thence by Flanders into Holland to his master; and, in February following [1649], your father was sent into Ireland by the king [Charles II], there to receive such monies as Prince Rupert could raise by the fleet he commanded of the king's. My husband sent for me and the little family I had thither. We went by Bristol very cheerfully towards my

---

* Fairfax retired to his Yorkshire house, Nun Appleton, where he employed the poet Andrew Marvell as tutor to his daughter. She later had the misfortune to become the wife of the 2nd Duke of Buckingham, whom Dryden described as 'stiff in opinions, always in the wrong; was everything by starts, and nothing long'. Devastatingly handsome in his youth, he eventually became 'worn to a thread with whoring'.

north star, that only had the power to fix me, and because I had
had the good fortune, as I then thought it, to sell [land worth]
£300 a year to him that is now Judge Archer, in Essex, for
which he gave me £4000, which, at that time, I thought a vast
sum. Be it more or less, I am sure it was spent in seven years'
time in the king's service, and to this hour I repent it not, I
thank God. Five hundred pounds I carried my husband, the
rest I left in my father's agent's hands, to be returned as we
needed it.

For six months, we lived so much to our satisfaction, that we
began to think of making our abode there during the war, for
the country was fertile, and all provisions cheap, and the houses
good, and we were placed in Red Abbey, a house of Dean
Boyle's, in Cork. My Lord of Ormond had a very good army,
and the country seemingly quiet; and, to complete our content,
all persons were very civil to us.

But what earthly comfort is exempt from change? for here I
heard of the death of my second son, Henry, and, within a few
weeks, of the landing of Cromwell, who so hotly marched over
Ireland, that the fleet with Prince Rupert was forced to set sail,
and within a small time after he lost all his riches, which was
thought to be worth hundreds of thousands of pounds, in one
of his best ships, commanded by his brother Maurice, who with
many a brave man sunk, were all lost in a storm at sea.

We remained some time behind in Ireland, until my husband could receive His Majesty's commands how to dispose of
himself. During this time I had, by the fall of a stumbling horse,
being with child, broke my left wrist, which, because it was ill-
set, put me to great and long pain, and I was in my bed when
Cork revolted. By chance that day my husband was gone on
business to Kinsale: it was in the beginning of October, 1649.
At midnight I heard the great guns go off, and thereupon I
called up my family to rise, which I did as well as I could in that
condition. Hearing lamentable shrieks of men, women, and
children, I asked at a window the cause; they told me they were
all Irish, stripped and wounded, and turned out of the town,
and that Colonel Jeffries, with some others, had possessed themselves of the town for Cromwell. Upon this, I immediately wrote

a letter to my husband, blessing God's providence that he was not there with me, persuading him to patience and hope that I should get safely out of the town, by God's assistance, and desired him to shift for himself, for fear of a surprise, with promise that I would secure his papers.

So soon as I had finished my letter, I sent it by a faithful servant, who was let down the garden wall of Red Abbey, and, sheltered by the darkness of the night, he made his escape. I immediately packed up my husband's cabinet, with all his writings, and nearly £1000 in gold and silver, and all other things both of clothes, linen, and household stuff that were portable, of value. Then, about three o'clock in the morning, by the light of a taper, and in that pain I was in, I went into the market-place, with only a man and maid. Passing through an unruly tumult with their swords in their hands, I searched for their Chief Commander Jeffries, who, whilst he was loyal, had received many civilities from your father. I told him it was necessary that upon that change I should remove, and I desired his pass that would be obeyed, or else I must remain there: I hoped he would not deny me that kindness. He instantly wrote me a pass, both for myself, family, and goods, and said he would never forget the respect he owed your father. With this, I came through thousands of naked swords to Red Abbey, and hired the next neighbour's cart, which carried all that I could remove; and myself, sister, and little girl Nan, with three maids and two men, set forth at five o'clock in October, having but two horses amongst us all, which we rode on by turns. We went ten miles to Kinsale, in perpetual fear of being fetched back again; but, by little and little, I thank God, we got safe to the garrison, where I found your father the most disconsolate man in the world, for fear of his family, which he had no possibility to assist. His joys exceeded to see me and his darling daughter, and to hear the wonderful escape we, through the assistance of God, had made.

But when the rebels went to give an account to Cromwell of their meritorious act, he immediately asked them where Mr Fanshawe was? They replied, he was that day gone to Kinsale. Then he demanded where his papers and his family were? At which they all stared one at another, but made no reply. Their general said, 'it was as much worth to have seized his papers as the town; for I did make account to have known by them what these parts of the country are worth.'

We within a few days received the king's order, which was that my husband should, upon sight thereof, go into Spain to Philip IV and deliver him His Majesty's letters; and by my husband also His Majesty sent letters to my Lord Cottington and Sir Edward Hyde, his Ambassadors Extraordinary in that court. Upon this order we went to Macrome to the Lord Clancarty, who married a sister of the Lord Ormond: we stayed there two nights, and at my coming away, after very noble entertainment, my lady gave me a great Irish greyhound, and I presented her with a fine bezoar-stone.*

From thence we went to Limerick, where we were entertained by the mayor and aldermen very nobly; and the recorder of the town was very kind, and in respect they made my husband a freeman of Limerick. There we met the Bishop of Londonderry and the Earl of Roscommon, who was Lord Chancellor of that kingdom at that time. These two persons with my husband being together writing letters to the king, to give an account of the kingdom, when they were going downstairs from my Lord Roscommon's chamber (striving to hold the candle at the stairs' head, because the privacy of their despatch admitted not a servant to be near my Lord Roscommon) fell down the stairs, and his head fell upon the corner of a stone and broke his skull in three pieces, of which he died five days after, leaving the broad seal of Ireland in your father's hands, until such time as he could acquaint His Majesty with this sad account, and receive orders how to dispose of the seals. This caused our longer stay, but your father and I being invited to my Lord Inchiquin's, there to stay till we heard out of Holland from the king, which was a month before the messenger returned, we had very kind entertainment, and vast plenty of fish and fowl. By this time my Lord Lieutenant, the now Duke of

---

* A stony concretion found in the stomachs of goats, etc., and thought to be a cure for all poisons.

Ormond's army was quite dispersed, and himself gone for Holland, and every person concerned in that interest shifting for their lives; and Cromwell went through as bloodily as victoriously, many worthy persons being murdered in cold blood, and their families quite ruined.

From hence we went to the Lady Honor O'Brien's, a lady that went for a maid, but few believed it: she was the youngest daughter of the Earl of Thomond. There we stayed three nights. The first of which I was surprised by being laid in a chamber, when, about one o'clock, I heard a voice that wakened me. I drew the curtain and, in the casement of the window I saw, by the light of the moon, a woman leaning into the window, through the casement, in white, with red hair and pale and ghastly complexion. She spoke loud and in a tone I had never heard, thrice, 'a horse'; and then, with a sigh more like the wind than breath, she vanished, and to me her body looked more like a thick cloud than substance. I was so much frightened, that my hair stood on end, and my night clothes fell off. I pulled and pinched your father, who never woke during the disorder I was in; but at last was much surprised to see me in this fright, and more so when I related the story and showed him the window opened. Neither of us slept any more that night, but he entertained me with telling me how much more these apparitions were usual in this country than in England; and we concluded the cause to be the great superstition of the Irish, and the want of that knowing faith, which should defend them from the power of the Devil, which he exercises among them very much. About five o'clock the lady of the house came to see us, saying she had not been in bed all night, because a cousin O'Brien of hers, whose ancestors had owned that house, had desired her to stay with him in his chamber, and that he died at two o'clock. She said, 'I wish you to have had no disturbance, for 'tis the custom of the place, that, when any of the family are dying, the shape of a woman appears in the window every night till they be dead. This woman was many ages ago got with child by the owner of this place, who murdered her in his garden, and flung her into the river under the window, but truly I thought not of it when I lodged you here, it being the best room in the house.'

We made little reply to her speech, but disposed ourselves to be gone suddenly.

By this time my husband had received orders from the king to give the Lord Inchiquin the seals to keep until further orders from His Majesty. When that business was settled, we went, accompanied by my Lord Inchiquin and his family, four or five miles towards Galway, which he did not by choice, since the plague had been so hot in that city the summer before, that it was almost depopulated, and the haven as much as the town. But your father hearing that, by accident, there was a great ship of Amsterdam bound for Málaga, in Spain, and Cromwell pursuing his conquests at our backs, resolved to fall into the hands of God rather than into the hands of men; and with his family of about ten persons came to the town, where we found guards placed that none should enter without certificates from whence they came.

An Irish footman that served us, said, 'I lived here some years and know every street, and likewise know a much nearer way than these men can show you, sir; therefore come with me, if you please.' We resolved to follow him, and sent our horses to stables in the suburbs: he led us all on the back side of the town, under the walls over which the people during the plague, which was not yet quite stopped, flung out all their dung, dirt, and rags, and we walked up to the middle of our legs in them, for, being engaged, we could not get back. At last we found the house, by the master standing at the door expecting us, who said, 'You are welcome to this disconsolate city, where you now see the streets grown over with grass, once the finest little city in the world'; and indeed it was easy to think so, the buildings being uniformly built, and a very fine market-place and walks arched and paved by the seaside for their merchants to walk on, and a most noble harbour.

At the beginning of February 1650 we took ship, and here now our scene was shifted from land to sea. We left that brave kingdom fallen, in six or eight months, into a most miserable sad condition, as it hath been many times in most kings' reigns, God knows why! for I presume not to say; but the natives seem to me a very loving people to each other, and constantly false to all strangers, the Spaniards only excepted. The country exceeds in timber and sea-ports, and great plenty of fish, fowl, flesh; and, by shipping, wants no foreign commodities. We pursued our voyage with prosperous winds, but with a most tempestuous master, a Dutchman, which is enough to say, but truly, I think, the greatest beast I ever saw of his kind.

When we had just passed the Straits [of Gibraltar], we saw coming towards us, with full sails, a Turkish galley well manned, and we believed we should be all carried away slaves, for this Dutchman had so laden his ship with goods for Spain, that his guns were useless, though the ship carried sixty guns. He called for brandy, and after he had well drunken, and all his men, which were near 200, he called for arms and cleared the deck as well as he could, resolving to fight rather than lose his ship, which was worth £30,000. This was sad for us passengers, but my husband bid us women be sure to keep in the cabin, and not appear, which would make the Turks think that we were a man-of-war, but if they saw women they would take us for merchants and board us. He went upon the deck, and took a gun and bandoleers, and sword, and, with the rest of the ship's company, stood upon deck expecting the arrival of the Turkish man-of-war. This beast, the captain, had locked me up in the cabin; I knocked and called long to no purpose, until at length the cabin-boy came and opened the door. I, all in tears, desired him to be so good as to give me his blue thrum cap* he wore, and his tarred coat, which he did. I gave him half-a-crown, and putting them on and flinging away my night clothes, I crept up softly and stood upon the deck by my husband's side, as free from sickness and fear as, I confess, from discretion; but it was the effect of that passion, which I could never master.

By this time the two vessels were engaged in parley, and so well satisfied with speech and sight of each other's forces, that the Turks' man-of-war tacked about, and we continued our course. But when your father saw it convenient to retreat, looking upon me, he blessed himself, and snatched me up in his arms, saying, 'Good God, that love can make this change!' and though he seemingly chid me, he would laugh at it as often as

* Made of coarse, shaggy cloth.

he remembered that voyage. In the beginning of March we all landed, praised be God, in Málaga, very well and full of content to see ourselves delivered from the sword and plague, and living in hope that we should one day return happily to our native country. Notwithstanding, we thought it great odds, considering how the affairs of the king's three kingdoms stood; but we trusted in the providence of Almighty God, and proceeded.

We were very kindly entertained by the merchants, and by them lodged in a merchant's house, where we had not been with our goods three days, when the vessel that brought us thither, by the negligence of a cabin-boy, was blown up in the harbour, with the loss of above a hundred men and all our lading.

After we had refreshed ourselves some days, we went on our journey towards Madrid, and lodged the first night at Velez Málaga, to which we were accompanied by most of the merchants. The next day we went to Granada, having passed the highest mountains I ever saw in my life, but under this lieth the finest valley that can be possibly described, adorned with high trees and rich grass, and beautified with a large deep clear river over the town. Here standeth the goodly vast palace of the king's, called the Alhambra, whose buildings are, after the fashion of the Moors, adorned with vast quantities of jasperstone; many courts, many fountains, and by reason it is situated on the side of a hill, and not built uniform, many gardens with ponds in them, and many baths made of jasper, and many principal rooms roofed with the mosaic work, which exceeds the finest enamel I ever saw.

From Granada the Fanshawes went to Madrid to try and raise a loan for Charles II from Philip IV of Spain, without success. Lady Fanshawe gave birth there to another daughter, who died fifteen days later. Then their wanderings continued.

We came to St Sebastian about the beginning of September, and there hired a small French vessel to carry us to Nantes: we embarked within two days after our coming to this town. I never saw so wild a place, nor were the inhabitants unsuitable, but like to like, which made us hasten away, and I am sure to our cost we found the proverb true, for our haste brought us woe. We had not been a day at sea before we had a storm begun, that continued two days and two nights in a most violent manner, and being in the Bay of Biscay, we had a hurricane that drew the vessel up from the water, which had neither sail or mast left, and but six men and a boy. Whilst they had hopes of life they ran swearing about like devils, but when that failed them they ran into holes, and let the ship drive as it would. In this great hazard of our lives we were the beginning of the third night, when God in mercy ceased the storm of a sudden, and there was a great calm, which made us exceeding joyful. But when those beasts, for they were scarce men, that manned the vessel began to rummage the bark, they could not find their compass anywhere, for the loss of which they began again such horrible lamentations as were as dismal to us as the storm past.

Thus between hope and fear we passed the night, they protesting to us they knew not where they were; and truly we believed them, for with fear and drink I think they were bereaved of their senses. So soon as it was day, about six o'clock, the master cried out, 'the land! the land!' but we did not receive the news with the joy belonging to it, but sighing said, God's will be done! Thus the tide drove us until about five o'clock in the afternoon, and drawing near the side of a small rock that had a creek by it, we ran aground. The sea was so calm that we all got out without the loss of any man or goods, but the vessel was so shattered that it was not afterwards serviceable.

We found ourselves near a little village about two leagues from Nantes. We hired there six asses, upon which we rode as many as could by turns, and the rest carried our goods. This journey took us up all the next day, for I should have told you that we stirred not that night, because we sat up and made good cheer, for beds they had none, and we were so transported that we thought we had no need of any. We had very good fires and Nantes white wine and butter, and milk, and walnuts and eggs, and some very bad cheese; and was not this enough, with the escape of shipwreck, to be thought better than a feast? I am

sure until that hour I never knew such pleasure in eating, between which we a thousand times repeated what we had spoken
when every word seemed to be our last.

As soon as it was day we began our journey towards Nantes,
and by the way we passed by a little poor chapel, at the door of
which a friar begged an alms, saying, that he would show us
there the greatest wonder in the world. We resolved to go with
him: he went before us to the altar, and out of a cupboard, with
great devotion, he took a box, and crossing himself he opened
it. In that was another of crystal that contained a little silver
box; he lifting this crystal box up, cried, 'Behold in this the
hem of St Joseph, which was taken as he hewed his timber!'
To which my husband replied, 'Indeed, father, it is the lightest,
considering the greatness, that I ever handled in my life.' The
ridiculousness of this with the simplicity of the man entertained
us till we came to Nantes. We met by the way good grapes and
walnuts growing, of which we culled out the best.

We hired a boat to carry us up to Orléans, and we were
towed up all the River of Loire so far. Every night we went on
shore to bed, and every morning carried into the boat wine and
fruit, and bread with some flesh, which we dressed in the boat,
for it had a hearth, on which we burnt charcoal: we likewise
caught carps, which were the fattest and the best I ever ate in
my life. And of all my travels none were, for travel's sake as I
may call it, so pleasant as this, for we saw the finest cities, seats,
woods, meadows, pastures, and champaign that I ever saw in
my life, adorned with the most pleasant River of Loire. We
arrived, about the middle of November, 1650, at Paris. We
went so soon as we could get clothes to wait on the queen-
mother and the Princess Henrietta. The queen entertained us
very respectfully, and after many favours done us, and discoursing in private with your father about affairs of state, he received
Her Majesty's letters to send to the king, who was then on his
way to Scotland.* We kissed her hand and went to Calais, with
resolution that I should go to England, to send my husband
more money, for this long journey cost us all we could procure.

---

* Her chronology is wrong here. Charles went to Scotland in June.

Anne Halkett

The unexpected defeat which the king's army had at Dunbar put everyone to new thoughts how to dispose of themselves, and none was more perplexed than I where to go or what to do. Again my Lady Dunfermline invited me to go north with her ladyship, assuring me of much welcome and that I should fare as she did, though she could not promise anything but disorder from so sudden a removal to a house that had not of a long time had an inhabitant. I had much reason to accept of this offer with more than an ordinary sense of God's goodness; for there could not have been a more seasonable act of generosity than this to a stranger that was destitute of all means that should assist me in a retreat.

Upon Saturday, the 7th of September, we left Dunfermline and came that night to Kinross, where we stayed till Monday. I cannot omit to insert here the opportunity I had of serving many poor wounded soldiers. As we were riding to Kinross I saw two that looked desperately ill, who were so weak they were hardly able to go along the highway; and enquiring what ailed them, they told me they had been soldiers at Dunbar and were going towards Kinross, if their wounds would suffer them. I bid them when they came there enquire for the Countess of D.'s lodging and there would be one there who would dress them. It was late, it seems, before they came, and so till the next morning I saw them not, but then they came, attended with twenty more. And betwixt that time and Monday that we left that place, I believe threescore was the least that was dressed by me and my woman and Ar. R., who I employed to such as was unfit for me to dress. Besides the plasters or balsam I applied, I gave every one of them as much with them as might dress them three or four times, for I had provided myself very well of things necessary for that employment, expecting they might be useful.

Amongst the many variety of wounds amongst them, two were extraordinary. One was a man whose head was cut so that the [?] was very visibly seen and the water came bubbling up, which when Ar. R. saw he cried out, 'Lord have mercy upon thee, for thou art but a dead man.' I seeing the man, who had courage enough before, begin to be much disheartened, I told him he need not be discouraged with what he that had no skill said, for if it pleased God to bless what I should give him he might do well enough. This I said more to hearten him up than otherways, for I saw it a very dangerous wound. And yet it pleased God he recovered, as I heard afterwards, and went frankly from dressing, I having given him something to refresh his spirits. The other was a youth about sixteen that had been run through the body with a tuke [a rapier]. It went in under his right shoulder and came out under his left breast, and yet he had little inconvenience by it, but his greatest prejudice was from so infinite a swarm of creatures that it is incredible for any that were not eye witnesses of it. I made a contribution and bought him other clothes to put on him and made the fire consume what else had been impossible to destroy.

Of all these poor soldiers there was few of them had ever been dressed from the time they received their wounds till they came to Kinross, and then it may be imagined they were very noisome; but one particularly was in that degree, who was shot through the arm, that none was able to stay in the room, but all left me. Accidentally a gentleman came in, who seeing me (not without reluctancy) cutting off the man's sleeve of his doublet, which was hardly fit to be touched, he was so charitable as to take a knife and cut it off and fling [it] in the fire.

When I had dressed all that came, my Lady D. was by this time ready to go away, and came to St Johnston that night where the king and court was. My Lord Lorne came to me and told me that my name was often before the council that day. I was much surprised, which his lordship seeing kept me the longer in suspense. At last he smiling told me there was a gentleman (which it seems was he that had cut off the man's sleeve) that had given the king and council an account of what he had seen and heard I had done to the poor soldiers; and representing the sad condition they had been in without that relief, there was presently an order made to appoint a place in several towns and chirugions [surgeons] to have allowance for taking care of such wounded soldiers as should come to them. And the king was pleased to give me thanks for my charity.

The New Usurpers
1651-8

Nothing could be more symbolic of the depth of Colonel Hutchinson's antipathy for Oliver Cromwell than his destruction of Nottingham Castle in May 1651 lest it be used by Cromwell as a means of oppressing the area. It is ironic that after the Restoration it was the Duke of Newcastle who bought the site of Nottingham Castle on its bluff above the town. In 1674 he began the building of a grand rectangular mansion, its outline familiar to many from the days when it was the trademark on all John Player cigarette packets.

From this point Hutchinson was 'reduced to an absolutely private condition'. He took no part in the campaign that culminated in Cromwell's 'crowning mercy', the Battle of Worcester in September 1651, exactly a year after Dunbar; he ceased to be a member of the Council of State and certainly had no time for the various 'pocket parliaments' and the rule of the major-generals to which Cromwell had to resort, after his forcible dissolution of the Long Parliament in April 1653 ended the Commonwealth and ushered in his Protectorate. As Lucy Hutchinson said, 'while the grand quarrel slept . . . both the victors and the vanquished were equal slaves under the new usurpers.' She did have the grace to say that Cromwell's ambitions were 'gallant and great', unlike, for example, General Lambert's who 'had nothing but an unworthy pride most insolent in prosperity and as abject and base in adversity'. Only with the succession of 'Tumbledown Dick' Cromwell after his father's death in September 1658 did Colonel Hutchinson re-enter public life.

Loyal servant to the Stuarts that he was, Richard Fanshawe came close to giving up his life for them when captured a few days after Worcester. He was lucky to be put on parole and could only get away to the Continent in 1658. One must admire the nerve and ingenuity shown by his wife in tricking her way out of the country so as to be able to follow him.

Lucy Hutchinson

The army being small, there was a necessity for recruits [early in 1651], and the Council of State, soliciting all the Parliament men that had interest to improve it in this exigence of time, gave Colonel Hutchinson a commission for a regiment of horse. He immediately got up three troops, well armed and mounted, of his own old soldiers, that thirsted to be again employed under him, and was preparing the rest of the regiment to bring them up himself; when he was informed, that as soon as his troops came into Scotland, Cromwell very readily received them, but would not let them march together, but dispersed them, to fill up the regiments of those who were more his creatures.

When the colonel heard how Cromwell used his troops, he was confirmed that he and his associates in the army were carrying on designs of private ambition, and resolved that none should share with them in the commands of the army or forts of the nation, but such as would be beasts, and be ridden upon by the proud chiefs. Disdaining, therefore, that what he had preserved, for the liberty of his country, should be a curb upon them [the inhabitants of Nottinghamshire], and foreseeing that some of Cromwell's creatures would at length be put in, to exercise him with continual affronts, in Cromwell's absence he procured an order for the removal of the garrison at Nottingham, which was commanded by his kinsman Major Poulton, into the marching army, and for the demolishing of the place; which accordingly was speedily executed [May 1651].

Cromwell's son-in-law, Ireton, Deputy of Ireland, would not

be wrought to serve him, but hearing of his machinations, determined to come over to England to endeavour to divert him from such destructive courses. But God cut him short by death, and whether his body or an empty coffin was brought into England, something in his name came to London, and was to be, by Cromwell's procurement, magnificently buried among the kings at Westminster. Colonel Hutchinson was, after his brother, one of the nearest kinsmen he had, but Cromwell, who of late studied to give him neglects, passed him by, and neither sent him mourning, nor particular invitation to the funeral, only the Speaker gave public notice in the House, that all the members were desired to attend it. Such was the flattery of many pitiful lords and other gentlemen, parasites, that they put themselves into deep mourning, but Colonel Hutchinson that day [6 February 1652] put on a scarlet cloak, very richly laced, such as he usually wore. Coming into the room where the members were, seeing some of the lords in mourning, he went to them to enquire the cause, who told him they had put it on to honour the general; and asked again, why he, that was a kinsman, was in such a different colour? He told them, that because the general had neglected sending to him, when he had sent to many who had no alliance, only to make up the train, he was resolved he would not flatter so much as to buy for himself, although he was a true mourner in his heart for his cousin, whom he had ever loved, and would therefore go and take his place among his mourners. This he did, and went into the room where the close mourners were; who seeing him come in, as different from mourning as he could make himself, the aldermen came to him, making a great apology that they mistook and thought he was out of town, and had much injured themselves thereby, to whom it would have been one of their greatest honours to have had his assistance in the befitting habit, as now it was their shame to have neglected him. But Cromwell, who had ordered all things, was piqued horribly at it, though he dissembled his resentment at that time, and joined in excusing the neglect; but he very well understood that the colonel neither out of ignorance nor niggardness came in that habit, but publicly to reproach their neglects.

At the time [April 1653] that the Parliament was broken up, Colonel Hutchinson was in the country, where, since his going in his course out of the Council of State, he had for about a year's time applied himself, when the Parliament could dispense with his absence, to the administration of justice in the country, and to the putting in execution those wholesome laws and statutes of the land provided for the orderly regulation of the people. And it was wonderful how, in a short space, he reformed several abuses and customary neglects in that part of the country where he lived, which being a rich fruitful vale, drew abundance of vagrant people to come and exercise the idle trade of wandering and begging. He took such courses that there was very suddenly not a beggar left in the country, and all the poor in every town were so maintained and provided for, that they were never so liberally maintained and relieved before or since. He procured unnecessary alehouses to be put down in all the towns, and if anyone that he heard of suffered any disorder or debauchery in his house, he would not suffer him to brew any more. He was a little severe against drunkenness, for which the drunkards would sometimes rail at him; but so much were all the children of darkness convinced by his light, that they were more in awe of his virtue than his authority. In this time he had made himself a convenient house, whereof he was the best ornament.

The only recreation he had during his residence at London was in seeking out all the rare artists he could hear of, and in considering their works in paintings, sculptures, gravings, and all other such curiosities, insomuch that he became a great virtuoso and patron of ingenuity. Being loth that the land should be disfurnished of all the rarities that were in it, whereof many were sent for sale from the king's and divers noblemen's collections, he laid out about £2000 in the choicest pieces of painting, most of which were bought out of the king's goods, which had been given to his servants to pay their wages.* To them the colonel gave ready money, and bought such good pennyworths,

* The most outstanding of these was Titian's *Venus del Pardo* which the colonel bought in 1649 for £600. He sold it to Cardinal Mazarin's agent in 1653 for £7000, and it is now in the Louvre.

that they were valued at much more than they cost. These he brought down into the country, intending a very neat cabinet for them; and these, with the surveying of his buildings, and improving by enclosure the place he lived in, employed him at home, and, for a little time, his hawks employed him abroad. But when a very sober fellow, that never was guilty of the usual vices of that generation of men, rage and swearing, died, he gave over his hawks, and pleased himself with music, and again fell to the practice of his viol, on which he played excellently well. Entertaining tutors for the diversion and education of his children in all sorts of music, he pleased himself with these innocent recreations during Oliver's mutable reign. As he had great delight, so he had great judgement, in music, and advanced his children's practice more than their tutors. He also was a great supervisor of their learning, and indeed was himself a tutor to them all, besides all those tutors whom he liberally entertained in his house for them.

He being now reduced into an absolutely private condition, was very much courted and visited by those of all parties, and while the grand quarrel slept, and both the victors and vanquished were equal slaves under the new usurpers, there was a very kind correspondence between him and all his countrymen.

In the interim Cromwell and his army grew wanton with their power, and invented a thousand tricks of government, which, when nobody opposed, they themselves fell to dislike and vary every day. First he calls a Parliament out of his own pocket, himself naming a sort of godly men for every county [Barebones Parliament], who meeting and not agreeing, a part of them, in the name of the people, gave up the sovereignty to him. Shortly after he makes up several sorts of mock parliaments, but not finding one of them absolutely to his turn, turned them off again. His wife and children were setting up for principality, which suited no better with any of them than scarlet on the ape; only, to speak the truth of himself, he had much natural greatness, and well became the place he had usurped. He at last exercised such an arbitrary power, that the whole land grew weary of him, while he set up a company of silly, mean fellows, called major-generals as governors in every country [Autumn 1655].

Some had at that time a plot to come with a petition to Cromwell, and, while he was reading it, certain of them had undertaken to cast him out of a window at Whitehall that looked upon the Thames, where others would be ready to catch him up in a blanket if he escaped breaking his neck, and carrying him away in a boat prepared for the purpose, to kill or keep him alive, as they saw occasion, and then to set up General Lambert.* This was so carried on that it was near its execution before the Protector knew anything of it. Colonel Hutchinson being at that time at London, by chance came to know all the plot. Certain of the conspirators coming into a place where he was, and not being so cautious of their whispers to each other before him, but that he apprehended something; by making use of which to others of the confederates, he at last found out the whole matter, without having it committed to him as a matter of trust, but which, carelessly thrown down in pieces before him, he gathered together, and became perfectly acquainted with the whole design. Weighing it, and judging that Lambert would be the worse tyrant of the two, he determined to prevent it, without being the author of any man's punishment.

After Colonel Hutchinson had given [General] Fleetwood† that caution, he was going into the country, when the Protector sent to search him out with all the earnestness and haste that could possibly be. The colonel went to him, who met him in one of the galleries, and received him with open arms and the kindest embraces that could be given, and complained that the colonel should be so unkind as never to give him a visit, professing how welcome he should have been, the most welcome person in the land. With these smooth insinuations he led him

---

* Major-General Lambert had succeeded Ireton as Lord Deputy of Ireland, and, in Lucy Hutchinson's words, 'too soon put on the prince'. Later Cromwell dismissed him, and he went 'to plot new vengeance at his house in Wimbledon, where he fell to dress his flowers in his garden, and work at the needle with his wife and his maids'.

† He married Henry Ireton's widow, thus becoming Cromwell's son-in-law.

along to a private place, giving him thanks for the advertisement he had received from Fleetwood, and using all his art to get out of the colonel the knowledge of the persons engaged in the conspiracy against him. But none of his cunning, nor promises, nor flatteries, could prevail with the colonel to inform him more than he thought necessary to prevent the execution of the design. 'But,' says he, 'dear colonel, why will not you come in and act among us?' The colonel told him plainly, because he liked not any of his ways since he broke up the Parliament, being those which would lead to certain and unavoidable destruction, not only of themselves, but of the whole Parliament party and cause.

After he had endeavoured, with all his arts, to excuse his public actions, and to draw in the colonel, he dismissed him with such expressions as were publicly taken notice of by all his little courtiers then about him, when he went to the end of the gallery with the colonel, and there, embracing him, said aloud to him, 'Well, colonel, satisfied or dissatisfied, you shall be one of us, for we can no longer exempt a person so able and faithful from the public service, and you shall be satisfied in all honest things.' The colonel made haste to return to the country. There he had not been long before he was informed, that notwithstanding all these fair shows, the Protector, finding him too constant to be wrought upon to serve his tyranny, had resolved to secure his person, lest he should head the people, who now grew very weary of his bondage. But before his guards apprehended the colonel, death imprisoned himself, and confined all his vast ambition and all his cruel designs into the narrow compass of a grave. His army and court substituted his eldest son, Richard, in his room, who was a meek, temperate, and quiet man, but had not a spirit fit to succeed his father, or to manage such a perplexed government.

The people, being vexed with the pocket parliaments and the major-generals of the counties, who behaved like bashaws [Turkish pashas], were now all muttering to have a free Parliament, after the old manner of elections, without pledging those that were chosen to any terms. Those at Richard's court, that knew his father's counsels to prevent Colonel Hutchinson from being chosen in his own country, advised Richard to prick him for Sheriff of the County of Nottingham. When the colonel went himself to London and went to the young Protector, Richard told him that since God had called him to the government, it was his desire to make men of uprightness and interest his associates, to rule by their counsels and assistance. The colonel, seeing him herein good-natured enough, was persuaded by a very wise friend of his to take it upon him, and returned well enough satisfied with the courteous usage of the Protector.

Ann Fanshawe

When your father arrived in Scotland [in 1651], he was received by the king with great expressions of great content; and after he had given an account of his past employment, he was by the king recommended to the Kirk party, who received him very kindly, and gave him both the broad seal and signet to keep. They several times pressed him to take the Covenant, but he never did, but followed his business so close, with such diligence and temper, that he was well beloved on all sides, and they reposed great trust in him. I now settled myself in a handsome lodging in London: with a heavy heart I stayed in this lodging almost seven months, and in that time I did not go abroad seven times, but spent my time in prayer to God for the deliverance of the king and my husband, whose danger was ever before my eyes. I was seldom without the best company, and sometimes my father would stay a week, for all had compassion on my condition. I removed to Queen Street, and there in a very good lodging I was upon the 24th of June delivered of a daughter: in all this time I had but four letters from your father, which made the pain I was in more difficult to bear.

I went with my brother Fanshawe to Ware Park, and my sister went to Balls, to my father, both intending to meet in the winter, and so indeed we did with tears. For the 3rd of September following [1651] was fought the Battle of Worcester, when the king being missed, and nothing heard of your father being dead or alive, for three days it was inexpressible what affliction I was in. I neither ate nor slept, but trembled at every motion I heard, expecting the fatal news, which at last came in their news-book, which mentioned your father a prisoner.

Then with some hopes I went to London, intending to leave my little girl Nan, the companion of my troubles, there, and so find out my husband wheresoever he was carried. Upon my coming to London, I met a messenger from him with a letter, which advised me of his condition, and told me he was very civilly used, and said little more, but that I should be in some room at Charing Cross, where he had promise from his keeper that he should rest there in my company at dinner-time; this was meant to him as a great favour. I expected him with impatience, and on the day appointed provided a dinner and room, as ordered, in which I was with my father and some more of our friends. About eleven of the clock, we saw hundreds of poor soldiers, both English and Scotch, march all naked on foot and many a horseback. At last came the captain and two soldiers with your father, who was very cheerful in appearance. After he had spoken and saluted me and his friends there, he said, 'Pray let us not lose time, for I know not how little I have to spare. This is the chance of war: nothing venture, nothing have; so let us sit down and be merry whilst we may.' Then taking my hand in his and kissing me, 'Cease weeping, no other thing upon earth can move me; remember we are all at God's disposal.'

Then he began to tell how kind his captain was to him, and the people as he passed offered him money, and brought him good things, and particularly Lady Denham, at Boarstall House, who would have given him all the money she had in her house, but he returned her thanks, and told her he had so ill kept his own, that he would not tempt his governor with more, but if she would give him a shirt or two, and some handkerchiefs, he would keep them as long as he could for her sake. She fetched him two smocks of her own, and some handkerchiefs, saying she was ashamed to give him them, but, having none of her sons at home, she desired him to wear them.

Thus we passed the time until order came to carry him to

Whitehall, where, in a little room yet standing in the bowling-green, he was kept prisoner, without the speech of any, so far as they knew, ten weeks, and in expectation of death. They often examined him, and at last he grew so ill in health by the cold and hard marches he had undergone, and being pent up in a room close and small, that the scurvy brought him almost to death's door.

During the time of his imprisonment, I failed not constantly to go, when the clock struck four in the morning, with a dark lantern in my hand all alone and on foot, from my lodging in Chancery Lane, at my cousin Young's, to Whitehall, in at the entry that went out of King Street into the bowling-green. There I would go under his window and softly call him. He, that after the first time expected me, never failed to put out his head at the first call; thus we talked together, and sometimes I was so wet with the rain, that it went in at my neck and out at my heels. He directed how I should make my addresses, which I did ever to their general, Cromwell, who had a great respect for your father, and would have bought him off to his service upon any terms.

Being one day to solicit for my husband's liberty for a time, he bid me bring the next day a certificate from a physician, that he was really ill. Immediately I went to Dr Bathurst, that was by chance both physician to Cromwell and to our family, who gave me one very favourable in my husband's behalf. I delivered it at the council chamber, at three of the clock that afternoon, as he commanded me, and he himself moved, that seeing they could make no use of his imprisonment whereby to lighten them in their business, that he might have his liberty upon £4000 bail, to take a course of physic, he being dangerously ill. Many spake against it, but most Sir Henry Vane, who said he would be instrumental, for aught he knew, to hang them all that sat there, if ever he had opportunity; but if he had liberty for a time, that he might take the engagement* before he went out. Upon which Cromwell said, 'I never knew that the engagement was a medicine for the scorbutic [scurvy].' They, hearing their general say so, thought it obliged him, and so ordered him

* An undertaking to be loyal to the Commonwealth.

his liberty upon bail. His eldest brother and sister Bedell, and self, were bound in £4000; and the latter end of November he came to my lodgings, at my cousin Young's. He there met many of his good friends and kindred, and my joy was inexpressible, and so was poor Nan's, of whom your poor father was very fond. I forgot to tell you, that when your father was taken prisoner of war, he, before they entered the house where he was, burned all his papers, which saved the lives and estates of many a brave gentleman.

In 1653, the Fanshawes went to live in Yorkshire, where Sir Richard occupied himself translating Camoens's long poem The Lusiad from the Portuguese. In 1654 they returned south. After Cromwell's death in 1658, Sir Richard went to France as tutor to the Earl of Pembroke's son.

My husband was overjoyed to get loose upon any terms that were innocent, so having seen his bonds cancelled, he went into France to Paris, from whence he by letter gave an account to Lord Chancellor Clarendon of his being got loose, and desired him to acquaint His Majesty of it, and to send him his commands, which was about April 1659. He did to this effect, that His Majesty was then going a journey, which afterwards proved to Spain; but upon his return, which would be about the beginning of winter, my husband should come to him, and that he should have in present the place of one of the Masters of Request, and the secretary of the Latin tongue. Then my husband sent me word of this, and bade me bring my son Richard, and my eldest daughters with me to Paris, for that he intended to put them to a very good school that he had found at Paris. We went as soon as I could possibly accommodate myself with money and other necessaries, with my three children, one maid, and one man. I could not go without a pass, and to that purpose I went to my cousin Henry Neville,* one of the High Court of Justice, where he was then sitting at Whitehall. I told him my husband had sent for me and his son, to place him there, and that he desired his kindness to help me to a pass:

* See the footnote on p. 239.

ne went into the then masters, and returned to me, saying, 'that by a trick my husband had got his liberty, but for me and his children upon no conditions we should not stir'. I made no reply, but thanked my cousin Henry Neville, and took my leave.

At Wallingford House, the office was kept where they gave passes: thither I went in as plain a way and speech as I could devise, leaving my maid at the gate, who was much a finer gentlewoman than myself. With as ill mien and tone as I could express, I told a fellow I found in the office, that I desired a pass for Paris, to go to my husband. 'Woman, what is your husband, and your name?' 'Sir,' said I, with many courtesies, 'he is a young merchant, and my name is Ann Harrison.' 'Well,' said he, 'it will cost you a crown.' Said I, 'that is a great sum for me, but pray put in a man, my maid, and three children.' All which he immediately did, telling me a malignant would give him five pounds for such a pass.

I thanked him kindly, and so went immediately to my lodgings. With my pen I made the great H of Harrison, two *ff*, and the rrs, an *n*, and the i, an *s*, and the s, an *h*, and the o, an *a*, and the n, a *w*, so completely, that none could find out the change. With all speed I hired a barge, and that night at six o'clock I went to Gravesend, and from thence by coach to Dover, where, upon my arrival, the searchers came and demanded my pass, which they were to keep for their discharge. When they had read it, they said, 'Madam, you may go when you please.' But says one, 'I little thought they would give a pass to so great a malignant, especially in so troublesome a time as this.' About nine o'clock at night I went on board the packet boat, and about eight o'clock in the morning landed safe, God be praised, at Calais.

Restoration
1659-60

In the power vacuum after the death of Cromwell, the Hutchinsons continued to be entangled with the Byrons, as in the Civil Wars. But they had just as much grounds to fear the likes of Generals Lambert and Fleetwood. This period of uncertainty within the country was resolved by General Monk marching down from Scotland, which he had governed during the Protectorate. Monk had begun his career as a royalist and had decided to end it as one too. Even though elected to the Parliament that invited Charles II to return, Colonel Hutchinson guessed only too well the danger that he might be offered up as a public sacrifice for his role in the death of the king's father. For the returning royalists, the Fanshawes among them, the good times began even before they set foot in England. Thanks to Pepys's Diary *we know that one of the first tasks Richard Fanshawe was called upon to perform back in England fell to him because of his literary and linguistic skills. Sir Edward Montagu (see p. 179), who was now General-at-Sea and to whom Pepys acted as secretary, had been instrumental in bringing Charles II over safely from Holland. His reward was to be raised to the peerage as Earl of Sandwich. 'My lord must have some good Latinist to make the preamble to his patent [of Nobility], which must express this late service in the best terms that he can ... Sir Richard Fanshawe hath done the General Monk's very well ... June 30th. Betimes to Sir Richard Fanshawe, to draw up the preamble to my lord's patent.' Monk became Duke of Albemarle.*

Lucy Hutchinson

The colonel was in himself more persuaded that the people's freedom would be best maintained in a free republic delivered from the shackles of their encroaching slaves in the army. This was now not merely muttered, but openly asserted by all but the army: although of those who contended for it, there were two sorts; some that really thought it the most conducible to the people's good and freedom; others, who by this pretence hoped to pull down the army and protectorian faction, and then restore the old family [the Stuarts]. It is believed that Richard Cromwell himself was compounded with, to have resigned the place that was too great for him; certain it is that his poor spirit was likely to do any such thing. The army, perceiving they had set up a wretch who durst not reign, also that the whole nation was bent against them and would not bear their yoke, found out some members of that glorious Parliament which they had violently driven from their seats [in April 1653] with a thousand slanderous criminations and untruths. To these they counterfeited repentance and opened the House doors for them. The Speaker, with some few members, as many as made a House, were too hasty to return into their seats, upon capitulation with those traitors who had brought the Commonwealth into such a sad confusion. But after they were met, they immediately sent summons to all the members throughout England, among whom the colonel was called up, and much perplexed, for now he thought his conscience, life, and fortunes were again engaged with men of mixed and different interests and principles. Yet in regard of the trust formerly reposed in him, he returned into his place, infinitely dissatisfied that any condescension had been made to the army's proposals.

During the late Protector's times the Lord Byron, thinking that no gentleman ought to be unprovided with arms in such an uncertain time, had provided himself with a trunk of pistols, which were brought down from London; but some suspicion of it having reached the Protector's officers, he durst not fetch the trunk from the carrier's himself, but entreated the colonel to send for them to his house, and secure them there. This the colonel did; but afterward, when my Lord Byron had entered into a conspiracy with the enemies of the Parliament, he knew that Colonel Hutchinson was not to be attempted against them, and was in great care how to get his arms out of the colonel's house.

The colonel, being of a very compassionate and charitable nature, had entertained into his service some poor people who on the enemy's side had been ruined. Among these, Lord Byron corrupted a gentleman who then waited on the colonel, as the man afterwards alleged; my lord said he offered himself. However it was, the plot was laid that fifty men, near the colonel's house, should be raised for him, and he with them should first come to the colonel's house, and take away my lord's arms, with all the rest of the colonel's that they could find. The chaplain, the waiting woman, and two servants more, were drawn into the confederacy. The colonel was then at the Parliament House, and only his wife and children at home, when, the night before the insurrection, Ivie (that was the gentleman's name) came to a singing-boy who kept the colonel's clothes, and commanded him to deliver him the colonel's own arms and buff coat.

The boy was fearful, and did not readily obey him, where-upon he threatened immediately to pistol him, if he made the least resistance or discovery of the business; so the boy fetched him the arms, and he put them on, and took one of the best horses and went out at midnight, telling the boy he was a fool to fear, for the next night, before that time, there would come fifty men to fetch away all the arms in the house.

As soon as the boy saw him quite gone, his mistress being then in bed, he went to the chaplain and acquainted him; but the chaplain cursed him for breaking his sleep. Then he went to the waiting gentlewoman, but she said she thought it would be unfit to disturb her mistress; so the boy rested till next day, when Ivie, having failed of his men, was come back again. Then the boy, finding an opportunity after dinner, told his mistress. When Mrs Hutchinson had heard that, she bade him keep it private, and called immediately a servant that had been a cornet of the Parliament's party, and bade him go to the county troop's captain, and desire him to send her a guard for her husband's house, for she had intelligence that the cavaliers intended some attempt against it. Mrs Hutchinson, ashamed to complain of her own family, thought of this way of security, till she could discharge herself of the traitor, not knowing at that time how many more such were about her. Then calling her gentlewoman, whom she thought she might trust, upon her solemn protestations of fidelity, she took her to assist her in hiding her plate and jewels, and what she had of value, and scrupled not to let her see the secret places in her house, while the false and base dissembler went smiling up and down at her mistress's simplicity. Meantime, the man that was sent for soldiers came back, bringing news that the cavaliers had risen and were beaten.

Colonel White rose, only to show his apostasy, and run away. The Lord Byron also lost himself and his companions in the forest, being chased by a piece of the county troop. And Mr Robert Pierrepont, the son of the late colonel, went out to make up the rout, and ran away, and cast away some good arms into the bushes to make his flight more easy.

Then also the coachman, who finding himself not well, had borrowed a horse to go to Nottingham to be let blood, came home, bringing with him a cravat and other spoils of the enemy, which he had gotten. For when he came to the town, hearing the cavaliers were up, he got a case of pistols, and thought more of shedding than losing blood, and meeting the cavaliers in the rout, it is said, he killed one of them; although this rogue had engaged to Ivie to have gone on the other side with him. Mrs Hutchinson not being willing, for all this, to take such notice of Ivie's treason as to cast him into prison, took him immediately to London with her, and said nothing till he came there. Then she told him how base and treacherous he had been; but to save her own shame for having entertained so false a person, and for her mother's sake whom he had formerly served, she was willing to dismiss him privately, without acquainting the colonel, who, if he knew, must punish him. So she gave him something and turned him away, and told her husband she came only to acquaint him with the insurrection, and her own fears of staying in the country without him. He, being very indulgent, went immediately back with her, having informed the Parliament, and received their order for going down to look after the securing of the country. His wife, as soon as she came down, having learned that the chaplain had been Ivie's confederate, told him privately of it, and desired him to find a pretence to take his leave of the colonel, that she might not be necessitated to complain, and procure him the punishment his treason deserved. He went away thus, but so far from being wrought upon, that he hated her to the death for her kindness.

The colonel having set things in order in the country, intended to have carried his family that winter with him to London; when just in that week he was going, news was brought that Lambert had once more turned out the Parliament, and the colonel rejoiced in his good fortune that he was not present.

Hereupon the colonel took measures to have some arms bought and sent him, and had prepared a thousand honest men, whenever he should call for their assistance; intending to improve his posse comitatus* when occasion should be offered. To provoke him more particularly to this, several accidents fell out. Among the rest, six of Lambert's troopers came to gather money, laid upon the country by an assessment of Parliament. The colonel [told them] that in regard it was levied by that authority, he had paid it, but otherwise would not; two of them only who were in the room with the colonel, the rest being on horseback in the court, gave him such insolent terms, with such insufferable reproaches of the Parliament, that the colonel drew a sword which was in the room to have chastised them. While a minister that was by held the colonel's arm, his wife, not willing to have them killed in her presence, opened the door and let them out, who presently ran and fetched in their companions in the yard with cocked pistols. Upon the bustle, while the colonel having disengaged himself from those that held him, had run after them with the sword drawn, his brother came out of another room. The soldiers pressing against a door that went into the great hall, the door flew open, and about fifty or sixty men

* The body of men which a sheriff was authorised to raise in his county.

appeared in the hall, who were there upon another business. For Owthorpe, Kinoulton, and Hickling, had a contest about a cripple that was sent from one to the other, but at last, out of some respect they had for the colonel, the chief men of the several towns were come to him, to make some accommodation, till the law should be again in force.* When the colonel heard the soldiers were come, he left them [the chief men] shut up in his great hall, who by accident thus appearing, put the soldiers into a dreadful fright.

When the colonel saw how pale they looked, he encouraged them to take heart, and calmly admonished them for their insolence, and they being changed and very humble through their fear, he called for wine for them, and sent them away. To the most insolent of them he said, 'These carriages would bring back the Stuarts.' The man, laying his hand upon his sword, said, 'Never while he wore that.' Among other things they said to the colonel, when he demanded by what authority they came, they showed their swords, and said, 'That was their authority.'

After they were dismissed, the colonel, not willing to appear because he was sheriff of the county, and had many of their papers sent him to publish, concealed himself in his house, and caused his wife to write a letter to Fleetwood, to complain of the affronts [which] had been offered him, and to tell him that he was thereupon retired, till he could dwell safely at home. To this Fleetwood returned a civil answer, and withal sent a protection, to forbid all soldiers from coming to his house. Notwithstanding all this pretended civility, Fleetwood and his counsellors were afraid of the colonel, and the protection was but sent to draw him thither, that they might by that means get him into their custody. But he, having intimation of it, withdrew, while men and arms were preparing, that he might appear publicly in the defence of the country, when he was strong enough to drive out the soldiers that were left in those parts. Three hundred of them were one night drawn out of Nottingham to come to Owthorpe for him, but some of the party gave him notice, and he being then at home, immediately went out of the house.

* The argument was over which village had the responsibility to look after the cripple.

It is true that at that time the colonel had met with Colonel Hacker, and several other gentlemen of Northampton and Warwickshire, and at the same time as Major Beque was to have reduced Coventry, and another colonel Warwick Castle, two regiments of horse should have marched to a place within seven miles of Colonel Hutchinson's house, where his men should have rendezvoused. The town of Nottingham at the same time was to have seized all the soldiers there, and they of Leicester the like. But just before it should have been put into execution the Parliament were restored to their seats, Lambert was deserted by his men and fled, and Monk was marching on southwards, pretending to restore and confirm the Parliament; insomuch that Colonel Hutchinson, instead of raising his country, was called up to his seat in Parliament. This insolent usurpation of Lambert's had so turned the hearts of all men, that the whole nation began to set their eyes upon the king beyond the sea, and think a bad settlement under him better than none at all.

Sir Anthony Ashley Cooper* at that time insinuated himself into a particular friendship with the colonel, and made him all the honourable pretences that can be imagined. Some days before the rising of that house, when it began to be too apparent which way Monk inclined, the colonel, upon the confidence of his friendship, entreated him to tell him what were Monk's intentions, that he and others might consider their safety, who were likely to be given up as a public sacrifice.† Cooper denied to the death any intention besides a Commonwealth; 'but', said he, with the greatest semblance of reality that could be put on, 'if the violence of the people should bring the king upon us, let me be damned, body and soul, if ever I see a hair of any man's head touched, or a penny of any man's estate, upon this quarrel.' This he backed with so many and such deep protestations of that kind, as made the colonel, after his treachery was apparent, detest him of all mankind, and think himself obliged, if ever he had opportunity, to procure exemplary justice on him, who was so vile a wretch as to sit himself and sentence some of those

* Later the Earl of Shaftesbury.
† As regicides, signatories of Charles I's death warrant.

that died. And although this man joined with those who laboured for the colonel's particular deliverance, yet the colonel, to his dying day, abhorred the mention of his name, and held him to be a more execrable traitor than Monk himself.

A new Parliament was to be chosen, and some time before the writs for the new elections came, the town of Nottingham, as almost all the rest of the island, began to grow mad, and to declare themselves so, in their desires of the king. The boys, set on by their fathers and masters, got drums and colours, and marched up and down the town, and trained themselves in a military posture, and offered many affronts to the soldiers of the army that were quartered there, which were two troops of Colonel Hacker's regiment. Insomuch that one night there were about forty of the soldiers hurt and wounded with stones, upon the occasion of taking away the drums, when the youths were gathering together to make bonfires to burn the Rump,* as was the custom in those mad days. The soldiers, provoked to rage, shot again, and killed in the scuffle two Presbyterians. The soldiers drew into the meadows near the town, and sent for the regiment, resolving to execute their vengeance on the town, and the townsmen again were mustering to encounter them. Mrs Hutchinson by chance coming into the town, and being acquainted with the captains, persuaded them to do nothing in a tumultuary way, however provoked, but to complain to the general, and let him decide the business.

One of the officers, more enraged than the rest, went away immediately to Monk, and complained to him of the malice of the Presbyterians and cavaliers against the soldiers. He, without asking more on the other side, signed a warrant to Colonel Hacker, to let loose the fury of his regiment upon the town. The colonel [Hutchinson], who had been by his wife informed of the disorders there, then went to the general, and prevailed with him for a countermand of all hostility against the town. They could not but look upon the colonel as their deliverer; and this being done a very few days before the election for the next Parliament; when the election day came, Mr Arthur Stanhope and the colonel were clearly chosen.

* Symbolising the remaining members of the Long Parliament.

The colonel and Mr Stanhope went up to the Parliament, which began on the 25th day of April, 1660; to whom the king sending a declaration from Breda, which promised, or at least intimated, liberty of conscience, remission of all offences, enjoyment of liberties and estates; they voted to send commissioners to invite him.

Ann Fanshawe

Upon the king's restoration, the Duke of York, then made admiral, appointed ships to carry over the company and servants of the king, which was very great. His Highness appointed for my husband and his family a third-rate frigate, called the *Speedwell*; but His Majesty commanded my husband to wait on him in his own ship. We had, by the States' order sent on board to the king's most eminent servants, great store of provisions: for our family, we had sent on board the *Speedwell* a tierce of claret, a hogshead of Rhenish wine, six dozen of fowls, a dozen of gammons of bacon, a great basket of bread, and six sheep, two dozen of neats' tongues, and a great box of sweetmeats. Thus taking our leaves of those obliging persons we had conversed with in The Hague, we went on board upon the 23rd of May, about two o'clock in the afternoon. The king embarked at four of the clock, upon which we set sail, the shore being covered with people, and shouts from all places of a good voyage, which was seconded with many volleys of shot interchanged. So favourable was the wind, that the ships' wherries went from ship to ship to visit their friends all night long. But who can sufficiently express the joy and gallantry of that voyage, to see so many great ships, the best in the world, to hear the trumpets and all other music, to see near a hundred brave ships sail before the wind with the vast cloths and streamers, the neatness and cleanness of the ships, the strength and jollity of the mariners, the gallantry of the commanders, the vast plenty of all sorts of provisions. Above all, the glorious Majesties of the king and his two brothers were so beyond man's expectation and expression.

The sea was calm, the moon shone at full, and the sun suffered not a cloud to hinder his prospect of the best sight, by whose light and the merciful bounty of God he was set safely on shore at Dover, in Kent, upon the 25th of May, 1660.

So great were the acclamations and numbers of people, that it reached like one street from Dover to Whitehall. We lay that night at Dover, and the next day we went in Sir Arnold Brem's coach towards London, where on Sunday night we came to a house in the Savoy. My niece, Fanshawe, then lay in the Strand, where I stood to see the king's entry with his brothers; surely the most pompous show that ever was, for the hearts of all men in this kingdom moved at his will.

The next day I went with other ladies of the family to congratulate His Majesty's happy arrival, who received me with great grace, and promised me future favours to my husband and self. His Majesty gave my husband his picture, set with small diamonds, when he was a child: it is a great rarity, because there never was but one.

Retribution
1660-4

In May 1660 Colonel Hutchinson admitted before his fellow Members of Parliament that 'he had made shipwreck of all things but a good conscience'. However, at first, and thanks in no small measure to his wife and her brother Sir Allen Apsley taking his defence into their own hands against his wishes, things seemed to go well for the colonel. But Charles II was unrelenting, convinced the colonel 'would do the same thing for him that he had done for his father'. In October 1663 he was arrested on the excuse of implication in a plot fomented by 'trepanners' or agents provocateurs in Yorkshire. The only one among his captors to behave with decency was the old Duke of Newcastle, who would not lend himself to the deceits and intrigues of the new era. For Lucy, her visits to her husband in the Tower of London brought her life full circle, since this was where she had spent her childhood.

The lack of a formal charge or trial did not prevent the colonel being transferred to Sandown Castle in Kent in May 1664, where his captors expected the unhealthy conditions would do their work for them. They were not disappointed.

Lucy Hutchinson

The Presbyterians were now the white boys, and according to their nature fell a-thirsting, and then hunting after blood, urging that God's blessing could not be upon the land, till justice had cleansed it from the late king's blood. First that fact was disowned, then all the acts made after it rendered void, then an inquisition made after those that were guilty thereof, but only seven were nominated of those that sat in judgment on that prince, for exemplary justice, and a proclamation sent for the rest to come in, upon penalty of losing their estates.

When Colonel Hutchinson, who was not there at the beginning, came in, he was told what they were about, and that it would be expected he should say something. He was surprised with a thing he expected not, yet neither then, nor in any like occasion, did he ever fail himself, but told them, 'That for his actings in those days, if he had erred, it was the inexperience of his age, and the defect of his judgment, and not the malice of his heart, which had ever prompted him to pursue the general advantage of his country more than his own. If the sacrifice of him might conduce to the public peace and settlement, he should freely submit his life and fortunes to their disposal; that the vain expense of his age, and the great debts his public employments had run him into, as they were testimonies that neither avarice nor any other interest had carried him on, so they yielded him just cause to repent that he ever forsook his own blessed quiet, to embark in such a troubled sea, where he had made shipwreck of all things but a good conscience. As to that particular action of the king, he desired them to believe he had that sense of it that befitted an Englishman, a Christian, and a gentleman.' The result of the House that day was to suspend Colonel Hutchinson and the rest from sitting in the House. Monk, after all his great professions, now sat still, and had not one word to interpose for any person, but was as forward to set vengeance on foot as any man.

Mrs Hutchinson, whom to keep quiet, her husband had hitherto persuaded that no man would lose or suffer by this change, at this beginning was awakened, and saw that he was ambitious of being a public sacrifice. Colonel Hutchinson not being of the number of those seven [to be tried for condemning Charles I to death], was advised by all his friends to surrender himself, in order to secure his estate, and he was very earnest to do it, when Mrs Hutchinson would by no means hear of it. At length, being accused of obstinacy, in not giving him up, she devised a way to try the House, and wrote a letter in his name to the Speaker, to urge what might be in his favour, and to let him know, that by reason of some inconveniency it might be to him, he desired not to come under custody, and yet should be ready to appear at their call. The letter was very well received; and upon that occasion all of all parties spoke so kindly and effectually for him, that he had not only what he desired, but was voted to be free without any engagement. His punishment was only that he should be discharged from the present Parliament, and from all offices, military or civil, in the state for ever. Upon his petition of thanks for this, his estate also was voted to be free from all mulcts and confiscations.

The colonel retired to a lodging further from Westminster, and lay very private in the town, not coming into any company of one sort or other, waiting till the Act of Oblivion were perfected, to go down again into the country. Only the gentlemen who were the late king's judges, and who were decoyed to surrender themselves to custody by the House's proclamation, after they had voted only seven to suffer, were now given up to trial, both for their lives and estates, and put into close prison; where they were miserably kept, brought shortly after to trial, condemned, and all their estates confiscated and taken away, themselves kept in miserable bondage.

Although the colonel was cleared both for life and estate in the House of Commons, yet he not answering the court expectations in public recantations and dissembled repentance, and applause of their cruelty to his fellows, the chancellor was cruelly exasperated against him, and there were very great endeavours to have rased him out of the Act of Oblivion. But then Sir Allen Apsley solicited all his friends, as if it had been for his own life, and divers honourable persons drew up a certificate, with all the advantage they could, to procure him favour.

Then the colonel went down into the country. He had not been long at home before a pursuivant from the council was sent to fetch him from his house at Owthorpe, who carried him to the attorney-general. He, with all preparatory insinuations, how much he would express his gratitude to the king and his repentance for his error, if he would now deal ingenuously, in bearing testimony to what he should be examined, sifted him very thoroughly; but the colonel, who was piqued at heart that they should thus use him, imagining that he would serve their turns in witnessing to the destruction of the rest, composed himself as well as he could, and resolved upon another testimony than they expected, if they had really called him to any. The attorney-general brought the warrant of [Charles I's] execution to the colonel, and would fain have persuaded him to own some of the hands, and to have imparted some circumstances of the sealing, because himself was present. But the colonel answered him, that in a business transacted so many years ago, wherein life was concerned, he durst not bear a testimony, having at that time been so little an observer, that he could not remember the least tittle. The attorney-general, very ill-satisfied with his private examination, dismissed him; yet was he served with a writ to appear in the court the next day.

The next day the court sat, and the colonel was fetched in and made to pass before the prisoners' faces, but examined in nothing; which he much waited for [longed for]. The sight of the prisoners, with whom he believed himself to stand at the bar, and the sight of their judges, among whom was that vile traitor [Ashley Cooper] who had sold the men that trusted him, had so provoked his spirit that, if he had been called to speak, he was resolved to have borne testimony to the cause and against the court. But they asking him nothing, he went to his lodging, and so out of town, and would not come any more into their court, but sent the attorney-general word he would witness nothing, and was sick with being kept in the crowd and in the press, and therefore desired to be excused from coming any more thither.

Presently after Mrs Hutchinson came to town, a kinsman of hers, fallen into the wicked counsels of the court, came to visit her one evening, and had been so freely drinking as to un-lock his bosom, when he told her that the king had been lately among them where he was, and told them that they had saved a man, meaning Colonel Hutchinson, who would do the same things for him that he had done for his father. The kinsman in great kindness advised her that her husband should leave England. She told him he could not conveniently, and the Act of Oblivion being passed, she knew not why he should fear, who was resolved to do nothing that might forfeit the grace he had found. But he told her it was determined that, if there was the least pretence in the world, the colonel would be imprisoned, and never be again let loose.

She advertised the colonel and persuaded him, being also advised to the same by other friends, to go out of England, but he would not: he said this was the place where God had set him, and protected him hitherto, and it would be in him an ungrate-ful distrust of God to forsake it. At this time he would have sold part of his estate to pay his debts, but the purchasers scrupled, desiring to see his pardon, which he not having, was fain to break off the treaty; and though all his friends laboured for it, the chancellor utterly refused it. There was a thousand pounds offered to one person to procure it, but it was tried several times and could not be passed, by reason of which he lost the oppor-tunity then of settling his estate. Yet a year afterwards a little solicitor shuffled it in among many others, and managed it so dextrously that it passed all the seals.

Before this time, in December 1660, Captain Cooper sent one Broughton, a lieutenant, and Andrews, a cornet, with a company of soldiers, who plundered his house at Owthorpe, while he was absent, of all the weapons they found in it, to his very wearing-swords, and his own armour for himself, although at that time there was no prohibition of any person whatsoever to have or wear arms. Also an order came down from the secre-tary, commanding certain pictures and other things the colonel had bought out of the late king's collection, which had cost him in ready money between £1000 and £1500, and were of more value; and these, notwithstanding the Act of Oblivion, were all taken from him.

After these troubles were over from without, the colonel lived with all imaginable retiredness at home, and because his active spirit could not be idle nor very sordidly employed, he took up his time in opening springs, and planting trees, and dressing his plantations; and these were his recreations, wherein he relieved many poor labourers when they wanted work, which was a very comfortable charity to them and their families. With these he would entertain himself, giving them much encouragement in their honest labours, so that they delighted to be employed by him. His business was serious revolving the law of God, wherein he laboured to instruct his children and servants, and enjoyed himself with much patience and comfort, not envying the glories and honours of the court, nor the prosperity of the wicked.

[Some time later there were] very strange suspicious signs of some great business on foot among the papists, who, both in Nottinghamshire and Leicestershire, were so exalted, that the very country people everywhere apprehended some insurrection. Among the rest, there was a light-headed, debauched young knight [called Golding], living in the next town to Owthorpe, who vapoured beyond all bounds, and had twelve pair of holsters for pistols at one time of the colonel's saddler, and rode at that time with half a dozen men armed, up and down the country. One of the colonel's maids going to Colston Bassett, to have a sore eye cured by a woman in the town, heard there that he had vapoured that the papists should shortly have their day, and that he would not leave one alive in the colonel's house. Whereupon he made strong shutters to all his low windows with iron bars; and that very night that they sat up, the house was attempted to be broken in, and the glass of one of the great casements broken, and the little iron bars of it crashed asunder. Mrs Hutchinson being up late, heard the noise, and thought somebody had been forcing the doors, but, as we since heard, it was Golding who made the attempt.

Upon the Lord's day, the 11th of October 1663, the colonel having that day finished the expounding of the Epistle to the

Romans to his household, and the servants being gone off out of the parlour from him, one of them came in and told him soldiers were come into the house. He was not at all surprised, but stayed in the room till they came in. [Their leader] told the colonel he must go along with them, after they had searched the house. They found no arms in the house but four birding-guns, that hung open in the kitchen, which being the young gentleman's, they left at that time. It was as bitter a stormy, pitchy, dark, black, rainy night as any that year; all which considered, the colonel desired that they would but stay for the morning light, that he might accommodate himself. They would not, but forced him to go along with them then, his eldest son lending him a horse, and also voluntarily accompanying him to Newark, where, about four o'clock in the morning, he was brought into the Talbot, and put into a most vile room, and two soldiers kept guard upon him in that room.

Tomson, the host of the inn, led a greater party of horse than those who had first seized the colonel, to Owthorpe, and coming in after sunset, to the affright of Mrs Hutchinson and her children, again searched their house more narrowly if possible than at first, with much more insolent behaviour, although they found no more than at first; but they took away the birding-guns they had left before. At night Tomson came up into the colonel's chamber, and behaved himself most insolently, whereupon the colonel snatched up a candlestick and laid him over the chaps with it. Mr Leke [one of the deputy-lieutenants for Nottinghamshire], being in the house, and hearing the bustle, with others, came in with drawn swords. The colonel took that opportunity to tell him that he stood upon his justification, and desired to know his crime and his accusers, and to be delivered out of the hands of that insolent fellow, and to have accommodation fit for a gentleman. Two days after they removed him to the next inn, where he was civilly treated, with guards still remaining upon him.

The 19th of October, Mr Leke, with a party of horse, carried the colonel to the Marquis of Newcastle's, who treated him very honourably; and then falling into discourse with him,

'Colonel,' saith he, 'they say you desire to know your accusers, which is more than I know.' And thereupon very freely showed him the Duke of Buckingham's* letter, commanding him to imprison the colonel, and others, upon suspicion of a plot; which my lord was so fully satisfied the colonel was innocent of, that he dismissed him without a guard to his own house, only engaging him to stay there one week, till he gave account to the council, upon which he was confident of his liberty. The colonel thus dismissed, came home, and upon the 22nd day of October a party of horse, sent only with a wretched corporal, came about eleven o'clock with a warrant from Mr Leke, and fetched him back to Newark. The next day, Mr Leke came to him and showed him a letter from my Lord Newcastle, wherein my lord wrote that he was sorry he could not pursue that kindness he intended the colonel, believing him innocent, for that he had received a command from Buckingham to keep him a close prisoner, without pen, ink, or paper; and to show the reality of this, with the order he sent a copy of the duke's letter, which was also shown the colonel; and in it was this expression, 'that though he could not make it out as yet, he hoped he should bring Mr Hutchinson into the plot.'

Because here is so much noise of a plot, it is necessary to tell what it hath since appeared. The Duke of Buckingham set to work one Gore, Sheriff of Yorkshire, and others, who sent out trepanners [*agents provocateurs*] among the discontented people, to stir them up to insurrection to restore the old Parliament, gospel ministry, and English liberty; which specious things found very many ready to entertain them, and abundance of simple people were caught in the net; whereof some lost their lives, and others fled. But the colonel had no hand in it, holding himself obliged at that time to be quiet.

Upon the 27th of October, Mr Leke, with the marquis's secretary, came to him and acquainted him that the marquis had received express orders from the king, to send him up in safe custody to London. Mr Leke finding him so ill, was so civil as

* He was Lord Lieutenant of the West Riding of Yorkshire where the Northern or Derwentdale Plot, in which Colonel Hutchinson was supposedly implicated, took place. See footnote on p. 196.

to permit him to go by his own house, which was as near a road, that he might there take accommodations for his journey, and be carried up at more ease in his own coach. The colonel about sunset was sent out of Newark, to stay for the rest at his own house. Being driven in the night by an unskilful coachman, the coach was overturned and broken; but about twelve o'clock at night they came home safe. Golding [his Catholic neighbour], the night before he went [from Owthorpe], sent him a pot of marmalade to eat in the coach, and a letter to desire that all grudges be forgotten, and high flattering stuff. As the colonel came by his door he came out with wine, and would fain have brought him into the house to eat oysters, but the colonel only drank with him and bid him friendly farewell, and went on, not guarded as a prisoner, but waited on by his neighbours. To divert his wife, he made himself sport with his guards, and deceived the way, till upon November 4th he was carried to the Tower and committed there close prisoner.

On Friday, November the 6th, he was sent for by Secretary Bennet,* to his lodgings at Whitehall, which was the first time he was examined, and the questions he asked him were: 1st. 'Where he had lived this four or five months?' To which he answered, 'Constantly at home, at his own house in Nottinghamshire.' 2nd. 'What company used to resort to his house?' He told him, 'None, not so much as his nearest relations, who scarcely ever saw him.' 3rd. 'What company he frequented?' He told him, 'None; and that he never stirred out of his own house to visit any.' Bennet said, 'That was very much.' 4th. 'Whether he knew Mr Henry Neville?'† He answered 'Very well.' 5th. 'When he saw him?' He said, 'To his best remembrance never since the king came in.' 6th. 'When he wrote to him?' He said, 'Never in his life.' 7th. 'When Mr Neville wrote to him?' He said, 'Never.' 8th. 'Whether any messages had passed between them?' He said, 'None at all.' 9th. 'Whether none had moved anything to him concerning a republic?' He

* Henry Bennet, Secretary of State, and later first Earl of Arlington.
† A fellow member of the Long Parliament and a fervent republican, who failed to get a pass for his cousin Lady Fanshawe to join her husband in France in 1659 (see p. 219).

answered, 'He knew none so indiscreet.' 10th. 'What children he had?' He said, 'Four sons and four daughters.' 11th. 'How old his sons were?' He said, 'Two were at men's estate, and two little children.' 12th. 'Whether his sons had not done anything to injure him?' He replied, 'Never that he knew of, and he was confident they had not.' 13th. 'Where he went to church to hear divine service, Common Prayer?' He said, 'Nowhere, for he never stirred out of his own house.' 14th. 'Whether he heard it not read there?' He answered, 'To speak ingenuously, no.' 15th. 'How he then did for his soul's comfort?' He replied, 'Sir, I hope you leave me that to account between God and my own soul.' Then Bennet told him his answers to these had cut him off of many questions he should have asked, and he might return. So he was carried back to the Tower.

Not long afterwards Colonel Hutchinson was in great haste fetched away from his dinner at the Tower, and told he should be examined in the king's own hearing. When he came to land at Whitehall Stairs, one Andrews, an officer, with two files of musketeers, was ready to receive him, and led him to Bennet's lodgings. The colonel, having stayed two hours, at last out comes Secretary Bennet! who, taking him to a window apart from Mr Andrews and the keeper, most formally begins thus: 'Mr Hutchinson, you have now been some days in prison, have you recollected yourself to say any more than when I last spoke to you?' Mr Hutchinson answered, 'He had nothing to recollect, nor more to say.' 'Are you sure of that?' said the secretary. 'Very sure,' said Mr Hutchinson. 'Then', said Bennet, 'you must return to prison.'

He was kept a close prisoner, and had no air allowed him, but a pair of leads [a bit of flat roof] over his chamber, which were so high and cold, that he had no benefit from them; and every night he had three doors shut upon him, and a sentinel at the outmost. His chamber was a room where it is said the two young princes, King Edward V and his brother, were murdered in former days, and the room that led to it was a dark great room, that had no window in it, where the portcullis to one of the inward Tower gates was drawn up and let down, under which there sat every night a court of guard. There is a tradition, that in this room the Duke of Clarence was drowned in a butt of malmsey; from which murder this room, and that joining it, where Mr Hutchinson lay, was called the Bloody Tower. Between Mr Hutchinson's chamber and the dark room there was a door, which Mr Hutchinson desired the lieutenant might be left open in the night, because it left a little necessary house [lavatory] open to the chamber, which he and his man had occasion of in the night, having gotten fluxes with their bad accommodations and diet. But the lieutenant would not allow it him, although, when that was open, there were two doors more shut upon him, and he could not have any way attempted any escape, but he must, if it had been possible to work through the walls, have fallen upon a court of guard.

The colonel endured his prison patiently till Candlemas [February 1664] when he sent his wife to Secretary Bennet. He told her he would not move for any more liberty for her husband than he had, unless he could be assured it might be done with more safety to His Majesty than he could apprehend from it. 'But,' said he, 'Mrs Hutchinson, I have some papers of yours which I would show, not to examine you, but to see whether you will inform me anything of them.' She told him she had curiosity enough to see anything that passed under her name; whereupon he called forth his man, who brought out a great bundle of papers, called examinations, taken at Grantham, of passages between Mrs Hutchinson and Mrs Vane. The papers she afterwards learned to have been some letters between Mrs Vane, one of Sir Henry Vane's* daughters, and one Mrs Hutchinson, a gentlewoman who used to come thither, filled with such frivolous intelligence of private amours and intrigues as young people used to communicate to their confidants.

Mr Henry Neville and Mr Salloway had been put into the Tower upon the same suspicion which they had of Mr Hutchinson—a northern plot, for which there was a peculiar assizes, and some men were executed. As soon as those assizes were

* Sir Harry Vane, after the death of John Pym, was the most outstanding figure in the Long Parliament. He was a fervent republican but not a regicide. This, however, did not allow him to escape Charles II's vengeance, and he had been executed in June 1662.

past, Mr Hutchinson sent to Mr Neville and Mr Salloway, that he thought it now time for them to endeavour their liberty, and therefore desired to know what course they intended to proceed in, that they might all take one way. They both sent Mr Hutchinson word that they looked upon him as the best befriended, and they were resolved to see first what success he had, and to make him their leading card. Hereupon he, fearful of doing anything which they could not, sat still deliberating, while they, without giving him the least notice, wrought their own liberties secretly, Mr Neville desiring to travel, and Mr Salloway making such a false, flattering petition, that no honest man could make such another, and a less after his would have but more exasperated. It took so, that immediately he had his liberty, both of them taking some oaths to confirm their loyalty, which were given them by the clerk of the Tower. They had a mind at court that Mr Hutchinson should have made such another petition. But when they found that, notwithstanding their hint, Mr Hutchinson would not follow his [Salloway's] example, their malice grew very bitter against him at the court, insomuch that a gentleman having treated with Mrs Hutchinson for a niece of his, to whom he was guardian, that would have been a convenient fortune for her son, the chancellor [Lord Clarendon] sent for the gentleman and peremptorily forbade him to proceed in the affair, and openly said, 'he must keep their family down'.

Mr Hutchinson was not at all dismayed, but wonderfully pleased with all these things, and told his wife this captivity was the happiest release in the world for him; for before, although he had made no express engagement, yet, in regard that his life and estate had been freely left him when they took away others, he thought himself obliged to sit still all the while this king reigned, whatever opportunity he might have. But now he thought this usage had utterly disobliged him from all ties either of honour or conscience, and that he was free to act as prudence should hereafter lead him. He thought not his liberty out of prison worth purchasing by any future engagement, which would again fetter him in obligations to such persons as every day more and more manifested themselves to be enemies

to all just and godly interests. He therefore charged his wife
that she should not make applications to any person whatsoever, and made it his earnest request to Sir Allen Apsley to let
him stand and fall by his own innocency, and to undertake nothing for him, which, if he did, he told him he would disown. Mrs
Hutchinson, remembering how much she had displeased him
in saving him before, submitted now to suffer with him, according to his own will.

The colonel, at last, with some other prisoners were deliberating to sue out a habeas corpus,* and in order thereunto sent to
the Lieutenant of the Tower to desire a copy of the warrant
whereby he stood committed, which indeed was so imperfect,
that he could not legally be kept upon that. There was neither
his Christian name nor any place of residence mentioned in it,
so that any other Hutchinson might as well have been kept
upon it as he. But the lieutenant refused to give him a copy,
and his jailer told the prisoner it was altered after they had kept
him four or five months in prison. Then the colonel wrote to
Bennet, but neither from him could he obtain any copy of his
commitment.

A few days after, the jailer brought the colonel a warrant to
tell him that he must, the next morning tide, go down to Sandown Castle in Kent. When he came to the castle [May 1664],
he found it a lamentable old ruined place, almost a mile distant
from the town, the rooms all out of repair, not weatherproof,
no kind of accommodation either for lodging or diet, or any
conveniency of life. Before he came, there were not above half
a dozen soldiers in it, and a poor lieutenant with his wife and
children, and two or three cannoneers, and a few guns almost
dismounted, upon rotten carriages; but at the colonel's coming
thither, a company of foot besides were sent from Dover to help
to guard the place, pitiful weak fellows, half-starved and eaten
up with vermin, whom the Governor of Dover cheated of half
their pay, and the other half they spent in drink. These had no
beds, but a nasty court of guard, where a sutler† lived, within a

---

* A writ to demand a prisoner be shown as well as the reasons for his
detention.
† A supplier of food and drink to the soldiery.

partition made of boards, with his wife and family, and this was all the accommodation the colonel had for his victuals, which were bought at a dear rate in the town, and most horribly dressed at the sutler's. For beds he was forced to send to an inn in the town, and at a most unconscionable rate hire three, for himself, his man, and Captain Gregory.* He had to get his chamber glazed, which was a thoroughfare room, having five doors in it, one of which opened upon a platform, that had nothing but the bleak air of the sea, whilst every tide washed the foot of the castle walls. This air made the chamber so unwholesome and damp, that even in the summer-time the colonel's hat-case and trunks, and everything of leather, would be every day all covered over with mould—wipe them as clean as you could one morning, by the next they would be mouldy again. Though the walls were four yards thick, yet it rained in through the cracks in them, and then one might sweep a peck of saltpetre off of them every day, which stood in a perpetual sweat upon them.

The worst part of the colonel's sufferings in this prison, was the company of this poor fellow prisoner [Gregory], and the colonel having no particular retreat, he could not wholly decline his company; and he being a carnal person, without any fear of God, or any good, but rather scandalous conversation, he could take no pleasure in him. Meanwhile, many of his friends gave caution to his wife concerning him, as suspecting him to be a trepanner, which we had afterwards some cause to fear.

The colonel's wife and her son and daughter went to Deal, and there took lodgings, from whence they walked every day on foot to dinner and back again at night, with horrible toil and inconvenience. Though they procured the captain's wife to diet them with the colonel, when they had meat good enough, yet through the poverty of the people, and their want of all necessaries, and the faculty of ordering things as they should be, it was very inconvenient to them; yet the colonel endured it so cheerfully that he was never more pleasant and contented in his whole life. When no other recreations were left him, he diverted himself with sorting and shadowing cockle-shells, which his

* A fellow-prisoner, removed from the Tower at the same time.

wife and daughter gathered for him, with as much delight as he used to take in the richest agates and onyxes he could compass, with the most artificial engravings, which were things, when he recreated himself from more serious studies, he as much delighted in as any piece of art. But his fancy showed itself so excellent in sorting and dressing these shells, that none of us could imitate it, and the cockles began to be admired by several persons who saw them. These were but his trifling diversions; his business and continual study was the Scripture, which the more he conversed in, the more it delighted him; insomuch that his wife having brought down some books to entertain him in his solitude, he thanked her, and told her that if he should continue as long as he lived in prison, he would read nothing there but his Bible.

On the 3rd of September, being Saturday, he had been walking by the sea side, and coming home found himself aguish, with a kind of shivering and pain in his bones, and going to bed did sweat exceedingly. On Monday another fit came upon him and after that he slept no more until his last sleep came upon him, but continued in a feverish distemper. As his daughter sat weeping with him, 'Fie, Bab,' said he, 'do you mourn for me as for one without hope? There is hope.' He desired his brother to remember him to Sir Allen Apsley, and tell him that he hoped God would reward his labour of love to him. While he was thus speaking with them, his spirits decayed exceedingly fast and his pulse grew very low. He fetched a sigh, and within a little while departed, about seven o'clock at night, the 11th day of September 1664.

His family, after they had gotten out the body, brought it with a handsome private equipage to Canterbury, and so forward towards London, meeting no affronts in their way but at one town, where there was a fair. The priest of which place came out, with his clerk in his fool's coat, to offer them burial, and they laid hold of the horses to stop their hearse. The attendants putting them by, the wicked rout at the fair took part with them and set upon the horsemen; but they broke several of their heads and made their way clear. They passed through Southwark, over the bridge, and through the whole heart of the city in the daytime, to their lodgings in Holborn, and had not one reviling word or indignity offered them all the way, but several people were very much moved at that sad witness of the murderous cruelty of the men then in power. From London he was brought home with honour to his grave through the dominions of his murderers, who were ashamed of his glories, which all their tyrannies could not extinguish with his life.

Further Reading

Lucy Hutchinson's *Memoirs of the Life of Colonel Hutchinson* was first published in 1806. The most recent edition, edited by James Sutherland, was published by Oxford University Press in 1973. There was also an Everyman Library edition in 1965. Ann, Lady Fanshawe's, *Memoirs* was first published in 1829. The most recent edition, edited by John Loftis, was published by Oxford University Press in 1979 in a double volume with the *Memoirs* of Anne, Lady Halkett, first published in 1875 by the Camden Society. *The Letters of the Lady Brilliana Harley* were also published by the Camden Society, in 1854. Alice Thornton's *Autobiography* was published by the Surtees Society in 1873. Priam Davies's account of the siege of Brampton Bryan is to be found in the Historical Manuscripts Commission, *Calendar of the Manuscripts of the Marquess of Bath*, I, pp. 1–33, published in 1904.

    Puritans and Roundheads by Jacqueline Eales, Cambridge University Press 1990, is subtitled 'The Harleys of Brampton Bryan and the Outbreak of the English Civil War'. *A Glorious Fame* by Kathleen Jones, Bloomsbury 1988, is a recent biography of the Duchess of Newcastle. Virginia Woolf's essay on the duchess is in *The Common Reader*, First Series, Hogarth Press 1925, while her essay on Lady Fanshawe is in *The Essays of Virginia Woolf*, vol. I, ed. A. McNellie, Hogarth Press 1986. *Portrait of a Cavalier* by Geoffrey Trease, Macmillan 1979, is a biography of the Duke of Newcastle. *The Weaker Vessel* by Antonia Fraser, Weidenfeld 1984, is subtitled 'Woman's Lot in Seventeenth-Century England'; *The Puritan Gentry* by T. J. Cliffe, Routledge 1984, 'The Great Puritan Families of Early Stuart England'; *Her Own Life* by Elspeth Graham, Routledge 1989, 'Autobiographical Writing of Seventeenth-Century Englishwomen'. *Newark on Trent: The Civil War Siegeworks*, HMSO 1964, covers the progress of the war in the area as well as the remaining physical evidence. *Literature and the English Civil War*, ed. Healy and Sawday, Cambridge University Press 1990, has an essay by N. H. Keeble entitled 'The Colonel's

Shadow: Lucy Hutchinson, Women's Writing and the Civil War'.

This War Without an Enemy by Richard Ollard, Hodder & Stoughton 1976, is an excellent short illustrated history of the Civil Wars. For greater detail there is *The Causes of the Civil War* by Conrad Russell, Oxford University Press 1990; *The Civil Wars of England* by John Kenyon, Weidenfeld 1988; and *The King's War* by C. V. Wedgwood, Collins 1958.

Index